Chaucer's Prosody

Chaucer's Prosody

A Study of the
Middle English Verse Tradition

IAN ROBINSON
Lecturer in English at the
University College of Swansea

λέγοιτο δ' ἂν ἱκανῶς εἰ κατὰ τὴν
ὑποκειμένην ὕλην διασαφηθείη
– *Nicomachean Ethics* A iii

CAMBRIDGE
AT THE UNIVERSITY PRESS
1971

Published by the Syndics of the Cambridge University Press
Bentley House, 200 Euston Road, London N.W.1
American Branch: 32 East 57th Street, New York, N.Y.10022

© Cambridge University Press 1971

Library of Congress Catalogue Card Number: 79–116841

I S B N: 0 521 07920 9

Printed in Great Britain
at the University Printing House, Cambridge
(Brooke Crutchley, University Printer)

For John Stevens

Saue for thy wisedom or this time as I wene,
With courtly misery I tangled should haue bene.
– Barclay's *Egloges*

Remarks a caricature of which is 'The poem is sad. The rhythms support this view' are useful or frustrating according to their phrasing or context. If there is nothing in the context to suggest that the rhythms are some separate, simple, uncontaminated thing, then we may well, as we often do, I believe, take remarks like this as the equivalent of 'Try reading the poem in the way my analysis of the meaning suggests. It goes well like that.' This is an effective mode of advocacy, of getting other people to see and appreciate what you think can be done with the poem, in a word useful criticism. But if there is a suggestion that the rhythms are a simple, separate, uncontaminated thing, then we might start looking for them and that is the way to unhappy frenzy.

– D. L. Sims, *Essays in Criticism*, vol. VI, pp. 351–2

Contents

Acknowledgements

My gratitude for particular facts and ideas is recorded in detail throughout the book; here I will mention only the main general and material debts. The oldest is to Professor J. G. Southworth, whose book *Verses of Cadence* first formulated my interest in the subject, and who was kindly unsparing in encouragement and criticism for a number of years. My ideas on rhythm developed largely from Professor D. W. Harding's essay 'The Rhythmical Intention in Wyatt's Poetry', and my sense of the later Chaucerian age is much indebted to Mr H. A. Mason's *Humanism and Poetry in the Early Tudor Period*. Parts of the book derive from papers read to the Conference of University Lecturers in English, the Cambridge University English Club, the Doughty Society of Downing College, the University of Reading English Society and the Literary and Philosophical Society of the University College of Swansea, and have been modified as a result, in the ensuing discussions, of remarks by people unknown to me.

My gratitude for as much detailed discussion as I wished to ask for is recorded in the dedication to my research supervisor at Cambridge, Dr J. E. Stevens. Mr Morris Shapira, Mr John Speirs, Mr H. A. Mason, Mr S. W. Dawson, Mr M. B. Mencher and Mr R. A. Andrews have all made comments on earlier drafts which in various ways affected the line of argument in this version. Mr Michael Black commented most usefully on later drafts of the book. I am grateful to my colleague Mr David Sims for the many conversations which more than anything else strengthened my belief in my own thesis and helped to refine my sense of the kind of argument I was engaged on: I am also particularly indebted to Mr Sims for extensive comment on Part One, and I believe that in so far as that part of the book is not a muddle the credit is his. I received some much-needed enlightenment about certain relevant problems concerning the nature of language from Mr Rush Rhees's seminars on Wittgenstein in the University College of Swansea. Finally I hope that a strong general debt to my Cambridge director of studies, Dr F. R. Leavis, will be apparent in my assumptions about the nature of literature and history.

I record grateful thanks for the state studentship which allowed me to begin work, to Churchill College, Cambridge, for the research fellowship which permitted its continuation, to the University College of Swansea for a research grant which enabled me to do some of the reading for Chapter 7, to the Cambridge English Faculty for the use of several photostatic copies of manuscripts and, for access to manuscripts or copies, to the usual British research libraries and to Mr John Fisher and the librarians of St John's, Trinity and Corpus Christi Colleges, Cambridge, the University of Durham and the University of Virginia.

Last but not least I must make acknowledgement to the two sets of examiners of the dissertations in which this work first found expression. Their unanimous disapproval convinced me that I must, after all, have something to say.

Note on Texts

ABBREVIATIONS

E.E.T.S. The Early English Text Society

M.E.D. *Middle English Dictionary*, ed. Kurath, Kuhn *et al.*
Ann Arbor (in progress)

N.E.D. The *New* (or *Oxford*) *English Dictionary*

S.T.S. The Scottish Text Society

The following PROSODIC MARKS are used throughout the book:

ᵕ   an unstressed syllable

′   a stressed syllable

ˋ   a syllable more stressed than ᵕ and / or less stressed than ′

∕   a division between phrases

ı   a division between feet

I   a division between half-lines

*   weak iambic foot

†   strong iambic foot

CHAUCER IS QUOTED, unless otherwise stated, from F. N. Robinson's second edition of his works, Boston, 1957, and line references to Chaucer follow the system (or in the case of *The Canterbury Tales* the older of the two systems) of that edition. Gower is quoted except where otherwise indicated from the E.E.T.S. reprint of G. C. Macaulay's edition of *Gower's English Works*, 2 vols, 1900–1; the book and line numbers of *Confessio Amantis* (abbreviated *Conf. Am.*) follow that edition. Details of all other editions are given on first quotation; London is the place of publication, except of periodicals, unless otherwise stated.

Canterbury Tales manuscripts are usually referred to by their short titles as in volume I of Manly and Rickert's *Text of 'The Canterbury Tales'*, Chicago, 1940, to which reference should be made for full descriptions. In a few cases manuscripts have changed owners and names since 1940 but there are advantages in trying to standardize the nomenclature.

Editorial PUNCTUATION has sometimes been removed in

quotations of medieval verse without further remark: the reasons for this are made clear later. Where punctuation has been added there is a note to say so.

The punctuation marks in manuscripts are of importance to the following argument and I have tried to reproduce them accurately, but there is no hard and fast line between the virgule (/) and the hairline descender with which some scribes liked to decorate the ends of words. It may be that the discretion I have had to exercise has told somewhat in favour of my case about the function of these marks; but I do not think that any possible bias can be serious enough to prejudice the argument.

Introduction

Anyone who wants to know the imaginative literature offered by our language sooner or later tries Chaucer, and is unlikely to be disappointed by what he finds.

This proposition may seem disconnected from the present work. Thought about a great poet does not usually take the form of academic discussion of his metre. It will be the task of this book to show why consideration of metres is a useful, perhaps a necessary part of Chaucer criticism; meanwhile I merely assert that unless the book is a provocation to thought about the poetry of Chaucer and his followers it has no right to exist even as a technical consideration of their prosody.

Chaucer, though one of our poets, is generally read in a peculiar bad way as if he were a foreign poet. A bad tradition of sounds and metres, though it offers to help us on our way to the poetry, gets between reader and poet; this tradition is, moreover, built into all the editions. This book too may be accused (with what justice it is not for me to say) of claiming to be indispensable, the only way into Chaucer. At least let it be clear at the outset that unless this book can, by undermining certain bad ways of reading and suggesting better ways, improve the common reading of Chaucer, it is not worth anybody's time. It is in following these ideas and ambitions that I hope to make clear why questions about metre are best seen as concerning the value of particular poems and poets.

One of the marks of attaining the higher levels of the educational system must have been, for many people, the privilege of reading Chaucer in the original. A further step is to be allowed to listen to, and encouraged to imitate, recordings of what Chaucer's poetry sounded like in his own age—for, whatever doubts teachers may have in their hearts, or may even manage to express, before they play the records, people do very often believe that they have heard the sounds of Chaucer's English. Some recordings are of course better than others, but the usual impression of these performances on the inexpert listener is, first, fascinated surprise at the queerness and quaintness of sounds in which English people actually at one time conversed in English, and secondly a milder surprise that the metre of Chaucer is so familiar. For there is nothing strange about the metre: its repetitive beat is as familiar as a nursery rhyme, and in the same style.

The noises in question were made in recording studios, often some years ago, but never in the Middle Ages. The recording I have most in mind is the old '78' by Professor H. C. Wyld.[1] Wyld took great pains to follow the metres and make the sounds prescribed by the authorities, but his labour somehow failed to lead to a good reading.

A 37   Me thynketh it acordaunt to resoun
     To telle yow al the condicioun
     Of ech of hem, so as it semed me,

says Chaucer early in the *General Prologue*, beginning to chat and establish the half-apologetic tone he later uses so well. In Wyld's reading the slow pace and simple metre lead to a grandness of style in which *resoun*, with its stress on the second syllable, seems to be the ancestor of *resound*. Sooner or later the question may arise in even the most reverent mind, Could Chaucer really have been read so woodenly in his own day? and if so is not any more lively modern reading simply an improvement? It might be said that Wyld is concentrating on the language not the poetry (and this and related distinctions are at the heart of the confusions to be discussed below), but if knowledge of fourteenth-century sounds and metres has no connection with good reading, the mere reader certainly has a right to ask why he should concern himself with such matters.

Yet it is generally agreed by the authorities that Chaucer's sounds and metres do matter (Chapter 1, below) and Wyld is in the centre of a generally accepted tradition which also has some important effects on all the editions of Chaucer. Follow all the instructions in any of the standard editions and you will produce something similar. But if the experts make Chaucer lifeless, or allow him to live only despite his sounds and rhythms, how can they be right?

We must ask how the tradition of reading exemplified in Wyld's recording came to be established, what assumptions that tradition rests on and whether or not they are true, and what questions it asks or fails to ask.

If the thesis of this work, that questions about the life of the

---

[1] 'Pronunciation of Chaucer's English', Linguaphone.

poetry are centrally relevant to all understanding of Chaucer's sound and metre, is accepted, then any value the book has must lie (since it belongs to criticism not to science) in its distance from the absolute, its necessary impermanence. It is comforting that if its arguments are accepted this work cannot succeed ten Brink's or Baum's as, in their sense, the authority on the subject.

The dominant tradition of Chaucer reading dates back to the seventeenth century and was securely established by the work of the great eighteenth-century editor, Thomas Tyrwhitt. In his day it was already a matter of concern to some scholars that Chaucer, in common with all his disciples and imitators, appeared to write lines that were not all metrically regular. The lines of *The Canterbury Tales* were of about the same length as iambic pentameters, but when read in modern English were frequently not iambic pentameters; similarly the verse of Hoccleve and Lydgate was often impossible to scan. A few irregularities in the text of Chaucer still survive the attentions of two centuries of editorial scholarship:

F 1207   But in his studie, ther as his bookes be

—this has a syllable too many at the caesura and doesn't sound like iambic pentameter. So perhaps it is not Chaucer's? Perhaps there was some scribal error? Unfortunately the line appears almost unchanged a little lower, which may suggest that on the contrary Chaucer liked it:

F 1214   Into my studie, ther as my bookes be.

And here is a line each of Hoccleve, Lydgate, Hawes and Barclay, English Chaucerians who will occupy us later:

Our right cristen kyng / heir and Successour...[1]
As auctours witnesse, this lond is desolat...[2]
And the .v. parte / is than memoratyfe...[3]
Yet nought had he kept to finde him cloth nor fode[4]

If there is any difficulty here it is not that these verses are simply unmetrical but that they come so close to metrical regularity. How

---

[1] *Hoccleve's Works*, E.E.T.S. 1892, etc., vol. I, ed. F. J. Furnivall, p. 41, line 2.
[2] *Duorum Mercatorum*, line 22. *Minor Poems of John Lydgate*, ed. H. N. MacCracken, E.E.T.S. 2 consecutively paginated vols. 1910 and 1934, p. 487.
[3] Stephen Hawes, *The Pastime of Pleasure*, line 1240; ed. W. E. Mead, E.E.T.S. 1928, p. 52.
[4] Alexander Barclay, *Egloges*, I, 145; ed. B. White, E.E.T.S. 1928, p. 5.

easy it would have been for any of the quoted lines to have appeared as regular iambic pentameter:

> In to my studie, ther my bokes be...

> Our cristen kyng, the heir and sǔccessour...

> As auctours seyn, this lond is desolat...

> And than the fift parte is memóratyfe...

> Yet nought he hadde to fynde him cloth nor fode...

The lines we have are so near to yet so far from metrical regularity: were these poets aiming at smoothness and failing?

It was felt by Tyrwhitt and his followers that Chaucer's verse ought to be metrically regular—I shall show that this feeling has always been the great inspiration of orthodox scholars—and Tyrwhitt succeeded in reducing much of Chaucer's verse to what he could accept as regularity, by two main procedures. The first, which will not concern us beyond a brief Appendix, was an argument based on notions of the metres of medieval French; the second was the reintroduction of what he took to be certain forgotten parts of the English of Chaucer's time. These were the sounding of whatever now mute final -e's were demanded by the metre, and the variable stressing of many words of two syllables (*hónour* or *honoúr*, etc.), also so as to produce regularity of metre. Tyrwhitt drew together and made respectable the surmises of earlier editors; the usual modern view of his achievement is that of C. F. E. Spurgeon: 'Tyrwhitt made possible...the rational study of Chaucer's own works by editing a careful and scholarly text of his Tales, and for the first time he definitely and clearly stated and proved the true theory of the poet's versification.'[1] But in Tyrwhitt's work we see at once one of the characteristics of the whole tradition, namely that the 'definite and clear statement and proof' depends on certain unexplored and, I shall argue, untrue assumptions about the nature of metre, and on the acceptance as

---

[1] C. F. E. Spurgeon, *Five Hundred Years of Chaucer Criticism and Allusion, 1357–1900*, Cambridge, 1925, vol. I, p. xi. (Miss Spurgeon liked the phrase 'definitely and clearly' and also says that Tyrwhitt 'definitely and clearly disposed for ever of the persistently erroneous view which was held of Chaucer's versification'. (*Ibid.* p. liv.) The works of Southworth have now made the rashness of this prophecy apparent.)

4

factual information about fourteenth-century English what is really literary criticism of modern English.

Tyrwhitt states some of his assumptions with the admirable lucidity of his century: 'In discussing this question we should always have in mind, that the correctness and harmony of an English verse depends entirely upon its being composed of a certain number of syllables, and its having the accents of those syllables properly placed.'[1] And: 'The offences against metre in an English verse, as has partly been observed before, must arise either from a superfluity or deficiency of syllables, or from the accents being improperly placed.'[2] So, since Chaucer was not ignorant of 'the strict laws of metre',[3] which are immutable, the duty of his editor, thinks Tyrwhitt, is to find means of making his verse metrical, which is *the same* as making it conform to his notion of modern English metre. So Tyrwhitt's reason for 'adopting in certain words a pronunciation different...from modern practice' is that 'the verse...may be made correct',[4] that is, we make the language archaic in order to make the metre modern. And there is every indication that Tyrwhitt's idea of modern English metre was just the commonplace one of his time, which it would hardly be unfair to describe as supposing that every iambic pentameter goes

De dum de dum de dum de dum de dum (de).

So too Tyrwhitt says '...nothing will be found of such extensive use for supplying the deficiencies of Chaucer's metre as the pronunciation of the *e* feminine...'[5] and he similarly proves the variable stressing of disyllables: 'These instances are all taken from the Riming syllables (where a strong accent is indispensably necessary) in order to prove beyond contradiction that Chaucer frequently accented his words in the French manner.'[6] This proof beyond contradiction hinges, however, on a question not of fact but of taste. It is not a fact, but an opinion—an opinion belonging with the opinion that all English pentameters go

De dum de dum de dum de dum de dum (de)

—that a strong accent is indispensably necessary in rhyming syllables in English verse. The questions, how we know that the

---

[1] T. Tyrwhitt, 'Essay on the Language and Versification of Chaucer', prefixed to *The Canterbury Tales*, 2nd edition, Oxford, 1798, vol. I, p. 53.
[2] *Ibid.* p. 55. [3] *Ibid.* p. 54.
[4] *Ibid.* p. 56. [5] *Ibid.* p. 57. [6] *Ibid.* p. 62.

laws of verse are unalterable and (even if they are) whether obeying them is so very simple, must at least be raised before one can agree that Tyrwhitt has definitely and clearly stated and proved anything.

Tyrwhitt was trying hard, under the guise of discovering Chaucer's English, to apply modern metres to Chaucer's English; and this is characteristic of all the scholars who follow him, down to the present day. Ten Brink's book,[1] still treated as a standard work on Chaucer's metre, argues consistently that where Chaucer's text does not contain 'the correct number of syllables' it is corrupt and should be emended to produce the right number: 'The MSS afford—especially in the Deeth of Blaunche—several verses which only violent slurring could reduce to the correct number of syllables, i.e. which contain a dissyllabic arsis. But the majority may easily be emended.'[2] But ten Brink never tells us how he knows what 'the correct number of syllables' is. His correctness is perhaps the same as Tyrwhitt's propriety, also somewhat mysterious. Similarly, after exhausting the possibilities of 'apocope, elision and slurring', ten Brink determines that any remaining 'redundant syllable at the caesura would have to be removed by emendation'.[3] One example of a line improved by reduction to the correct number of syllables is about the Prioress and her dogs,

A 148   But soore wepte she if oon of hem were deed,

which becomes

          But sore wepte, if oon of hem were deed

—this 'would be metrically superior to the one transmitted and would not be less compatible with the linguistic usage of the poet'.[4] But is it not simply a worse line, and is not ten Brink therefore applying ideas of metrical correctness, for which he has shown no evidence, in support of a critical misjudgement?

---

[1] B. ten Brink, *The Language and Metre of Chaucer*, revised by F. Kluge, translated by M. Bentinck Smith, 1901. For an account of the development of Tyrwhitt's theory in the nineteenth century see J. G. Southworth, *Verses of Cadence*, Oxford, 1954, Chapter 2.

[2] *Op. cit.* p. 209.

[3] *Ibid.* p. 217. Cf. also ten Brink's treatment of 'suppression of the anacrusis' and 'dissyllabic anacrusis', both of which are 'emphatically repudiated' by means of emendation, *ibid.* pp. 215–16.

[4] *Ibid.* pp. 217–18.

Tyrwhitt and ten Brink's case for reading Chaucer metrically depends wholly on their certainties about metre; but if we ask for the evidence on which they found their certainty, we may be long finding it. Their tradition continues, however. A. H. Licklider makes well some of the necessary objections to the arguments of the Tyrwhitt school: 'It is assumed, too, that our modern ideas of accent were perfectly familiar to the poets of the fourteenth and fifteenth centuries, and any deviation from that standard is denounced as "wrenched accent". The student thus attempts to fit Tennyson's coat to Lydgate's back and is horrified to find the Monk of Bury bursting through.'[1] But Licklider himself falls into the same assumptions: 'Whatever the origin of the heroic line in English poetry, it is undisputed that Chaucer once for all established its use, and that the form he gave to it was accepted then and is now as the norm.'[2] But what if one disputes? How can one know that the heroic line was the same for Chaucer as for us? It is not even certain that Licklider's idea of the heroic line would be widely accepted as a true picture of any English poetry, for his idea of the 'norm' is even more rigid than ten Brink's, and the verse is made to fit the norm by a complicated system of 'archaisms, contractions and resolutions, secondary accents, romance stresses',[3] etc., which has much in common with the one in which at about the same time Miss Foxwell was attempting to confine Wyatt.[4] Licklider is even worried when a word is metrically stressed at one place but unstressed at another, as in Hoccleve's line

$$\breve{}\, /\quad \breve{}\, /\quad \breve{}\, /\quad \breve{}\, /\quad \breve{}\, /$$
O wilt thow so wilt thow make it so strange[5]

Even scanned like that there would be no real difficulty; Hoccleve's point would be to vary the phrase with the different stress. But the real trouble is the imposition of the 'norm'. Licklider scans another line:

$$\breve{}\, /\quad \breve{}\, /\quad \breve{}\, /\quad \breve{}\, /\quad \breve{}\, /$$
But help is noon help and confort been dede

—but surely it goes better:

$$\breve{}\, /\quad \breve{}\, /\quad /\quad \breve{}$$
But help is noon. Help and confort been dede.

[1] A. H. Licklider, *Chapters on the Metric of the Chaucer Tradition*, Baltimore, 1910, p. 10.   [2] *Ibid.* p. 26.   [3] *Ibid.* p. 11.
[4] Cf. A. K. Foxwell, *A Study of Sir Thomas Wyatt's Poems*, 1911. Cited and discussed by Mitchell, see below, p. 192.

This is an effective line but with a trochaic third foot. But Licklider, like the other scholars discussed, organizes his beliefs about Middle English to confirm his beliefs about modern English metre, and is never strengthened in either of them by convincing readings of poetry, old or modern.

Complete continuity with Tyrwhitt can still be found as recently as 1960 in a dissertation by Dr E. W. Stone, who writes: 'It is well for the beginning student to have right at the start a clear concept of Chaucer's regular iambic line...'[1] But Dr Stone presents no evidence for believing that the clear concept is true, and offers no advice about where, before he reads the poet, the student should get his clear concept from. This seems to be 'the sort of ecstatic enthusiasm which starts straight off with absolute knowledge, as if shot out of a pistol'.[2] Dr Stone also writes, 'A certain amount of deviation from the fixed metrical pattern is expected; but when the addition of syllables results in verses of imprecise rhythm, one suspects he is not reading the lines as Chaucer intended them.'[3] But unless the researcher tells us how the metrical patterns come to be fixed there must always remain the suspicion that he has fixed them himself. Dr Stone's claim for his 'new method' is that 'lines lying beyond the bounds of poetry have been reclaimed through the practices of elision or/and contraction'[4]—that is, some lines have been turned into poetry by being made metrically satisfactory to the ear of the modern academic. This new method is just Tyrwhitt's.

In the same way one modern standard work assumes that we know Chaucer's metre before we have read a line of the poet: 'Occasionally, a poet will change meters absolutely. Thus, the very first line of Chaucer's *Canterbury Tales* shows not the expected alternating pattern of unstressed then stressed syllables, but the reverse of that scheme.'[5] The point here is, of course, that the assumption is modified by the actual verse. But what makes it right for us to bring an expected pattern to Chaucer in the first place? And if we do, may the expectation not be strong enough to distort the kind of modification the verse forces on us? In this case

[1] E. W. Stone, *Chaucer's Prosody, Examination Based on a New Method*, University of Denver Ph.D. dissertation, 1960, p. 84.

[2] G. W. F. Hegel, *The Phenomenology of Mind*, translated by J. B. Baillie, 1910, p. 25.

[3] Stone, *op. cit.* p. 1.   [4] *Ibid.* p. 100.

[5] K. Shapiro and R. Beum, *A Prosody Handbook*, New York, 1965, p. 31.

the distortion could be the replacement of one assumption by another, namely, that all we have to do is to turn the expected pattern back to front.

Numbers of industrious Germans produced dissertations from 1850 onwards based on the same metrical assumptions and open (for all their wealth of documentation) to exactly the same objections as Tyrwhitt and Stone, namely, that the answers to all the real problems about what metre is and does are taken for granted.[1]

Mr E. T. Donaldson is, similarly, quite sure that we begin with knowledge of Chaucer's metre and that that tells us how to pronounce his lines.[2]

The most influential modern inheritor of the Tyrwhitt tradition is, however, Professor P. F. Baum, the discussion of whose work[3] will have to occupy a number of these pages. Baum shares the most important of Tyrwhitt's assumptions. On page 11 (having already got as far as the word *finally*) Baum offers this as self-evident truth: 'But finally now, however he may have come to it, Chaucer's line is a series of five iambs.' This may indeed be true, but a metaphor used persistently by Baum makes it a dogma and those who dissent, heretics. Once again there is no evidence or argument. Professor Baum does hint at some of the difficulties neglected by his predecessors. Will Chaucer's metre tell us how to read his verse in fourteenth-century English? Baum, in a passage we must mention later (below, p. 57), realizes that it will not. But after glimpsing difficulties Baum constantly returns to the safety of the orthodox tradition. 'One thing may be said with security, that modern English versification starts with Chaucer. With him it was almost a *de novo* creation.'[4] Would not security have been made doubly secure by some presentation of the evidence for this contention? Again, Baum writes of *The Canon's Yeoman's Tale*: 'I repeat, it is not that all these [metrically irregular] lines are bad or that they resist scansion—some of them are very good when read for their rhetorical effect, regardless of meter—it is that their continual recurrence disturbs the ear conditioned to metrical regularity and the intelligence [*sic*] because the prose rhythm is inadequately

[1] Cf. for instance, O. Bischoff, 'Über zwasilbige Senkung und epische Cäsur bei Chaucer', *Englische Studien*, vols. xxiv and xxv, 1898–9; F. Bock, *Metrische Studien zu Hoccleve's Versen*, Wilheim, 1900; E. Hampel, *Die Silbenmessung in Chaucers fünftaktigen Verse*, Halle, 1898.
[2] See his retort to Southworth in *PMLA*, 1948; see Bibliography.
[3] P. F. Baum, *Chaucer's Verse*, Durham, N.C. 1961.
[4] *Ibid.* p. 11.

9

subdued to the prepared pattern.'[1] In that case may there not be something inappropriate about the prepared pattern? Or is there *no* connection between metre and the way a line is read? At such questions Baum could only reiterate his faith that finally now Chaucer's line is a series of five iambs, and we are back with our first response to Wyld: if so, *tant pis*.

The case for reading *The Canterbury Tales* as iambic pentameter is always a literary–critical one with a direct bearing on reading, but is hardly ever recognized as such. The argument is always of the form: good poets write metrically, Chaucer is a good poet, therefore Chaucer writes metrically.

But what good metre is may be disputed, and against the tradition from Tyrwhitt to Baum, the establishment line as it may be called, there has been a longstanding opposition. Tyrwhitt was subjected to telling criticism twenty years after his death by Dr G. F. Nott, the editor of Wyatt and Surrey and the founder of a rival tradition of reading our medieval poets which survives into the present day in such writers as Professor J. G. Southworth on Chaucer or Professor D. W. Harding and Mr H. A. Mason on Wyatt.

Nott denied that the Middle English poets wrote iambic pentameters; he saw their lines instead as 'rhythmical', a word not fully clear in his work, but which may mean that he thought of these lines as composed of half-line phrases rather than feet. Nott's great contribution to this study was his understanding of the importance of manuscript punctuation (which is often used to indicate phrase-divisions, see Chapter 7, below); and his remarks on manuscript punctuation are still the best I know.[2] Nott has always received the treatment reserved by the orthodox for heretics, and to Southworth's collection of unintelligent anti-Nott remarks[3] I can add, for instance:

For a specimen of modern criticism I take Isaac D'Israeli...'In the most ancient MSS of Chaucer's works the caesura in every line is carefully noted.' This extraordinary assertion [which is true] has been carried yet further by Dr Nott in his preface to Surrey's *Poems*; but it is not necessary at the present day to quote Dr Nott.[4]

---

[1] *Ibid.* p. 132.

[2] G. F. Nott, 'Dissertation', in vol. I, *The Works of Henry Howard, Earl of Surrey, and of Sir Thomas Wyatt, the Elder*, 2 vols. 1815.

[3] J. G. Southworth, *Verses of Cadence*, pp. 15–16.

[4] Sir George Young, *An English Prosody on Inductive Principles*, Cambridge, 1928, p. 90.

Baum has an oddly similar refusal to discuss Nott. He quotes Nott and continues, 'It would be as easy as it would be pointless to talk back to Dr Nott...'[1] One might have been more convinced of the ease if the talking had been done.

C. S. Lewis also argued in a well-known essay that the 'fifteenth century heroic line' is not iambic pentameter. His warnings against assuming what we are trying to prove ought to have had more effect: 'Even in Wyatt the stumbling-blocks occur far more often in what seem to be decasyllabics than in his lyric metres. I say "what seem to be decasyllabics" because that is precisely the point on which we must not begin by begging the question.'[2] But Lewis's own solution of the problem of how to read Chaucer and the Chaucerians falls into the same trap of imposing preconceived ideas on them. He thinks they go like nursery rhymes or like William Allingham's poem 'The Fairies', and he invites us to read the famous lyric

> He came al so still
> Ther his moder was
> As dew in April
> That falleth on the grass

in the same metre as the nursery-rhyme

> Pease pudding hot
> Pease pudding cold
> Pease pudding in the pot
> Five nights old.

Lewis only quotes the first two lines of the latter and may have had some less thumping version in mind, but he leaves no doubt of how he wants the medieval poem read. He accents it like this:

> He came al so still
>
> Ther his moder was
>
> As dew in April [sic]
>
> That falleth on the grass

The marked metre can be applied to the verse only because it is so strongly external: it is being forced on to the verse rather than discovered in it, and the result is an insensitive reading.

---

[1] *Chaucer's Verse*, p. 119.
[2] C. S. Lewis, 'The Fifteenth Century Heroic Line', *Essays and Studies*, vol. XXIV, 1938, p. 28.

The modern leader of the opposition to the Tyrwhitt establishment is Professor J. G. Southworth, who, in two books and a succession of articles listed in the bibliography, has maintained a long, vigorous and entertaining if not altogether coherent onslaught on what he likes to call 'the goddam iamb'. Southworth's two main insistences are that nothing can be learned of how to read Chaucer from a study of the medieval poetry of France or Italy, and that Chaucer's verse and that of his disciples must be read 'rhythmically'. Southworth seems to me to have made the first of these cases so conclusively that there has been no need to add anything beyond a short Appendix. But about what he means by 'reading rhythmically' Southworth suffers from a vagueness and confusion that makes his work less influential than it should be. He often quotes manuscripts, using a musical notation to show how he thinks they should be read; but though one very often agrees with his reading it has to be objected to him as much as to ten Brink that he nowhere gives any connected account of why he reads in the way he does. Southworth is as far from giving an airing to any of the basic questions as his opponents in the establishment. Southworth's real distinction is that he has come to realize that mathematical demonstration is not possible in this subject; he has abandoned the word-counts he started with and appealed instead for agreement about how the verse of these poets moves—the typical procedure of literary criticism. But as a critic Southworth leaves something to be desired, both theoretically and practically. His basic idea that 'the rhythms of poetry are based on the rhythms of prose'[1] is in almost equal measure stimulating and crude because he never asks *how* they are founded and what difference the foundation makes; and he is inclined to make lists of poets as if they are all the same sort of evidence: 'The scholar whose ear has become attuned to the music of modern rhythms as manifested in the work of Eliot, Pound, Williams, Stevens, Ransom, Marianne Moore, Auden, Spender and Thomas...'[2] It is true that some acquaintance with modern poetry would have helped the establishment tradition to escape its damaging stiffness, but I also want to object that if my ear is attuned to Eliot it may well be put out of tune by Dylan Thomas.

Southworth's books are so bitty and inconsequential that they have been brushed off by the establishment, and Baum, feeling

[1] *Verses of Cadence*, p. 4. [2] *Ibid.*

no need to treat Southworth more seriously than Nott, dismisses him in an appendix of characteristically avuncular tone which begins, 'Appendix 1. The Rhythmical or Four-Beat Heresy. There is a heresy—Professor Southworth would call it a Myth— which holds that Chaucer's five-stress line was not five-stress at all and not iambic...'[1] This naturally does not lead into an argument, the reader's impression being that Southworth is rejected only because of his unorthodoxy. Yet with all his limitations, Professor Southworth has put heavily into his debt all who want to read Chaucer, for he has rescued the subject of Chaucer's rhythms from what he calls (following Raleigh) 'the long sleep of decided opinion'.

And I am happy to report that in recent years Southworth's work has made real inroads on the general acceptance of the orthodox tradition. Scholars are now often less confident than they were ten years since that the last word on Chaucer's metre was said by ten Brink, and this in itself is a great improvement. But no clear alternative has emerged and, for example, in the *Introduction to Chaucer* that best represents intelligent modern opinion, the advice about metre is strangely confused. The basic position is still the old establishment's: 'The basic line of Chaucer's verse in nearly all *The Canterbury Tales* is the same as that of Shakespeare's blank verse or of Pope's heroic couplets: the iambic pentameter or line consisting of five feet.'[2] But Mr Spearing also says: 'But, as in Shakespeare or Pope, great variation is possible within this basic pattern: feet may be reversed, extra unstressed syllables may be added, and the result will be very different from the stiff regularity of the basic line.'[3] What then is it that makes us take the basic line as basic—especially if, being 'stiffly regular', it is bad verse? Still,

---

[1] Baum, *Chaucer's Verse*, p. 117. Cf. 'The first proposition, that the sun is the center and does not revolve about the earth, is foolish, absurd; false in theology and heretical, because expressly contrary to Holy Scripture.

'The second proposition, that the earth revolves about the sun and is not the center, is absurd, false in philosophy, and, from a theological point of view at least, opposed to the true faith.'
—quoted in H. Kesten, *Copernicus and his World*, New York, 1945, p. 316.

[2] M. Hussey, A. C. Spearing and J. Winny, *An Introduction to Chaucer*, Cambridge, 1965, p. 100.

[3] *Ibid.* p. 101. As an example of a stiffly regular basic line we have been offered:

> A Knight ther was and that a worthy man

which it seems to me is only stiffly regular (with heavy stresses on 'was' and 'that') in an insensitive reading.

so far this is reasonably clear as a development of the traditional position. But on the other hand we find this, which follows Southworth: 'Indeed, it is often possible to hear, behind the five foot pattern (borrowed from French or Italian), a different rhythm based on that of Old English alliterative verse, and consisting of two half-lines separated by a slight pause, and each containing two heavily-stressed syllables.'[1] This must raise the crucial question of the effect on reading. If there are these two rhythmic systems, how do they co-operate in the rhythms we actually read? Unfortunately Mr Spearing does not move from the possible to the actual; he doesn't tell us what difference the presence of an alliterative element might make, and so his direct advice about metrical reading hides its confusions behind scholarly hedges:

> In reading Chaucer aloud, it is probably better not to attempt a mechanical division into feet and stressed and unstressed syllables, but simply to follow the natural rhythm of each phrase as it might be spoken, while at the same time keeping in mind the basic × / × / × / × / × / pattern. Like other English poets, Chaucer produces some of his most effective verse by playing off the actual rhythms of speech against the 'ideal' pattern of metrical regularity: the expectation of regularity is built up so that it may be defeated as well as fulfilled.[2]

'Aloud' and 'probably' and 'simply' are various red herrings— alas! our problems are not simple. But if we are to follow the natural rhythm of each phrase as it might be spoken (presumably in modern English) we are begging the question of the difference of verse from speech, how it might affect the phrasing that what we are reading is verse. So it is not clear from this account why we should keep the 'basic pattern' in mind. What will that do for us? It will apparently allow us to play off the actual rhythms of speech against the pattern. But why should we? The 'expectation of regularity' (whose building-up is not shown) must refer not to the pattern but to actual readings: so, if the expectation is defeated, the verse is unmetrical. And what about the alliterative element? Is that just to be kept in mind, too, and if so, what good will that do?

The advice in the series of texts following the *Introduction* is similarly unhelpful: 'It is not now thought that the later works of Chaucer were written in a ten-syllable line from which no variation was permissible. The correct reading of a line of Chaucer is now seen to be more closely related to the correct reading of a compar-

---

[1] *Ibid.*   [2] *Ibid.*

able line of prose with phrasing suited to the rhythms of speech.'[1] But what, in that case, makes Chaucer verse? How are lines of prose comparable with lines of verse? Mr Spearing's confusion is certainly a step forward from ten Brink's certainty, but clearly there is a long way to go.

The English Chaucerians notoriously present similar rhythmic problems. 'Is Lydgate's verse metrical or not?' and 'how should he be read?' are questions that have intrigued generations of scholars and are of less interest to the common reader only because he has first to answer the prior question *why* to read Lydgate. But whereas Chaucer has traditionally been forced into metre, the alternative course is usually taken with the Chaucerians, who are dismissed as unmetrical. 'Hoccleve's metre is poor. So long as he can count ten syllables by his fingers, he is content...He constantly thwarts the natural run of his line by putting stress on a word that shouldn't bear it.'[2] And 'A large portion of this verse... is, e.g. in...Hawes' *Pastime*, sheer doggerel, guiltless of rhythm, and conscious only of an approaching rhyme.'[3] (See also Chapter 3, below.) Here too, however, the opposition has made much progress and in the case of Wyatt (see Chapter 11) may perhaps now be established. Here too though the modern alternatives can be unclear. Mr Mitchell's new book on Hoccleve[4] is admirably free from the Licklider straitjacket but takes this freedom somewhat too easily to mean that all the problems are solved. Concerning the Chaucerians too there are questions that need discussion.

In the body of this book doctrines of establishment and opposition will be considered where necessary: the immediate point is that the establishment and opposition are not so far apart as they would wish to appear. Both fail to ask some necessary questions, and the result for the average scholar or the common reader tends to be confusion about how to read. Tyrwhitt and his followers *and* Nott and *his* followers have always claimed to be putting Chaucer back into his century by reintroducing parts of his English but have in fact always been making Chaucer's metres modern, more

---

[1] A. C. Spearing (ed.), *The Knight's Tale*, Cambridge, 1966, p. 81.

[2] F. J. Furnivall, *Hoccleve's Works*, vol. i, p. xli. E.E.T.S. 1892.

[3] E. P. Hammond, in *English Verse between Chaucer and Surrey*, Durham, N.C. 1927, p. ix.

[4] J. Mitchell, *Thomas Hoccleve, A Study in Early Fifteenth Century English Poetic*, Urbana, Illinois, 1968. See below, p. 192.

like the ones found in modern English poetry. Hence the odd
mixture of familiar metre and strange sound in Wyld *et al.* The
two sides differ, however, as to what they like in modern English
poetry: Baum is for Tennyson and Shelley, Southworth for Blake
and Eliot. If forced to make the choice I would opt for Southworth's poets rather than Baum's, but if it is at all possible
I would prefer Chaucer to be himself. It may be necessary to
argue in the first place from modern English rhythms, but unless
we can reach something different and believe it to be Chaucer
there seems little point in the exercise.

I do not regard as mistaken the traditional belief (missing in
Mr Spearing's paragraph) that a right reading of a poet depends
on a right sense of metrical regularity; and I shall not even try to
deny that that must be, in ways to be explored, a sense of modern
English. But I do wish to show that that right sense of right metre
is a very subtle thing that demands, firstly, more clarity about the
general questions involved than is usually to be found, and
secondly, real literary criticism; for the metres are not, in Mr Sims's
phrase, 'some simple, separate, uncontaminated thing', but an
essential part of particular poems, with whose understanding they
are inseparably connected. There is no way, I shall argue, of
separating an understanding of Chaucer's metres from an appreciation of his poetry. If so it will be a relevant objection to his
authority *on metre* that Professor Baum can be a very insensitive
critic. Agreeing with Edith Sitwell's remark about the 'bucolic
clumsiness of Chaucer's heroic couplets' he writes: 'Compared
with the finesse of cameo detail which is the rewarding achievement of Pope, Chaucer's couplets may be coarse. The tempo of his
narrative, even of his descriptions, seldom leaves time for subtle-
ties. He was not a miniaturist.'[1] A man who believes the portrait
of the Prioress to be written in coarse couplets, or *The Franklin's
Tale* to be unsubtle, or the end of the *Dunciad* to offer only a
finesse of cameo detail, is not qualified to write about the rhythms
of Chaucer or of Pope.

For the most part, in truth, Chaucer's versification is skilful rather than
masterly. He was not so much a virtuoso as a good craftsman, and as he
said in another context *craft is al who so that do it kan* (E 2016). But this
only places him among the great majority of English poets. The excep-

[1] *Chaucer's Verse*, p. 53.

tions are few and such specialists as Tennyson and Swinburne and Robert Bridges are usually regarded with suspicion.[1]

I shall not be arguing that Chaucer is a metrical specialist, whatever that may be, but that he is more than a good craftsman (a phrase which fits Lydgate better). Chaucer is not a metrical specialist but an artist, and the way to refute Baum is to show that words obey Chaucer's call, that the rhythms are one mark of his having come into his strength.

So the question whether the best way to read Chaucer is to begin with a clear concept of his long line as a succession of five iambs, to be read with medieval sounds, is an open one; so is the question whether Chaucer should be read more or less like prose. These are among the questions which if we are to make progress in this study we must think about with whatever clarity we can muster.

It does seem to me that the writers on our subject have failed to ask some necessary questions and have unwarrantably assumed the answers to others, and that this has prevented them from giving us as much help in reading as they should have done. The questions fall into groups which I shall discuss in the following chapters. The first group is: What can we know of Middle English? What need we know to read Chaucer? And how do we acquire the necessary knowledge? The second: Is there any point in distinguishing rhythm and metre? Has metre a function—can it tell us how to read? How do particular lines embody a metrical form and what is following a rule here? And the final group: Is there a gap between Chaucer and his disciples, or between Chaucer and us? A question underlying all these is: What certainty can we hope for here?

I am far from claiming that any answers I give to these questions will be absolutely true; on the contrary my main contribution will be the conviction that we are in the world of literary criticism where the best one can hope for is to say (in Dr Leavis's formula) 'This is so, isn't it?' hoping for a reply of the form 'Yes, but...' If it can be established that this, rather than any descriptive science, is the right mode of discourse, that will be a worthwhile advance, an advance that will necessarily show at the same time that no account of Chaucer's rhythms can convince unless by inspiring the reader to agree that this is what Chaucer ought to be like to read.

[1] *Ibid.* p. 111.

17

It has been necessary in the course of the work to tackle some formidable technical problems, and some technical vocabulary has made its way in, unbidden: but it goes with my case that the common reader is the best judge of the subject and that the most relevant expertise is that of reading English poetry. So, in the hope of taking a common reader or two with me, I have kept specialized terminology to a minimum.

Part One: Criteria

I

What do you need to Know to read Chaucer?

Before page one of the editions of Chaucer commended by schools and universities there are always some pages of editorial matter giving the reader the linguistic information the editor thinks he must possess before he can read the poet. This prefatory course of instruction in Chaucer's language usually consists of some grammar, tables of the vowel-sounds of fourteenth-century English, and diagrams or other illustrations of Chaucer's chief metres. Metres will be the concern of the rest of this work: it will be convenient to take first the question whether we must read Chaucer with the vowel-sounds of his century rather than our own. This is always assumed by scholars.

'The brief grammatical outline that follows', says Professor Robinson in the best one-volume edition of Chaucer, 'is intended to supply the reader or student with such knowledge of Chaucer's sounds and inflections as is necessary for the intelligent reading of the verse.'[1] This necessary information appears under the heading 'Language and Meter' and introduces 'Pronunciation', mainly a table of vowel-sounds followed by an account of inflections, which leads to a section on 'Versification'. Similarly ten Brink's book (called in English translation *The Language and Metre of Chaucer*) gives comparable facts in more detail, presumably for the same purpose of providing the information without which the poet cannot be read. S. E. Moore writes, 'All teachers desire that their students shall learn to read Chaucer aloud...with a fair degree of approximation to Chaucer's own pronunciation.'[2] To satisfy this desire of all teachers he too gives information about vowel-sounds. W. W. Skeat takes it for granted, both in his monumental seven-

---

[1] *Ed. cit.* p. xxx.
[2] S. E. Moore, *Historical Outlines of English Phonology and Morphology*, 2nd edition, Ann Arbor, 1929, p. v.

volume edition and in his still useful Oxford Standard Authors text, that we shall read Chaucer with fourteenth-century vowel-sounds, and says of his table in the latter, 'By help of these symbols it is possible to explain the meaning of the M.E. symbols employed by the scribes in Chaucer's Tales'.[1] A. C. Baugh sums up the editorial case for insisting on this information: 'But in addition to [sic] understanding the language, the student should learn to read Chaucer's poetry with a reasonable approximation to fourteenth-century pronunciation. This is essential not only to an appreciation of the music of Chaucer's lines, but to the rhythm of the verse and the correctness of many lines.'[2]

In all these and numerous others not quoted the assumption is that to read Chaucer well we must read him in his own English and that we shall read in the English of the fourteenth century by reproducing its vowel-sounds. Produce the sounds and understand them and you will be reading the language—this idea is so deeply rooted in the minds of medievalists, and looks so full of common-sense, that it ought to be worthwhile if once in a century or so somebody asks if it is true. For after all, many people read Chaucer before the development of historical phonology, and many since do not obey the editorial instructions: are we to say that they are necessarily missing something vital?

The insistence on the old vowels tends, I think, to lead away from Chaucer's poetry rather than into it, and I shall try to say why. It is also true that this way of proceeding treats Chaucer's language as dead. You begin a dead language by being introduced to the local tradition of its sounds which, unlike the sounds of a living language, cannot be modified by a visit to native speakers of the language. Whether Chaucer must or ought to be treated as a writer in a dead language is at least worth asking.

In the first place, if we need to know the sounds of fourteenth-century English before reading Chaucer, we can never read Chaucer, because the necessary knowledge cannot now be obtained.

This statement is not intended as the declaration of a one-man war on historical phonology: the case is not quite the emperor's new clothes nor the walls of Jericho. Ignorance, it is true, is some

---

[1] *The Complete Works of Geoffrey Chaucer*, ed. W. W. Skeat, Oxford, 1912, p. xxiii.

[2] *Chaucer's Major Poetry*, ed. A. C. Baugh, 1964, p. xxiii.

safeguard here; for the ignorant man cannot suffer from the scholar's occupational hazard of forgetting the irreversible pastness of the past, the evanescence of the speech of six hundred years since which has, in the obvious ways, gone for ever. It is true that the professionals sometimes forget that in Middle English we have a written language without a spoken base, except in so far as we speak it now, and that therefore whatever we know of the sounds of Middle English cannot be known with the kind of sureness we easily attain with any living language. It is even true that scholars can be found *preferring* to work on the corpus of a dead language because it can be known finally—with the finality of death—and that in their analytical enthusiasm they can overlook the incompleteness of their final knowledge.

Nothing prevents the linguist from attempting a description of the Latin of Cicero or the Old English of Alfred. His task will be more complex, in such a case, because he will have to discover a system of phonemes behind the writing which reflects it only to an imperfect degree. On the other hand his work may be facilitated by the fact that the extant works of Cicero or Alfred form a well-defined whole which can easily be submitted to statistical procedures, enabling us to draw precise conclusions... These conditions of work present such advantages that one is tempted to recreate them in dealing with a contemporary language, by setting up a 'corpus', that is to say a collection of utterances recorded on tape or taken down from dictation. Once this collection has been made, it is regarded as inviolable...[1]

And it is possible to lose sight of the obvious fact that 'Here we are more or less "predicting" backwards (although the prediction can never be verified); and for the most part can only give a fairly loose and probabilistic description. The further we go back the more speculative the description will become.'[2] S. E. Moore thought, on the contrary, that the further we go back into the past the surer we are, and says that 'it is generally possible to determine [*sic*] the Middle English pronunciation of a *native* English word from a knowledge of its pronunciation in Old English'.[3] Skeat, who also offers to demonstrate Middle English sounds by way of Anglo-Saxon, tries to determine the Middle English vowels in a related way by saying (forgetting that each language has its own sound-system) that they 'were nearly as in French and [*sic*] Italian. They

---

[1] A. Martinet, *Elements of General Linguistics*, 1964, p. 39.
[2] R. M. W. Dixon, *What is Language?* 1965, p. 13.
[3] Moore, *op. cit.* p. 98.

can be denoted by phonetic *invariable* symbols'.[1] He also calmly remarks, 'the pronunciation of M.E. and of Anglo-French vowels did not materially differ'.[2] But how on earth can he have known whether these differences were 'material' or not? Even a modern authority like Professor Gimson can get into an occasional muddle about how much we really know: 'The further back we go into history the scantier the evidence of spoken forms becomes. Our conclusions will, therefore, be based on information mostly of an indirect kind; yet such is the agreement generally amongst the various types of evidence that the broad lines of sound change can be conjectured with reasonable certainty.'[3] The category of certain conjecture, certainly an odd one, betrays an uneasiness about our knowledge. It is true, finally, that if historical phonology is a science, as its practitioners like to call it, it is the unique instance of a science that could *conceivably*, and by its own rules, be quite wrong.

But, I repeat, I am not trying to attack historical phonology: what historical phonology *can* tell us of the sounds of the past has been amassed and codified with the thoroughness traditional to the discipline. And what we *know*—the probabilities it would be perverse to deny—are the 'broad lines of sound change', deduced from two heads of evidence, comparison of the sounds of living languages so as to reconstruct their history, and the spellings of manuscripts. The first is excellent evidence but can, of course, give results of only very approximate accuracy. The second, which to anyone who has not considered the problems looks so obviously final, is useful when combined with the other evidence but can of itself tell us nothing whatever. It may be worth reminding the reader that marks on paper without a key give no information about sound. 'The history of English spelling is one thing and the history of English pronunciation quite another.'[4] So when Gimson

[1] *The Complete Works of Geoffrey Chaucer*, ed. W. W. Skeat, 2nd edition, Oxford, 1899, vol. VI, p. xxv.

[2] *Ibid.* p. xxx.

[3] A. C. Gimson, *An Introduction to the Pronunciation of English*, 1962, p. 72. Both Gimson and Dixon assume that our knowledge of past sounds becomes less● certain in direct proportion to the lapse of time, which is an oversimplification.

[4] H. C. Wyld, *A Short History of English*, 1914, p. 94. The need to distinguish spelling- from sound-change, first argued by August Friedrich Pott and used against A. J. Ellis by Payne (cf. *Verses of Cadence*, Chapter 2), is still not universally recognized. It would be helpful if scholars would write of spelling-change, rather than sound-change, when that is what they mean.

writes 'Spelling forms can also help us to deduce the pronunciation of the ME period...Generally speaking, it may be said that the letters still had their Latin values and that those letters which were written were meant to be sounded'[1] he is going beyond what we know. *If* we know the Latin values of letters and if (which seems unlikely) English used the same sounds, then we can read the sounds of Middle English. But the spellings alone will not remove the 'if's.

What we can know of the sounds of Chaucer's language, the broad sounds given by historical phonology, is not the knowledge we need for reading or speaking, that is, not knowledge of the language. An essential part of knowing the sounds of a language is knowing where one sound stops and another starts, which phonetically differentiable sounds count as the same phoneme, or what sounds one can and cannot get away with without sounding strange. It is just this knowledge, the limits of the vowels in use, that historical phonology cannot give us but which we certainly need if we are to use the fourteenth-century vowel system. The editions confuse the broad probabilities of historical phonology with the kinds of sound languages really use. (The sounds offered by Skeat's edition are so broad as to make the difference between the sounds of French and Italian immaterial.)

It may be that Wyld's recording would not have seemed ridiculous to Chaucer except in style (though there are other possibilities) but as far as probabilities go—which is here not very far—it seems likely that modern renderings of medieval vowels would have seemed to Chaucer odd or flat or unidiomatic, without being positively wrong. This seems a small reward for abandoning one's own language.

Secondly, even if one grants the accuracy and necessity of the information about vowels given by editions of Chaucer, it would still be very far from knowledge sufficient to allow us to read Middle English. Since the development of modern linguistics it is hardly venturesome to remark that there is much more to the sound of a language than its vowels and consonants. There are also its conventional patterns of pitch and stress—the 'prosodies' or rhythms—without which there is no language. One can imagine whole conversations in which one participant relies wholly on intonation and stress:

[1] Gimson, *op. cit.* p. 74.

A. Mrs Jones is dead.
B. Hm? [the voice rising by about a semi-tone
A. Mrs Jones is dead.
B. Hm? [surprised: a rise of a ninth
A. They say she left half a million.
B. Hm! [up an octave and down again
A. It all went to the Dogs' Home.
B. Hm! [*staccato* on one note
A. But then she always was a bit batty.
B. Hm-hm. [drops a third between *hm*'s

Each of these *hm*'s is different, but beyond the indications of ' ? ' or ' ! ' there is no ordinary typographical way of differentiating them; the knowledge of how to say them is assumed, not written; but, for instance, if a good novelist writes 'hm' we shall read the right one. The vowel-sounds of these *hm*'s don't matter, and some can equally well appear as a whistle. (My second and third examples combine to form the wolf-whistle.) In sentences intonation differentiates meaning, too.

She was wearing her old blue coat.[1]

Unless for some private reason you are reading perversely you have taken this sentence as a plain statement, with the stresses, pauses and intonations that make it so. But equally, with the addition of a punctuation mark to indicate a change of tune, the same words can be read as a question:

She was wearing her old blue coat?

The different intonation conveys the different meaning. Various other questions can be asked by varying stress and intonation, and the different tones can be indicated (not recorded) in print by the use of *italics*:

She was wearing her old blue coat?
She was wearing *her* old blue coat?
She *was* wearing her old blue coat?
She was *wearing* her old blue coat?

and so on. The variations are numerous and conventional, but not spelled out by the letters, outside learned works of phonetics. Nobody can get these tunes from writing, but nobody can use well these bits of English without knowing the tunes. Intonation is of obvious importance for speaking or reading a language.

---

[1] I got this sentence some years ago from Mr J. L. M. Trim's interesting Cambridge lectures, where he played different games with it.

There is simply no way of knowing, in any scientific sense, how English intonation has changed since Chaucer's time. The few scholars who realize the importance of this for our study take one of two alternatives. Either they merely record the fact and ignore it, as when Baum says 'We assume a knowledge of the individual vowel and consonant sounds, but of the structural patterns of his [Chaucer's] spoken language...we know very little',[1] or they assume that things haven't changed much, as when Mr John Thompson writes: 'The reader will note here that I proceed as though the sixteenth century speaker had much the same voice as ours. The sounds of the language have changed, somewhat, but in the absence of evidence to the contrary, I assume that the basic structure of the language, in the formation of phrases by sound-patterns, was the same.'[2] Either way out leaves us with a diminished confidence that we can read Chaucer as he was read in his own time.

But thirdly, and most important, even if we could reproduce fourteenth-century sounds and rhythms so as to read Chaucer in a way that would not have seemed strange to him, it would still not follow that by doing so we should now be reading in Chaucer's language, because those sounds were for him the sounds of English, whereas for us they are something quite different. An example may make clearer this rather difficult but essential point.

Shakespeare too used different sounds from ours, and we can know what they were both more certainly and more accurately than we can know Chaucer's.[3] But Shakespeare is hardly ever performed with the sounds of his own time. We almost always leave him his seventeenth-century costume but modernize him at this much more basic level. The reason for doing so seems to me a very good one; it is that the performance of Shakespeare in the original sounds is a way of destroying, not preserving, the life of his language. Daniel Jones's record of a bit of *The Tempest* in con-temporary sounds[4] does not speak for us the language of Shake-speare by reproducing its sounds, because the sounds are those of a part of our own English, but an inappropriate part. Shakespeare's sounds belong to a countrified and archaic English in which his plays cannot now be performed; it would be absurd to declaim

---

[1] *Chaucer's Verse*, p. 108.
[2] J. Thompson, *The Founding of English Metre*, 1961, p. 16.
[3] For the evidence for this statement see E. J. Dobson, *English Pronunciation 1500–1700*, 2nd edition, Oxford, 1968.
[4] 'Pronunciation of Early XVIIth Century English', Linguaphone.

To be or not to be, thaat is the quehstion,
Whehther 'tis noobler in the mooind to zoofer
The slengs and aarows of aowtrayjuice vortoon...

But for Shakespeare these were the sounds of his English. He heard them in the haunts of the gentry as well as in the street: they were naturally the sounds in which his plays were performed. The meaning of language depends on the whole situation of its use, and to reproduce Shakespeare's meaning in his own sounds would be to be alive in Shakespeare's England, which is impossible.

There is no separating the sounds of a language from the rest of it (sound is an aspect of language not *vice versa*, *pace* one school of linguists). The linguist can detach and study sounds in isolation from the rest of language only in so far as he ceases to be a linguist: when the sounds are studied apart from their language the discipline is not linguistics but physics. So the great wish of the historical phonologists, to make our knowledge of the sounds of old language external and demonstrable, is at the same time a retreat from the study of language itself. Language is only understood from the inside. It may well be that the merest fourteenth-century London parrot could make Chaucer's sounds better than we can; but understanding a language is following the meaning of its sounds, and conversely the sounds in which we understand a language are, for us, the sounds of that language.

The sounds of Shakespeare's poetry are the ones in which the poetry has as much of its full meaning as possible. For us the sounds of Shakespeare are the sounds of modern English; for listeners and readers five hundred years hence they will be (in the unlikely event of the survival of English civilization) the sounds of *their* English.

This is only to say that knowledge of a language must be internal. There is no way of freeing linguistic knowledge from this situation. Knowledge of fourteenth-century English as a language can never be more 'objective' than knowledge of modern English; if this seems to be an insistence on the obvious, the necessity will become more apparent as the work progresses.

So it could be that by reproducing Chaucer's original sounds we are distracting attention from the life of his language. And the question whether to opt for fourteenth-century sound, quaintness and, at best, a kind of historical accuracy, is the same as the question whether Middle English is a dead language. There is an

English literature only as far as there is a group of authors who are normally read in standard English, though not necessarily otherwise connected. Shakespeare is read in modern standard English; on the other hand the Anglo-Saxon poets cannot be read in modern English because their language is too decisively different. The dividing line between what can belong to modern English and what can't falls, then, somewhere between Shakespeare and *The Battle of Maldon*, but precisely where may be to some extent as much a matter of choice as of observation. (In any case such a line could hardly be very definite.) It is possible to treat Chaucer as belonging, like *Beowulf*, to a dead language; but it might also be possible to treat him as, like Shakespeare, one of our writers, belonging to our literature; and my case will be that where we have the choice it is overwhelmingly better to opt for the living.

The performance of Shakespeare in modern English pronunciation shows that, however things have changed, he still belongs to our language. The only alternative to treating Chaucer's English as a dead language, beginning by mastering a sound-system for it and by learning its grammar and metres, and perhaps by translating passages into English, must be to keep his poetry alive in a comparable way by performing it as part of our own language. And if Chaucer's English is a variety of our language we can begin reading it by simply opening the book, without editorial guidance.

So I offer a first piece of advice to the reader of Chaucer: do not be persuaded by the authority of the scholars into using archaic sounds unless you can make them natural and feel at home in them.

This advice is opposed to that of J. M. Manly. Manly is alone among the editors of Chaucer in treating the question of his sounds in what seems to me the right way, realizing that it has to do with tone and style. Unfortunately his argument is simply mistaken.

The grammar of past forms of speech we can easily determine and discuss; it appears in the writings. But the pronunciation has disappeared; we can ascertain it only with great labor and difficulty, and even then only approximately. Still it is astonishing how much we can find out with patience and ingenuity, and we are getting steadily nearer to the reality. If Chaucer could hear a good student read his poetry, the pronunciation would probably seem like that of a foreigner, but he would, we hope, be able to understand what he heard. At any rate, to read his poetry with the pronunciation established by scholars makes possible the maintenance of a uniform tone and atmosphere, whereas the pronunciation of it as modern English, with an occasional extra syllable, makes it sound like the babbling of a child, or like a rustic dialect.[1]

I will not make the possible objections to the opening of this paragraph, with which I am in broad agreement. My objection is to the stylistic judgements at the end: this is literary criticism— Manly is talking the right language—but it is bad literary criticism. Why should a modified modern English sound rustic, which the old English sounds *certainly* do? But more important, why should one aim at a uniform tone for Chaucer? On the contrary, uniformity of tone is one of the most cripplingly disadvantageous results of using the old sounds. If a uniformly antique tone comes first how can the astonishingly rich range of Chaucer's tones be preserved? Is not Manly's ambition to make Chaucer decorous and reduce the Knight, the Reeve and the Pardoner to the same level? Whatever the difficulties of reading Chaucer in modern English, they are worthwhile if uniformity of tone is avoided.

This is not to say the difficulties are not real. Many of Chaucer's words have disappeared, many of his rhymes do not now rhyme, and to make his verse metrical we have to pronounce vowels that would now be silent and change the modern stressings of words. But this is true to a lesser degree with Shakespeare also. (Think of the dissyllabic *-ion* ending or names like Mílan.) A good actor will naturalize the old parts of Shakespeare in modern English; and though this may not always be possible with Chaucer it might be the thing to aim at.

But it is not my intention to persuade anyone to abandon any particular sound-system for Chaucer, provided only that he feels at home with it; I only wish to show that no particular system has any relevant scientific authority and that the one traditionally taught has the great disadvantage of keeping bad company, in that it is used by people whose prime concern is not the life of the poetry.

Reading medieval poetry has much in common with performing medieval music. In both cases we begin with black marks on a page, whose meaning may be in dispute, and in both cases experts can understandably be tempted into seeing as the most important questions those concerning what sounds, whether of the human

[1] *The Canterbury Tales*, ed. J. M. Manly, n.d. p. 89.

voice or of instruments, are the right interpretation of the marks. But a medieval score played with the most authentic instruments is not necessarily music, and the noise made is not necessarily a re-creation of the work of art the score records. A score can only be shown to be a notation of music if the music is really performed. A good performance convinces the listener that the work is being allowed to be itself: at the same time performance makes it belong to music and to be understood, so to speak, in the language of music. For this the authenticity represented by shawms, rebekkes and so on is secondary to the authenticity of imaginative sympathy with the piece.

And yet...the sounds of a language do belong so closely, perhaps so indissolubly, to that language: we feel that the connection between French and the sounds of French is more than arbitrary, that if French happened to use the sounds of German it would be a quite different language. (Cf. J. R. Firth's famous dictum that it is part of the meaning of a Frenchman to sound like a Frenchman, and Leo Spitzer's essay 'Linguistics and Literary History'.[1]) Burns loses very much in any English accent. Here, of course, we are on the verge of one of the most chasmal problems in linguistics and philosophy: how meanings get attached to particular sounds. But turning back from the void we can at least say that we know *what* the English lose of Burns: we can know it by visiting Scotland. But Chaucer's sounds and Shakespeare's sounds are not now fully alive anywhere; we only have their descendants. We must have lost a lot of Shakespeare. But in contrast with Burns we cannot get it back by recreating Shakespeare's sounds: that is to lose also those more important parts of Shakespeare's language that are still alive. After all it is still possible to read Shakespeare or Herbert with some enjoyment and understanding as an English author. And foremost among the parts of their language we can still have are the rhythms. The point of the present work will be, of course, to say something similar of Chaucer.[2]

[1] Leo Spitzer, *Linguistics and Literary History*, Princeton, 1948.
[2] So too vowel-sounds do matter in poetry.

> Sweet day, so cool, so calm, so bright,
> The bridal of the earth and sky,
> The dew shall weep thy fall tonight,
> For thou must die

—part of the way Herbert's verse works, and an important part, is its play with *d*

31

But having asserted that we can have no knowledge of the intonations of Shakespeare's or Chaucer's English even in the way that we can have a reliable 'broad transcription' of their vowel-sounds, am I not now flatly contradicting the assertion? I hope not; I hope to show that we can develop all necessary knowledge of Chaucer's rhythms. But it will not be the same kind of knowledge as physical knowledge of vowel-sounds and will not be verifiable in the same ways: linguistic knowledge must here be the same as the capacity to read poetry, and to show that we can know Chaucer's rhythms will be the same as showing that Chaucer can still be read in English. (If that looks obscure it will be a later task to make it plain.)

For the alternative to seeing Middle English as a dead language is to explore it as an unfamiliar province of modern English. If we begin in modern English that will mean, as to pronunciation, beginning with modern vowels and modern rhythms. How then will it be Chaucer we are reading if we are reading neither the vowels nor the rhythms he intended? At first we shall be reading modern meanings into his words too, which is even worse. But the attempt to treat Chaucer as part of our English is bound to lead immediately to stumbles: *his* English, his difference from ours, begins to trip us at once, and continues to do so until we are thoroughly familiar with him—and, depending on how it goes, this might be a sign both that Chaucer belongs to us and that he is different, himself, which is as it should be. This is like (though not in every way like) an English child meeting a Scottish child for the first time. The different language can be, more or less, understood, it isn't foreign, but sounds and words are both strange. If the children go on meeting for a year they may get quite used to the difference and even begin picking up turns of phrase from each other. (We can quote Chaucer.) Reading Chaucer is in a different way like picking up a new technical jargon—different because we don't use Chaucer in the same way but like in that learning a technical vocabulary is not so much memorizing a list

plus vowel: *day, bridal, dew, die*. Perceiving the progress of these sounds in the rhythm of these lines is a great part of understanding the verse. But surprisingly enough the particular vowels used do not matter very much. English 'accents' are largely differentiated by their vowel-sounds, but this poem would make its point very similarly in any one of them. Perhaps Cockney has a certain advantage over Herbert's own sounds in that it would make *day* very similar to *die*. But the poem also works in modern standard English. Any of these sets of vowels is certainly different from the one Herbert used.

32

of its terms as beginning with one's own language, tripping over strange uses, gradually becoming familiar with what the strangenesses are doing, then linking them to make the new system an extension of the original language.

If we can acclimatize Chaucer in modern English it is by extending modern English to allow the life of Chaucer's different language. This applies at all linguistic levels.

A 1   Whan that Aprill with his shoures soote...

This is more or less English—certainly not any other language, anyway—but noticing the strangenesses is simultaneous with identifying it as English: it is only our language in so far as it is not quite ours. There are odd spellings, and we may not realize that 'soote' is the same as 'sweet'. 'Whan that' is not our syntax and we may misunderstand it at first. 'Aprill' may look feminine, but takes a masculine pronoun where we would anyway have 'its'. And so on. But for all that, a native English speaker is likely to grasp the sense and movement of the line with not much more difficulty than he grasps the lines of, say, Hugh MacDiarmid or W. B. Yeats.

The way into Chaucer is a kind of familiarization which makes us, for example, get used to ordinary words in new senses. *Truth* is a familiar English word, and, knowing only how it is used at present, one can make some preliminary sense of its meanings in Chaucer. But it is only by getting to know Chaucer well, from the inside, that one understands his use of the word. F. N. Robinson's glossary says: '*Trouthe*, truth; troth, promise; fidelity', which is better than some attempts and shows that the word had a different range in the fourteenth century from now: we have no word to equal all those senses. But to be at home with Chaucer's range of uses one goes on reading his poetry. To take only the two key places for *trouthe* we find the moral ballade of the same name, and *The Franklin's Tale*. *Trouthe* shows that the quality is more than the absence of lies or of troth-breaking; it is seen in the refrain line as a positive, saving virtue:

And trouthe shal delivere, it is no drede.

In *The Franklin's Tale* the word gets defined in the best way of all, by being attached to the story, so that following the story and understanding the word fall together. Trouthe is what saves the

marriage of Dorigen and Arveragus when it is put to the test.
When they agree to keep *trouthe* (F 1479 Trouthe is the hyeste
thyng that man may kepe) a delivering power is released into the
story, and the characters begin to vie with each other in *gentilesse*,
another word whose meaning we learn in similar ways. Knowing
what Chaucer means by *trouthe* we are then equipped to modify the
knowledge by seeing what *Sir Gawain and the Green Knight* and
Piers Plowman do with the word.

So we read and think about the places in Chaucer that depend
on understanding words like *trouthe* and *gentilesse* and in the end
we may begin to understand them. Then we can read them without
every time noticing (or, worse, failing to notice) their difference
from modern English. When they cease to be unfamiliar or quaint
we have extended our language to include them.

But it is our language we extend: it is still our own language
because the sense we make of the parts of Chaucer that are different
depends on our finding ourselves naturally at home with the many
parts that are the same. It is still possible to find oneself at home in
Middle English, taking tone and movement quite naturally.

For example, *Piers Plowman* is even further from us than Chaucer,
partly for metrical reasons; yet it is possible merely by reading the
poem to make some necessarily fine perceptions of tone, just as if
it were a poem in modern English. In Passus VI of the B-text Piers,
in a famous passage, calls in Hunger to bring the wasters to heel.
The passage works first by the forcefulness, surely apparent to
any reader, of the savage onset of Hunger:[1]

173   ' Now by the peril of my soule ' quod Pieres · ' I shal apeyre ʒow alle '
     And houped after Hunger · that herd hym atte firste
     ' A-wreke me of thise wastoures ' quod he · · ' that this worlde schendeth '
      Hunger in haste tho · hent Wastour bi the mawe
     And wronge him so bi the wombe · that bothe his eyen wattered
     He buffeted the Britoner · aboute the chekes
     That he loked like a lanterne · al his lyf after
     He bette hem so bothe · he barste nere here guttes

But thereafter the passage begins to depend on changes of tone,
sometimes rapid and subtle, but not beyond the apprehension of
the modern reader. The first change comes when Piers's temper
subsides:

[1] *Piers Plowman* is quoted from the edition of W. W. Skeat, 2 vols., Oxford,
1886.

183 'Suffre hem lyue' he seyde · 'and lete hem ete with hogges
Or elles benes and bren · ybaken togideres
Or elles melke and mene ale' · thus preyed Pieres for hem

We take there the change to a wry kind of pity for the wasters. But Piers does not rest here: he goes further and now tries to persuade Hunger to go away again 'into his own erde', but asks Hunger to tell him, before he goes, how to 'amaistrien' the 'beggeres and bidderes'—without, he implies, having to starve them to death. But Hunger can of course only offer himself as the remedy, and his domineering preaching style is now unmistakable:

215 'Here now' quod Hunger · 'and holde it for a wisdome
Bolde beggeres and bigge · that mowe her bred biswynke
With houndes bred and hors bred · holde vp her hertis'

But Langland makes the point even clearer, for in answer to Piers's further request for medical information, Hunger becomes outrageous:

255 'Зet I prey зow' quod Pieres · 'par charite and зe kunne
Eny leef of lechecraft · lere it me my dere
For somme of my seruauntz · and my self bothe
Of al a wyke worche nouзt · so owre wombe aketh'
'I wote wel' quod Hunger · 'what sykenesse зow eyleth
Зe han maunged ouer moche · and that maketh зow grone'

Here the savage comedy is plain: the people thus addressed are starving, and the violence of starvation has been well created at the beginning of the episode. But Hunger's cruel remedy has its comic side, brought out by his over-confidence, which allows him to go off into an attack on one of the author's pet hates, doctors who are more dangerous than diseases. So Piers, having failed to get rid of Hunger by direct request, tries flattery.

277 'By seynt Poule' quod Pieres · 'thise aren profitable wordis
Wende now Hunger whan thow wolt · that wel be thow euere
For this is a louely lessoun · lorde it the forзelde'

Piers's thanks are insincere. This can be said flatly because the language can convey the insincere tone, the gingerly politeness with the real wish 'wende now' all wrapped up in the thanks. But Hunger retorts in his usual bold way,

280 'Byhote god' quod Hunger · 'hennes ne wil I wende
Til I haue dyned bi this day · and ydronke bothe'

And so on.

To read in this way, to make sense of the passage, it is not necessary to introduce any rhythms not found in modern English. I have allowed the passage to express its changes of tone by taking the phrase-lengths indicated by the punctuation and shaping the phrases as I would in modern English. This is not, of course, a demonstration that Langland would have shaped the phrases in the same way. But there is at least no impediment in his language to a modern rhythmic shaping: on the contrary the modern rhythms it suggests are lively and precise. The rhythm, unlike the spelling and diction and syntax, is not one of the things that trip us. Perhaps it ought (and we must return to the question in the next chapter) but it doesn't.

At any rate it may now begin to be clear why if I am to show that Chaucer belongs with the English poets the present study must be of his rhythms. *If* the continuity of the language is such that the rhythms we read now are the ones Chaucer or Langland would have used to express their meaning, rhythms, rather than sounds, are the way into their language. We must ask whether we naturally make good sense of Chaucer by reading him with the rhythms of our own language. If so there will be no need to begin with information about sounds, metres or even words; there will be no difference in kind between reading Chaucer and reading any other English poet. If the poet's language is English, the literate English speaker has all the information he needs to begin reading.

But unless Middle English can differentiate itself from modern English, including, it may be, in its rhythms, we can have no real confidence that we are not translating it. If I insist that Middle English must be an extension of our own language, that can only be a precondition for asking how it can have its own life today and take us, in an extension of our own language, into its different world.

This cannot be done by offering the beginning student clear concepts of metre (see next chapter) or charts of strange noises: we have to work from within our knowledge of English. The procedure is only possible if we assume, in Mr Thompson's already quoted words, that the basic structure of the language was the same. The grounds for supposing the assumption to be true, and that Chaucer's language is basically ours, is that the assumption works by allowing us to read Chaucer. The important thing is to realize that 'it works' is the demonstration appropriate to this subject.

2

Rhythm and Metre

Even if metre can ever tell us how to read a poet it cannot do so quite in the way the Tyrwhitt tradition assumes; it cannot provide 'the beginning student' (Dr E. W. Stone, above, p. 8) with a clear concept of Chaucer's metre in advance of any acquaintance with his verse. It is necessary to show why this is so. The editions will usually give us a diagram, e.g.

ᴗ / | ᴗ / | ᴗ / | ᴗ / | ᴗ / (ᴗ)

and tell us to apply it to Chaucer (or, even less usefully, assume the diagram and tell us not to apply it to Chaucer; Spearing, above, p. 14). If we assume, naturally enough unless warned, that 'ᴗ' and '/' represent some fixed or absolute quantity of stress, the results on reading can be disastrous. For example, after stating that 'most of Chaucer's lines, if read naturally and with a proper regard for grammatical endings, have an obvious rhythm',[1] and warning us that 'the metrical accents varied in strength, unimportant words receiving only a secondary stress',[2] F. N. Robinson prints the lines about the Clerk from the *General Prologue* like this:

> / / / / /
> A CLERK ther was of Oxenford also,
>
> / / / ‖ / /
> That unto logyk hadde longe ygo.
>
> / ‖ / / / / ‖
> As leene was his hors as is a rake,
>
> / / / / ‖
> And he nas nat right fat, I undertake,
>
> / / ‖ / / /
> But looked holwe, and therto sobrely.
>
> / / / / /
> Ful thredbare was his overeste courtepy;
>
> / / / / ‖
> For he hadde geten hym yet no benefice,
>
> / / / / ‖
> Ne was so worldly for to have office...[3]

---

[1] Robinson, *ed. cit.* p. xxxv.   [2] *Ibid.* p. xxxvi.

[3] *Ibid.* e‖ = sounded -e, ẹ = unsounded -e.

37

But what is this supposed to do for us? Robinson does not say, and his warning that some stresses are 'secondary' (without saying which) will hardly be enough to prevent the reader trying to follow his marks from pulling the stresses towards equality with each other. He uses equal marks, after all, and doesn't explain them: if they are not meant to indicate roughly equal stresses it is not easy to see what they are meant to do. And in that case there are no rules about how rough 'roughly' should be. A. C. Baugh in the rival text takes a more cavalier line with the declaration that 'There is no need to explain the elementary principles of prosody. All of Chaucer's verse is iambic in movement ($\smile$ ´), most of it with either four or five stresses to the line.'[1] (Examples follow.) Many bad readings result from attempts to understand and follow editorial advice by applying the diagram of iambic pentameter to Chaucer's verse. This chapter tries to explain why such advice is a hindrance rather than a help, and this gives an opportunity of asking what is meant by the words *rhythm* and *metre*. The question will not, of course, be answered; but later investigations may look clearer in the light of the discussion.

I

Rhythms join sounds in language in ways comparable to those in which grammar and syntax join words. Rhythm is the connecter of sounds in both speech and music: properly speaking the rhythm of music is the phrasing, the relation of notes to each other by variations of stress and length as well as of pitch. One of the functions of this relating to each other of sounds in speech is to express syntax, as I shall show.

In English speech, rhythm works by the patterning of sound around certain stressed sounds; stress is then the principal agent of speech-rhythms, and affects all levels of language from emotional expressiveness to grammar and syntax. Stress, or emphasis, is not the same as loudness,[2] a whisper can be stressed; but a stressed sound always gives the impression to the listener of receiving more emphasis—whether because of its different length,

---

[1] *Chaucer's Major Poetry*, ed. Baugh, p. xl.

[2] It is necessary to say so because the very influential group of linguists led by Professors Trager and Smith want to say that degrees of speech-stress are simply degrees of loudness, on a more or less fixed scale.

pitch, loudness, chest-impulse or other distinction—than the other sounds in its immediate context.

I shall call the unit of rhythm in English speech 'the phrase'. The vagueness of this term is a great advantage and will save us from losing ourselves in the fascinating disputes about chest-pulses and tone-groups that enliven contemporary linguistics. A phrase has one main stress, perceptibly greater than any other stress in the phrase, and 'balanced' (as I shall call it) against the rhythms of preceding and succeeding phrases. A phrase may be of one or more syllables.

$$\acute{\text{Cat}}$$

The word spoken in isolation has one main stress. So has

$$\acute{\text{Pussy}}$$

spoken alone. In isolation the rhythm of this word depends on its second vowel having less stress than its first. If the two words are combined we still have only one phrase, viz.

$$\overset{/\quad\cup\quad\backslash}{\text{Pussy-cat}}$$

Here one part capable of having a phrase-stress is subordinated to another capable of having a phrase-stress, so that 'cat' receives more stress than '-sy' but less than 'pus-'. If there is more than one phrase in an utterance, each will have its own stress-pattern, and the phrases will balance and affect one another in a further pattern:

$$\overset{\cup\ \cup\ \backslash\quad/\quad\cup\ /\ \cup\ \backslash}{\text{I have just seen / a pussy cat}}$$

Linguists differ in their ways of describing speech-stresses and phrases, and about the different functions in phrases of loudness and intonation. But the alternative ways of talking about stress are, I think, different abstractions rather than different observations. I prefer to talk of phrases and their main and subordinate stresses, but it would make as good sense to see 'I have just seen a pussy cat' as a continuous though varied stress with two stress-peaks (in which case the possible length of a single unit of stress would be limited by the breath). In any description the language would be seen to make its rhythms by building contrastive patterns of stress.

Real uses of language can use different observations of differentiation of stress. If we found in *The Times*, 'Mrs Cross remarked to our correspondent that she wished to join the choir invisible of those immortal dead who live again in lives made nobler by their presence' we should not be obliged particularly to notice that the second syllable of 'invisible' is more stressed than the first and third: that would be taken for granted. But if one sees that the passage becomes verse, the contrast becomes functional and has to be noticed: the perception of metre can depend on distinctions that need not be noticed in prose.

Different traditions of speech or writing often specify different phrase-lengths. The units of Anglo-Saxon poetry are its half-lines, each consisting of two smaller phrases with a main stress: this balancing of the two stresses in the half-line and then the two half-lines in the verse defines the rhythmic tradition. The phrases of Middle English alliterative verse are also joined into larger half-line phrases, but the latter are usually longer than the half-lines of Anglo-Saxon verse. The phrases of biblical English of the seventeenth century are much shorter than those of Henry James's last novels.

Different phrase-rhythms made by different stress-patterns can alter meaning (as commonly understood, syntax and lexis) as decisively as different words. Is Henry James's novel *The Áwkward Àge* or *The Àwkward Áge*? The different phrases, made by selecting different syllables as the stress-peak, have different meanings; no doubt the ambiguity was James's point. Or that sentence of Mr Trim's we played with above can be made to yield many different unambiguous senses by the alteration of its stress-patterns. One rather casual and ordinary way of saying it would be to split it into two phrases thus:

She wăs wearĭng her / old blue coat

where the first phrase only just achieves a main stress and balances the second with its three strong stresses culminating in the last and strongest. But if we alter it to

She was wearing / her old blue coat

reversing the pattern so that the second phrase has its run of unstressed syllables (which could be indicated in print by italicizing *was*) the changed stress-pattern expresses a different sense and the sentence becomes, perhaps, an assertion in reply to the suggestion that she wasn't. 'She was wearing. . . ' can deny that anyone else was, and 'She was wearing her. . . ' might say in the right context that the coat worn was not her own. 'She was wearing. . .'—not doing something else with it. And so on. In these places the perception of rhythm is the perception of grammatical and syntactic relations.

It can also be the perception of tone. Speech establishes the exact shade of tone through what is done with the phrase-rhythms. Our sentence can be turned into a furious assertion by making it into one phrase and speaking it with the right stresses and intonation:

She was wearing her old blue coat [*crescendo*]

A sentence like 'My dear, how can you possibly suppose that was what I meant?' can vary between tenderness, contempt and anger, depending on its rhythms, the exact way of joining its sounds. The speaking establishes the shade of meaning and of feeling.

But with the expression of feeling it may be thought we have gone beyond rhythm as at present defined, the relating of sounds. Emotion is expressed through sound quality and through context (silence can be a highly emotional expression) as well. My point, however, is that rhythm is one of the areas where pre-linguistic expressiveness and language are not sharply distinct. Rhythm has the functions in syntax I have described: but it is also true that a dog can stress a series of barks into rhythmic units, and that the phrasing of the dog, together with the peculiar quality of the barks, express its emotional state. Or, to put it differently, stress comes from the body as well as the mind; part of the effect of heavy stress is as of a physical expression. Rhythm partakes of the nature of gesture. One could almost say that stress comes straight from the heart. So different rhythms may affect all levels of language from a howl to a complex sentence.

Rhythms are necessary to language; without them language would be meaningless. It is possible to understand a series of syllables unrelated to each other by stress, but only by going through a kind of translation process and supplying the rhythm.

No native English or North American reader of poetry has the slightest difficulty with the rhythms of *Piers Plowman*. The reason for this astonishing fact—a fact always ignored by authorities on our subject but which, properly used, ought to be of prime importance to it—is that for the modern reader *Piers Plowman* goes naturally into rhythms very like the ones we use in talking. As we read it, alliterative verse seems to work by a succession of rhythmic phrases, two in each line, which are balanced internally and against each other by the relation of their stresses. Each half-line seems to be the kind of phrase, made of two small phrases, discussed above; each line normally takes a breath. If I can read 'I have just seen a pussy cat' in the rhythms of English speech I can also read *Piers Plowman*.

B Prologue 1   In a somer seson · whan soft was the sonne

                       ˘

            I shope me in shroudes · as I a shepe were

                            ˘

            In habite as an heremite · vnholy of workes

                     ˘

            Wend wyde in this world · wondres to here

The half-line is then a big phrase which relates two smaller phrases to each other as well as, as a whole, relating itself to the other half-line:

            In a somer / seson · whan soft / was the sonne

I shall use 'phrase' for the half-line, the coalescence of the two smaller units, as well as for the smaller units themselves. (If the alliterative line consists of two half-lines each of two simple phrases, an alternative description would be to call it—before further definition—a 'four-beat' line: this is again a difference of abstraction not observation.)

But though *Piers Plowman* goes so easily in the rhythms of modern English we quickly see a metre in it. Alliterative verse is easily distinguishable from prose even when, as is so often the case in the fourteenth century, there is no alliteration (alliteration being no more a necessary adjunct of alliterative verse than rhyme is of iambic pentameter). The metre is the length of the phrases and the expectation of two beats per phrase. It is possible for this expectation to affect the rhythmical shaping, as when a half-line seems to have three or more stresses when we expect it only to have two. This is where I diverge from the perceptive account in Professor Lawlor's book[1] and follow instead Professor Borroff, who writes of *Sir Gawain and the Green Knight*: 'It is my belief that there are in fact no extended lines...if by an extended line is meant one containing five chief syllables of equal rank. In all the first half-lines, however heavy, it is possible to subordinate one out of three stressed syllables—or in certain cases two out of four—so that two syllables will receive major emphasis.'[2] But alliterative verse generally avoids such tensions, and both Professor Borroff and Miss Daunt have shown how characteristic it is for alliterative verses to work with phrases that are ordinary syntactic units, to be pronounced with whatever rhythms they would have in speech or prose. The latter says, '*Old English verse is really conditioned prose*, *i.e.* the spoken language specially arranged with alliteration, but arranged in a way that does no violence to the spoken words'[3] and 'poetry, at that time, was made with *pieces of language*, groups of spoken language arranged to run easily and not monotonously on the breath.'[4] I agree that alliterative metre is just a traditional selection and formalization of speech-rhythms. The alliteration itself is best seen as an extension and regulation of a normal speech-aid: if the syllables bearing the main stress alliterate, the rhythmic patterns are made more unmistakable; and the half-lines are joined more easily (phrase-rhythm being a divider as well as a uniter) if the alliteration carries over. These 'pieces of language' may be some-what formalized or tidied by the metre: we may be more inclined to pronounce each half-line with two beats than we should the same words in prose.

But in any case it is a deeply-ingrained habit of English speech and prose to work in two-beat phrases. The vows of the marriage service could appropriately be written as alliterative verse:

> to have and to hold · from this day forward
> for better for worse · for richer for poorer
> in sickness and in health · to love and to cherish
> till death us do part...

---

[1] J. Lawlor, *Piers Plowman, an Essay in Criticism*, 1962, pp. 190–1.

[2] M. Borroff, '*Sir Gawain and the Green Knight*', *A Stylistic and Metrical Study*, New Haven and London, 1962, p. 198.

[3] Marjorie Daunt, 'Old English Verse and English Speech Rhythm', *Transactions of the Philological Society*, 1946, p. 57.

[4] *Ibid.* p. 60.

So could this piece of quite ordinary, good, flowing periodic prose:

    * The education of our hero · Edward Waverley
       was of a nature · somewhat desultory.
    * In infancy · his health suffered
    * or was supposed to suffer · (which is quite the same thing)
       by the air of London. · As soon therefore
    * as official duties · attendance on Parliament
       or the prosecution · of any of his plans
       of interest or ambition · called his father to town...[1]

But the great question is how we know the rhythms we naturally use in alliterative poetry are right. Could it not be that, since each half-line is usually a unit of syntax, we are seeing the syntactic shape of the original but expressing it in our own quite different rhythms? How unlikely that a rhythmic system disused for 400 years should suddenly come alive for any modern reader who opens *Piers Plowman*! How can we be *sure* the rhythms we read are the ones Langland wrote?

At its crudest, the answer is the one given at the end of the last chapter: 'It works.' Our reading with meaningful modern rhythms stays without difficulty within the boundaries marked by the half-lines of the original. Perhaps Langland read these phrases with different rhythms. But we do know, quite finally and certainly, that the poem can have a life in modern English expressed in a metre which, though it goes naturally in modern English, is not quite like anything in modern English verse, a metre which nobody would think of applying to the original if it did not at least seem to be found there and to work in modern English, and a metre which makes sense and allows the poem to live. I showed in an analysis of one passage that it is not difficult for such a reading to take us with considerable depth and subtlety into the poem. This establishes the confidence in being right that is appropriate to the occasion. It is reasonable in literary criticism to believe that at least we are not hopelessly wrong when we get from a poem a better sense than we can flatter ourselves we have inadvertently ourselves put in. And we are capable of receiving Langland's liveliness, whether in his language or not. But the contentious phrase here is 'in literary criticism', for that is, of course, the mode of discourse to which this argument must belong. There is nothing scientific about such a

---

[1] *Waverley*, vol. I, chapter 3. * Lines identifiable as regular members of one of Sievers's five types.

demonstration of the power to read a poem. Nothing is proved: proof is never a possibility in criticism. No two readings of a line or phrase will ever be quite the same, and there will always be room for better readings and danger of worse, even for changing one's mind quite basically about how a passage goes, in a way that linguistic scientists hardly ever do.

With all this, nobody who has ever really read a poem will think that the idea of a right reading is nonsense; and the confidence of having achieved a right reading, though it may be mistaken, is first-rate evidence in literary criticism, especially if an audience can be got to agree. No other kind of certainty can be offered in the present work. And it is better to offer the chancy and perhaps wrong insights of the critic if they are appropriate to the subject than the veriest fact which has no relevance and cannot advance understanding. I submit, as a proposition of central importance to this study, that our general agreement on how the lines of *Piers Plowman* move is good evidence that we are right, in so far as it gives us a great poem to read. The real 'proof' that we are right is our liveliness of response to the poem.

It will here be objected (experience tells me) that I am abandoning discipline in favour of reliance on 'subjective' impressions. But it is not unreliable or 'subjective' to say that any knowledge we have of the rhythms of Middle English is a development of our experience of the rhythms of modern English, and that there can be no verifiable scientific demonstration of it. The world is not properly divisible into the subjective and objective. 'The use which is here made of words like..."objective" and "subjective"... whose meaning is assumed to be familiar to everyone, might well be regarded as so much deception.'[1] Reading a poem is neither objective nor subjective; rather it takes place in Dr Leavis's 'third realm', 'the realm of that which is neither merely private and personal nor public in the sense that it can be brought into the laboratory or pointed to. You cannot point to the poem; it is "there" only in the re-creative response of individual minds to the black marks on the page. But—a necessary faith—it is something in which minds can meet.'[2] I cannot prove to you that Langland goes as I say in the way I could prove Pythagoras's theorem: on the other hand reading Langland like that is not a private whim of

[1] Hegel, *Phenomenology of Mind*, ed. cit. p. 76.
[2] F. R. Leavis, *Two Cultures?* 1962, p. 28.

mine; large numbers of thoughtful people agree, and the prime evidence for their agreement, the feel of a work of art, can be as valid in its way as any other argument. 'In studying this subject we must be content if we attain as high a degree of certainty as the matter of it admits. The same accuracy or finish is not to be looked for in all discussions.'[1] It is on similar grounds that we know *King Lear* is a tragedy. And in any use of language whatever, comparable criteria can be invoked: it is only if language seems not to make sense that we usually stop to ask whether there may not be some mistake.

Our study is the attempt to be conscious about the mysterious, hidden life of poetry. The marvel of mere sound's rising into significance is not explicable by linguistic science, and can only be glimpsed by the occasional inspiration of the philosopher (all the best linguistics from Aristotle to Wittgenstein is really philosophical speculation[2]) or the occasional insight of the literary critic in his sympathy with a poet. The discipline we need here is not that of any science, but of criticism—the long, hard, infrequently successful effort to tell the truth about impressions, perceptions and beliefs, whose only guarantee is the faith that people can in fact sometimes read poetry well. But I do not concede that criticism is inferior to scientific disciplines; criticism has its own strengths in its own places, of which this is one; and if our subject is not part of literary criticism then it must be beneath the notice of criticism.

We can sometimes be sure we have read a poem, and it is perfectly fair to base certain arguments about its language on that sureness (the point might be to work from the poem to its language as a way of coming back to the poem again). So it would be possible, though not necessary for our own concerns, to base a circular argument about the rhythms of fourteenth-century English on our reading of Langland: we might argue that since these are the rhythms that make sense they are very likely the ones he used.

---

[1] Aristotle, *Nicomacean Ethics*, Book I, Chapter 3; Penguin translation by J. A. K. Thomson, 1953, p. 27.

[2] The remark of Wittgenstein appropriate here is: 'Understanding a sentence is much more like what really happens when we understand a tune than at first sight appears. For understanding a sentence, we say, points to a reality outside the sentence. Whereas one might say "Understanding a sentence means getting hold of its content; and the content of the sentence is *in* the sentence".' L. Wittgenstein, *The Blue and Brown Books*, Oxford, 1958, p. 167.

I do not intend to do much with the argument, because it would be of no particular concern of those whose interest is in reading the poets: it could only place in a historical context what we know already. It is also an argument rather tricky to handle. J. R. Firth uses a similar argument about the rhythms of eighteenth-century English speech. He quotes 'God forbid you should stop your hand when correction is necessary! and surely it must be so on such an occasion as that was, though I don't suppose the dear child meant the harm she did', and comments, 'It is clear that the prosodies are very like those of present-day speech'.[1] No: what is clear is that to read the passage *now* we read with present-day rhythms: but whether people phrased in the same way then is the point at issue. (Some slight evidence to the contrary might be the difficulty one occasionally has in making sense of Jane Austen's copious italics.) Southworth commits the same error on page 38 of *Verses of Cadence*. And when Professor Gordon writes, 'With Old English versification as a guide we can turn confidently to Old English prose secure in the knowledge that our rendering of its stresses is based on something more certain than a subjective reading. The rhythm we discover is the prose rhythm of today',[2] one has to object (as well as that the certainty is misplaced) that there is no guarantee that we are 'discovering' the rhythms of today, because we are ourselves importing them—no guarantee, that is, except the 'subjective' arguments about making sense which I have tried to deploy.

Piers Plowman is a good example of a poem we can read by allowing its rhythms to come back to life again, reasonably confident they are *its* rhythms, not just our own foisted on it. I want, of course, to try something similar with Chaucer; but Chaucer's case is more difficult because we are apt to begin by thinking we know his metre and using it to tell us how to read. Langland's metre does not usually conflict with the way we shape and stress speech or prose, but Chaucer's metre is thought to be external to his verse. Before we can do anything with Chaucer's metre it will then be necessary to ask some questions about what metre does. (I do not wish to distinguish what it does from what it is.)

[1] J. R. Firth, *Papers in Linguistics, 1934–51*, Oxford, 1957, p. 207.
[2] I. A. Gordon, *The Movement of English Prose*, 1966, p. 17.

III

Poetic metre is often thought of as giving a second rhythmic system to replace or alter that of speech. This is a view of metre that derives from dancing or music and which leads into some traps when applied simply to spoken verse.

Diagrams of metre might do quite well as a way of beginning to talk about metre in music. If the composer gives a time-signature and uses bars the performer does know the metre before beginning to play, even though there is still a rather mysterious cottoning-on process as the first few notes and the metre are fitted together. Time in music (not *tempo*, which is speed) tells the performer that main stresses will recur or be implied at equal intervals of time, and bar lines tell him where to begin a stress. (This statement is of course only very crudely true: there are volumes of exceptions and modifications to be made before it could fully stand, and some music lives by the exceptions—*rubato*, for instance, can ruin a piece or make it successful, and the relation of this slowing of the rhythmic scheme to the above simple assertion is problematic— but there is enough crude truth in what I say to satisfy our purpose.) The individual phrases of the music are built so as not to contradict the metre. Syncopation, the appearance of a stress at an unexpected place, is possible because the metre tells one what to expect.

When a composer sets the words the music can (though it need not) completely replace speech-rhythm. By creating a melody the composer controls all the aspects of speech that belong to rhythm: the intonation becomes the tune, and the stresses and pauses depend not on the language but the music. Composers habitually take liberties with the phrasing of texts. Nahum Tate gave Purcell the awful couplet

> Ah Belinda, I am press'd
> With torment not to be confess'd

than which there could hardly be a more mechanical and inexpressive use of rhythms. 'Press'd' (of course press'd into service for the rhyme) gets the main emphasis, which only brings out its ridiculousness, while in the next line stress falls on those key terms 'not' and 'be'. Purcell, even in the extreme case of setting aside his music, rescues and improves the verse by phrasing it like this:

Ah, ah,
Ah, Belinda,
I am press'd with torment.
Ah, ah,
Ah, Belinda,
I am press'd with torment not to be confess'd.

A composer can even if he wishes change the stress-patterns of words, which is very unusual in spoken verse: Handel, Bach and Mozart all stress *allelúia* or *alléluía* at will. (Purcell's best things, on the other hand, always make use of the language, 'heightening' it in music, which is no doubt one reason why Hopkins loved Purcell.) When the first verse of Bishop Ken's evening hymn is sung to Tallis's Canon it has rhythms different from any that might go into a good reading:

♩ |♩ ♩ ♩ ♩ |♩ ♩ ♩
Glory to Thee my God this night

♩ |♩ ♩ ♩ ♩ |♩ ♩ ♩
For all the blessings of the light:

♩ |♩ ♩ ♩ ♩ |♩ ♩ ♩
Keep me O keep me King of kings

♩|♩ ♩ ♩ ♩|♩ ♩ ♩
Beneath Thine own almighty wings

Nobody would recite it like that, with the stresses of equal intensity at equal intervals of time.

But some English verse is spoken in a similar time-metre, and time is an element of varying importance in many metres. Children use time-metres when chanting to accompany games with metrical movements, like skipping:

| Sally's in the | kitchen | doing a bit of | knitting
| In came the | bogey man and | out popped | she

(where the bar-line indicates the descent of the skipping-rope). Reciting any verse, children tend to make the metre prominent and musical in this way; but some of them grow out of it later.

It is rather unusual for adult English verse to rely principally on time-metre. But, for instance, we read Chesterton's 'Lepanto' as if the main stresses were of equal intensity and equidistant in time ('equal' to the ear, that is, not necessarily to instruments in language laboratories) and the unstressed syllables are compressed within their allotted proportion of the time:

> Strong gongs groaning as the guns boom far
> Don John of Austria is going to the war

—where 'gongs' occupies the same time as '-ning as the' and as 'boom'.

The longer a line, the more likely a time-metre is to take over from speech-rhythms. Poulter's measure has to be taken as a time-metre, for that alone can prevent its dissolving into prose: any freedom of phrasing would make the metre imperceptible, so unless one reads in strict time, poulter's measure does not exist:

> Wrapt in my carelesse cloke ‖ as I walke to and fro
> I se how loue can shew what force there reigneth in his bow
> And how he shoteth eke ‖ a hardy hart to wound
> And where he glanceth by agayne that litle hurt is found.[1]

—where ‖ is a pause as long as one foot.

Even in verse which is not organized in a simple time-metre, time can have importance. Yeats achieves some of his nobility of manner by sometimes including in an iambic line an extra syllable, which is kept in order by the time: the effort needed to fit the extra syllable to the metre is used to express the dignity:

> The ceremony of innocence is drowned...[2]

> Before the indifferent beak could let her drop.[3]

In the above examples of simple time-metre, metre completely replaces the phrase-rhythms of speech. A similar almost complete replacement can be found at what is sometimes thought to be an opposite extreme, the verse of Walt Whitman. His lines seem to be composed of phrases like alliterative verse rather than of feet like time-metres; yet the effect of long successions of short phrases tends to be to make the main stress of each of the same intensity

---

[1] *The Poems of Henry Howard Earl of Surrey*, ed. F. M. Padelford, no. 26, lines 1–4; reprint New York, 1966, p. 78.

[2] 'The Second Coming'.

[3] 'Leda and the Swan'. This looks a very Italianate effect; if Chaucer had really been imitating Italian I would have expected to find similar things in his verse. But though Chaucer certainly includes extra syllables, his high style does not seem to depend on this time movement.

and at more or less equal distances of time, so that the phrases are turned into feet and the movement belongs rather with poulter's measure than with, for example, Shakespeare's blank verse. (Perhaps this is just to say that Whitman is not a very good writer, not doing what he intends with his medium.)

The púre contrálto síngs in the órgan lóft,

The cárpenter drésses his plánk, the tóngue of his fóreplane whístles its wíld

ascénding lísp,

The márried and únmarried chíldren ríde hóme to their Thánksgiving

dínner...[1]

Something similar can also happen in prose.

'What do people listen for?'
'The sea wind in the heat,' she said thoughtfully; 'and the crowing of the cock in the night of pain; and, in life, the footsteps of the beloved who never comes; or when he does come, goes on the instant.'[2]

Here too the phrases become feet, the stress of each foot being the same as the beat of the phrase, and the whole turns into a kind of beat-metre. The explanation why Whitman and poetic prose can thump may come clearer if we look at this other quite important word, *beat*.

There is a kind of English verse in which the stresses of metre and speech-phrase always coincide. In this kind of verse the foot and the phrase are the same. (This is not quite the same as the description of alliterative verse, to which the idea of the foot is not necessary.) I shall distinguish this kind of verse by saying that its metre consists of a certain number of beats per line with an indefinite number of unstressed syllables. Coleridge thought he had invented this metre, as also did Hopkins. *Christabel* is a good example:

'Tis the middle of night by the castle clock,
And the owls have awakened the crowing cock;
Tu——whit!——tu——whoo!
And hark, again! the crowing cock,
How drowsily it crew...
Four for the quarters, and twelve for the hour;

[1] *Song of Myself*, 15.
[2] John Masefield, *Sard Harker*, Part Three.

Ever and aye, by shine and shower,
Sixteen short howls, not over loud;
Some say, she sees my lady's shroud.

Here every metrical stress (except in the fifth quoted line, which is not in beat-metre) is a new chest-pulse, that is, the main stress of a simple speech-phrase; so here there can be no tension between the metre and speech-rhythm. This can apply to Whitman if each beat is taken as also the main stress of a foot.

But iambic pentameter is no more beat-metre than it is time-metre. Whatever iambic pentameter is, it certainly cannot be defined as a five-beat line (though of course it *may* have five beats). If a beat is the phrase-stress, iambic pentameter can have any number of beats from two to eight or more, but is usually, I think, following Northrop Frye,[1] a four-beat line. 'Beat' could not be of much help in defining iambic pentameter because in pentameter the stress of a foot need not be the same as the stress of a phrase. After all this is iambic pentameter:

Is this a Dagger, which I see before me,
The Handle toward my Hand? Come, let me clutch thee:
I have thee not, and yet I see thee still.
Art thou not fatall Vision, sensible
To feeling, as to sight? or art thou but
A Dagger of the Minde, a false Creation,
Proceeding from the heat-oppressed Braine?[2]

Here the stresses are certainly not of equal intensity or equidistant in time; indeed some of the metrically unstressed syllables receive a heavier stress than some of the metrically stressed syllables; and there is no fixed number of beats or phrase-stresses in these lines, though most have four. The verse may modify the rhythms of speech but it does not completely replace them. If in much of the best English verse the metre does not fully replace speech-rhythms it is necessary to ask what it does do, and why, even, one need bother about it at all.

It is under the influence of ideas of musical metre or beat-metre that such diagrams as

$$\cup\, /\, \cup\, /\, \cup\, /\, \cup\, /\, \cup\, /\, (\cup)$$

or as

De dum de dum de dum de dum de dum (de)

---

[1] Cf. *The Anatomy of Criticism*, Princeton, 1957, pp. 251 ff.
[2] *Macbeth*, II, i.

are misinterpreted. What are these diagrams *for*? What in particular do they tell the reader to do? The general assumption of the
Tyrwhitt tradition is that we take the diagram as a model and
imitate it as nearly as we can when reading the particular lines of
Chaucer. We make the lines approximate to the model, and if they
won't, we pronounce them unmetrical. Alternatively the diagram
can be seen as a rule which we obey by speaking the lines as much
like it as we can. (Another way of seeing it, as an abstraction of
what all pentameters have in common, I immediately dismiss,
because not all pentameters are at all like the model.) The significance of '∕' and '◡' is rarely explained, and in the absence of
explanation the natural thing is to take one stress as the same as
another, that is, of equal intensity, and one foot as the same as
another, of equal duration. In that oft-quoted line

> De dum de dum de dum de dum de dum

the stressed syllables certainly are equal and equidistant.
   Talk of ideal pentameter makes

> De dum de dum de dum de dum de dum

not *a* pentameter but *the* pentameter. This is the philosophers'
point that it is a mistake to suppose that the one thing we can be
sure is a metre long is the standard metre rod kept in Paris. That
is not a metre long, it is the metre, by which other lengths are
measured. But what sense could it make to say that

> De dum de dum de dum de dum de dum

'measures' all pentameters? That would just lead straight to all
the confusions about ideal metre: we can never understand what
the *function* of this paradigm is, unless to say mistakenly that we
try to bring the real close to the ideal.
   It is true that the last quoted line is an iambic pentameter,
though it is not, despite its universal popularity, of sufficient
distinction to be made a touchstone. It is true that most pentameters are roughly like the diagram even when the diagram is
interpreted as a time-metre; it is true that in many pentameters the
stresses are roughly equal and equidistant. (It is also true that
successive phrase-stresses in speech are often of about the same
intensity.) It is true that in reading pentameters we are following

53

rules which are also followed in the diagrams, and this could be demonstrated by breaking them to read, for instance,

$$\acute{/} \; \smile \; \smile \; \acute{/} \; \smile \; \smile \; \acute{/} \; \smile \; \smile \; \acute{/}$$
De dum de dum de dum de dum de dum

It is even true that when scanning a line one tries to read it with the stress-patterns of the model. But scanning is not reading; and for all the elements of truth in all these descriptions I shall contend that these diagrams and models are more of a hindrance than a help, because they appear to be giving advice about reading while really obscuring the essential questions about what metrical reading is.

One might, if mischievously inclined, suggest an anomalist theory of metre which could very likely have as much truth as the diagrams and be usefully corrective. The anomalists are due to come into fashion again as grammarians, so why not here too? One would then define iambic pentameter as Wittgenstein defines (or shows to be indefinable) *game*, by giving large numbers of examples of pentameters, then saying words to this effect: 'These lines are all iambic pentameter. There is no single thing they all have in common except at the level of useless generality, e.g. they are all English. There is no unifying core of iambicity. They do not all go de dum de dum de dum de dum de dum, even roughly. But each is like one or more of the others in some ways, though unlike in others. The very complex web of likenesses is the extent of the term. Now: you have seen many iambic pentameters: all other pentameters are in some ways (though not others) like some (but not others) of these. You must develop your sense of what is and what is not iambic pentameter by growing more accustomed to this web of similarity.' Such a procedure would be, after all, an ostensive definition of 'iambic pentameter', and the final section of this work will largely consist of numbers of examples. It is surely ironical that the scholars who when speaking of metres begin by postulating ideals are the very ones who in general follow St Augustine and the rest in the belief that language is learned by ostensive definitions. I refrain from elaborating these notions here only because they would not be of any immediate help to a reader, except perhaps in further undermining the acceptance of the rigid Ideal.

If the diagrams are models or blue-prints or specifications, they don't work. If they are rules they omit the essential information about how to follow them. At best they can only be the kind of rule Wittgenstein compares to a signpost. The diagram of iambic pentameter might say, 'Make the lines more or less like this'. But it is just *how much* more or less that we need to know, and that the diagram cannot say. That is why it would be preferable to give, say, 200 examples of iambic pentameter rather than the one model line: iambic pentameters go more or less like each other, but the reader has no obligation to make them more like

> De dum de dum de dum de dum de dum

than like

> See see where Christ's blood streams in the firmament.

The models imply 'and so on'. They tell us to make other lines like this one: but it would be obviously better if 'and so on' could follow a large number of examples covering more of the range. It was all very well for men of Tyrwhitt's generation, or even of ten Brink's, who seem to have been quite happy to stress metre at the expense of rhythm and to make all iambic pentameters very like the model. But now that we read verse differently it is harder to see the point of the model.

Metres are found only in lines of verse, and no particular line is an embodiment of the model, except the model itself. Other lines can be reduced to the model only by losing the particular rhythms that make them themselves. It is normally in their difference from the model that they are expressive. Lines of verse are more or less like the model, but that is all; and if so, the function of the model is obscure.

The difficulty of connecting the model with lines of real verse has, of course, long been recognized by writers on the subject; they tend to concentrate on the problem of why metrical stress is not always the same as speech-stress (or why, in the Trager–Smith scheme of linguistics, which has had a great influence, metre seems to recognize fewer degrees of stress than speech).[1] In

c 288   'Harrow' quod he, 'by nayles and by blood!'

the first syllable of *nayles* receives the same *metrical* stress as *and*. But as the line is read *nayles* has a stress enormously greater than

---

[1] Cf. G. L. Trager and H. L. Smith, Jr., *An Outline of English Structure*, Washington, 1956, and E. L. Epstein and T. Hawkes, *Linguistics and English Prosody*, *Studies in Linguistics, Occasional Papers*, no. 7, Buffalo, 1959.

and. Observations like this have traditionally led writers on metre to postulate an ideal pentameter with five equal and equidistant stresses but which no actual line ever quite embodies: 'The vital thing in English verse is the perpetual conflict between the law of verse and the freedom of the language; each is incessantly though insignificantly violated for the purpose of giving effect to the other.'[1] But this only raises, in a confusing way, all our questions about how to recognize metre and what it is to follow a metrical rule. Patmore's remarks may be close enough to common experience to allow us to see, more or less, what he is getting at, but this is an unhelpful way of putting it: for a law that is incessantly violated cannot control language—is not, that is, really a law—but on the other hand, a violation that is insignificant is also imperceptible, since rhythms are functional. Again, 'The simple fact [beware of simple facts in books on metre] is that the accents of refined English verse do not fall regularly.'[2] But if there is *no* regularity, what is it that we are calling metre? The natural outcome of this line of confusion is the Idea of the metre: 'The actual movement of the verse does not exactly correspond with the ideal rhythmic scheme deep down in our minds; it plays about— but never wholly forsakes it.'[3] This ideal rhythmic scheme seems to be a sort of inward metronome, beating time with equidistant equally stressed strokes, like a preclassical conductor of an orchestra, and the verse we read is supposed to 'counterpoint' the ideal scheme, perhaps in the way Bing Crosby's crooning plays about but never wholly forsakes the melody it is not quite expressing. 'It is common ground that poetic rhythm depends for its effects on variations from a norm which appears often enough unvaried[4] to provide a mental background against which the variations form a counterpoint.'[5] Cf. 'The one inescapable fact is that variation cannot exist without a norm...'[6] Mr Thompson also

---

[1] Coventry Patmore, quoted in E. P. Hammond (ed.), *English Verse between Chaucer and Surrey*, Durham, N.C., 1927, p. 19.

[2] E. A. Sonnenschein, *What is Rhythm?* Oxford, 1925, p. 97.

[3] C. M. Lewis, quoted in *English Verse between Chaucer and Surrey*, p. 19.

[4] C. S. Lewis in 'The Fifteenth Century Heroic Line' shows that the 'norm' *never* appears unvaried, and Lascelles Abercrombie made the similar observation that 'It is only as varieties of the pattern that the lines of verse exist'. (*Principles of English Prosody*, 1923, p. 109.)

[5] A. J. Bliss, *The Metre of Beowulf*, Oxford, 1958, p. 108.

[6] Seymour Chatman, *A Theory of Meter*, The Hague, 1965, p. 207.

uses the phrase 'the counterpoint of speech and metrical pattern'.[1] But these supposed ideal rhythmic schemes are quite, quite undemonstrable. If I deny the existence of any such scheme there is no way of showing it me. I do not object to the location of the ideal 'deep in the mind': I merely observe that in these descriptions it remains in the mind without affecting any events: it is altogether disconnected from the reading of the verse. The objection is practical as well as logical. I really am not conscious when reading Shakespeare of any inward metronome, and having discussed the matter with friends I report that some do think of themselves as varying an ideal metre when reading verse, others don't. The latter class, those unconscious of any ideal, are not in my experience worse readers than the former and do not seem to misunderstand metre.

The idea of the Idea of metre bypasses our question of what metre does. If it only ticks away without affecting reading, its measurement is like that of a gas-meter, of no immediate concern to the cook. An identical refusal to explore the possible function of metre is the great failing of Professor Baum's *Chaucer's Verse*. After discussing Chaucer's departures from iambic pentameter Baum has one page about how to reproduce them in modern reading, after which he gives the advice, 'So much granted, it becomes a matter of drawing the line, and for that each reader must follow his own predilection, with such guidance as he can acquire from a sympathetic reading of the texts'.[2] That is all. But if at the vital point where metre intersects with reading we are all quite free to draw our own lines, there is no apparent reason why people should publish books on the subject. On the other hand if we are discussing some kind of linguistic rule or control there are certain bounds beyond which we are not free to follow our own predilection. (A reading may imply another reading by deliberately avoiding it, and a metre may similarly be implied by being left uncreated. There is also, of course, an infinite number of good ways of reading any line of poetry. But there is also an infinite number of bad and impermissible ways, of ways outside the rules. We are concerned with the range permitted by whatever rules there may be. Within that range the individual must do the best he can: but it is important that the range should be defined as well as possible.)

[1] *The Founding of English Metre*, p. 16.   [2] *Chaucer's Verse*, p. 22.

Perhaps the way forward is to try to be more precise about the meaning of 'metrical stress'. Is any metrical stress absolute and equal to the other metrical stresses in the same line, or is metrical stress, like speech-stress, comparative? (I need not raise the question of whether the comparisons of stress in speech are between four fixed levels, as held by Trager and Smith: all linguists at any rate agree that stress works in speech by contrasts.) The fact that when scanning a line we mark only two levels of stress, stressed and unstressed syllables, could fit either alternative. But nobody in fact reads Shakespeare as if his verse contained only two degrees of stress, therefore—simply enough—metrical stress must be comparative.[1] A metrically stressed syllable is not one that more or less attains the stress of the inward ideal metronome, it is simply *more* stressed; and the environment within which the comparison is made is the foot, which is why the foot has always been a necessary concept in metrics. A metrically stressed syllable is more stressed than the other syllables in the same foot. (Though even this is not *always* true: there are iambic feet in which the stresses are to all intents and purposes equal.) It need not be the main stress of a phrase, except in beat-metre. So if one says that a syllable is metrically stressed one need have said nothing about its absolute degree of stress (if there is such a thing) or about its degree of stress in comparison with other syllables beyond the foot. The way in which one stressed syllable is the same as another is that each lies in the same comparative relationship with other syllables. Hence stressed and unstressed syllables are not, as generally supposed, as it were the *atoms* of metre, existing if necessary quite happily on their own. Stressed and unstressed syllables only exist in relation to each other. The foot is the smallest unit in metre; the stressed and unstressed syllables are parts that derive from this whole. Or, to change the metaphor, the foot is the *gestalt* apart from which it makes no sense to talk of stressed or unstressed syllables. To read metrically is to recognize and form certain foot-patterns of stress made by the comparison within the foot of lesser stress with greater. This contrasts with the procedure of alliterative verse or prose, where stress is comparative within the phrase and one need not think of feet.

This is only to say that the foot is the unit of metre as the phrase

---

[1] This position is worked out at greater length by Epstein and Hawkes in *Linguistics and English Prosody*.

is the unit of speech and prose rhythms, that when we read verse we have to notice the foot-unit which might or might not be noticeable in the same words spoken as prose. That is the way in which metre 'measures' differently from speech. But metre need not be an enemy of speech-rhythms, and if there is tension between phrases and metre it must be resolved before the verse is spoken. So far from conflicting with speech-rhythms, metre justifies itself by co-operating with them as an additional controller or pointer of speech.

When one thinks of stress as comparative within a quite restricted environment, the phrase or the foot, some of the confusions resulting from a belief in ideal metre dissolve, and it becomes less difficult to think about how to recognize metres and how to read in them.

If you open a book of verse and begin to read, the poet—unlike the composer when you open the music and begin to play—gives you no metrical information except whatever is implied by the words he has written down and the way they are printed. How do you know what to do about the metre? or, if you believe in the Ideal, when does the metronome start ticking?

The appearance of the print on the page is often all the information one needs to begin reading metrically. If the experienced reader doesn't know from the author's name what the metre is, he opens the book and recognizes the metre from the lengths and shapes of the lines, and begins reading it as what it looks like. Presuppositions of this kind can be very strong (see below, Chapter 7). But if it is a metre not immediately recognizable? Or if one stumbles and realizes one is reading the wrong metre? In the first case the reader treats the first line as if it were prose, while being at the same time alert (perhaps not deliberately) for metrical patterns; and the metre emerges from the first line if it is iambic pentameter or any of the octosyllabic metres, or from the first twenty lines the first time you read *Piers Plowman*. The metre is recognized as repeated stress-patterns (feet or half-lines); the points of recognition are not stresses of similar intensity (though they occur, of course) so much as repeated stress-relationships, in iambic pentameter, for instance, and with many varieties, five repetitions of the lesser-greater relationship, '$\smile$ $/$'. In this way it is impossible to know a poet's metre before you know his poetry, though there is certainly only a very small time-lag between beginning to know his poetry and knowing his metre, and the knowledge of the poetry would not get far without the metre. The look of a page is only a good hint: it may be wrong. The only test of the metre is in reading. (And if the look of the page gives you the right hint about the metre it is because you do already know the poetry in the sense that you suppose correctly that it is like other poetry you have read.)

One has to recognize or discover a metre in verse; but once found, the metre affects the reading. We read 'in the metre', and go on doing so unless the poet goes off into a different one. But reading metrically is not necessarily pulling the stress-patterns towards some ideal: the metre may rather help the reader to choose between alternative patterns all of which could occur in prose. Metre then is an additional control, another way of showing the reader how to shape and stress. Metre chooses from the rhythmic alternatives the one that creates the metre. If Yeats had written, 'I had this thought a while ago: my darling cannot understand what I have done, or what would do in this blind, bitter land', it would not occur to the reader to place a main stress on 'understand' and pause after the word. There is no reason *not* to: the reading is one of the possibilities of the language, but not the one suggested by the prose. As verse, however, the metre selects and insists on this possibility, giving a precise emotional effect (the effect in particular that that stress and slowing have, and which the critic's adjectives can only crudely approximate to) which prose wouldn't. The verse heightens and controls the language. So as verse the passage is altogether more expressive:

> I had this thought a while ago:
> My darling cannot understand
> What I have done, or what would do
> In this blind, bitter land.[1]

Any written language is rhythmically ambiguous, i.e. can be read with a variety of different rhythms, but 'one great part of a writer's skill consists in so framing his sentences that an ordinarily intelligent reader cannot make nonsense of them by reading them, aloud or to himself, with the wrong intonation or tempo'.[2] Metre is an additional aid to rhythmical accuracy .The good poet will see to it

---

[1] 'Words'.
[2] R. G. Collingwood, *The Principles of Art*, Oxford, 1938, p. 265.

that the metrical choice from the possible rhythms is the one he needs to express his meaning.

The nearest I can get to making sense of the notion of ideal metre is to think of it in terms of expectation and call it 'a willingness to create the metre'. There certainly is metrical expectation: when we are into a poem we expect the metre to continue and read the poem so as to make it do so.

Verse is *unmetrical* if it arouses expectations which the reader cannot fulfil. If there are no metrical expectations the question of metre doesn't arise; but it is possible to be continually aroused to expectations (like Saintsbury reading Lydgate) which are thwarted, whether intentionally or not, either by the poet or the reader. Jonson intentionally writes unmetrically in some of Nano's speeches:

> Now, room for fresh gamesters, who do will you to know,
> They do bring you neither play nor university show;
> And therefore do intreat you, that whatsoever they rehearse,
> May not fare a whit the worse, for the false pace of the verse.[1]

Browning seems unintentionally unmetrical in 'The Lost Leader':

> Still bidding crouch whom the rest bade aspire;
> Blot out his name then, record one lost soul more,
> One task more declined, one more footpath untrod,
> One more triumph for devils and sorrow for angels,
> One wrong more to man, one more insult to God!

There is no way of making the metre we find in the first two lines co-operate with the language in the third and following lines; the tension—the attempt to find a metrical way of reading—is still unresolved as the words are spoken. In successful English verse there may be a tension between the expectations of metre and speech-rhythm as we are forming the verse to speak, but the tension is resolved in the spoken verse in a compromise or co-operation between the two rhythmic systems, in which the metre is recognizably present (or else the verse is not metrical) and the speech-rhythms are not unacceptably distorted (or else the piece is not spoken English). (It does not affect this point that a reading may be intended to suggest other readings which it is not.)

But we should be careful of too easily dismissing as unmetrical

---

[1] *Volpone*, I, i.

verse which does not go right at first reading, of having too simple or explicit expectations. Would the following be unmetrical?—

> The curfew tolls the knell of day's parting,
> The lowing herd o'er the lea slowly winds...

No. It follows rules that are not merely arbitrary and could conceivably lead to expressiveness. If trochaic substitution were permitted in the third and fifth feet both those lines would be regular iambic pentameter. The first could be called unmetrical only if it were insisted that the fifth foot must be '∪ /'. But though it is a dogma from Tyrwhitt onwards that the fifth foot must be iambic, there are examples of the trochaic inversion of that foot.

> Madness in great ones must not unwatched go.[1]

> Man never is, but always to be blest.[2]

> Religious, punctual, frugal, and so forth.[3]

And, as Mrs Anne Samson remarked to me, it makes a good reading to take Keats's line as

> No hungry generations tread thee down.[4]

Once one sees verse stress as comparative within the foot, many striking lines which everybody feels to be successful verse but which are traditionally unscannable, become simply regular, and one can see the metre as an aid to their expressiveness.

> See, see, where Christ's blood streams in the firmament.[5]

The phrase-rhythms of this line are the basis of its power. They go, with some possible variations,

> See see / where Christ's blood / streams / in the firmament

These phrase-divisions are not themselves metrical, and it is by hearing them and not the metre that the line can seem unmetrical. But the metre is there too with its complementary pattern:

> See see where Christ's blood streams in the firmament

[1] *Hamlet*, III, i.
[2] Pope, *Essay on Man*, I, 96.
[3] Pope, *Moral Essays*, III, 343.
[4] 'Ode to a Nightingale'.
[5] Marlowe, *Dr Faustus*, last scene.

I mark the first foot as an iamb although it contains two similar stresses because it is normal in English for a repeated mono-syllable to be somewhat more stressed on repetition: enough, here, to make the iamb perceptible. In speech it would be possible to stress the first syllable more than the second, but the metre in any case chooses the iambic alternative and makes sure that this part of the line is at its most expressive. The main metrical contribu-tion, however, to the line's power is its concentration of stress on 'streams'. This word receives the main stress of a phrase and is the high point in the rhythmic contour of the line; the metre confirms and reinforces the strength of its stress by making it also the second syllable of what I shall call a 'strong iamb'. If an iambic foot begins with a strongly stressed syllable one may suspect a trochaic substitution; but if the foot turns out to be iambic after all its second syllable must be very strongly stressed to be percept-ibly *more* strongly stressed than the first. So a strong iamb can juxtapose two strong stresses with perfect metrical regularity.[1] The effect in this line is to put three heavily stressed syllables next to each other and to make the third the culmination of stress in the line—which is also the best way for these words to make their impact.

Donne similarly uses metre to point the speech-sense of his words. How do we know, in the line

> Call countrey ants to harvest offices[2]

that Donne despises the country? One of the possible answers is metrical. This line too starts with a strong iamb. 'Call', an

---

[1] Pope, who is not usually accused of unmetrical activities, often uses strong iambs to good effect, and also the other extreme, the weak iamb whose stresses are both very light. The effectiveness of the lines

> Lo! thy dread Empire, CHAOS! is restor'd;
> Light dies before thy uncreating word
>
> (*The Dunciad*, IV, 653–4)

comes from two successive strong iambs in the first line together with a weak iamb in the fourth foot and, in the second line, another strong iamb at the beginning. Cf. also the *Essay on Criticism*, 360 ff., and Pope's *Iliad*, XXIII, 138–41, the latter discussed by Winifred Nowottny, *The Language Poets Use*, 1962, p. 3. Words-worth too is a master of these movements: the force of this line comes from its use of a weak iamb then a strong iamb then the trochee: three successive stresses:

> [an acorn...at once]
>
> To the bare earth dropped with a startling sound.
>
> (*The Prelude*, I, 85.)

The Sunne Rising'.

imperative, is normally stressed, and it is only when we get to the second syllable that we realize the foot is not the very common trochaic inversion, that although 'call' is stressed, 'country' is even more stressed to make the iambic pattern. This chooses for 'country' an unusually strong stress which we might not give it in prose, and which is reinforced by the alliteration. One natural English sense of this unusual stress is contempt: the hint given by the metre only needs the context of the poem to confirm it. Again, in

> At the round earths imagin'd corners, blow
> Your trumpets, Angells, and arise, arise
> From death...

the sudden rhetorical onslaught on the reader is created by the concurrence of speech-rhythms and metre. The first quoted line has two phrases, the second being the single word 'blow', which balances the whole of the rest of the line whose phrase-stress is on 'corners'. This unusually great emphasis on 'blow' is forcefully confirmed by the metre. The line begins rather jerkily with a weak iamb (two not much stressed syllables of which the second is only marginally, or perhaps only in the imagination, more stressed than the first) and a strong iamb, after which it settles into a more obviously marked iambic pattern, with a certain effect of getting into its stride. The last foot begins with the end of the word 'corners' which continues strongly the speech-pattern of the rest of the line, so the last foot is divided by the pause between the phrases: this encourages us to increase the metrical stress, for it is when a metre is least obviously regular that it needs to be most carefully made in reading. The word 'blow', at the end of a line with enjambement, also has its metrical stress increased as a self-defence against loss of metre. So both the phrases and the metre conspire to place a quite unusually heavy stress on 'blow'—the metre reinforces the point of the speech-rhythms and makes them more forceful and precise than they could have been in prose. It is not easy to imagine the line as prose, but as verse it places the decisive stress just where the poem needs it. (Donne's sermons are often rhythmically ambiguous, needing the virtuoso performance of the writer himself: but the verse almost always tells the reader how it should move.) There are as many good reasons for writing metrically as there are good lines of verse: but all the reasons have to do with success in expression.

64

Failure to control metre can make the expression unsuccessful. Tillyard quotes the opening of a poem entered as an original composition in the English Tripos,

> When I was young, my God, when I was young,

and says: 'I take it the writer meant it to be read as

> /   /   /   /   /
> When I was young, my God, when I was young,

but it is hard not to read it as

> /   /
> When I was young—MY GOD when I was young

and to picture the desperate excesses of this prematurely ruined undergraduate.'[1] The reason for the irresistible misreading is that the metre itself indicates which of the possible speech-rhythms to choose. Both versions are metrical but the wrong one is more obviously and naturally iambic. The confirmation of the wrong reading is that it gives a more interesting sense. To get at the author's intended stressings one has (a) to introduce two trochaic substitutions without there being any apparent demand from the language to do so and (b) to go solemn.

In these examples the metre does not tell us anything about phrase-lengths. It organizes the lesser ups and downs of stresses within phrases, which the phrases themselves need not do. So the phrases, though important for what the poet is doing, are not themselves part of the metre: there is no consistent phrase-expectation as in alliterative verse. But the metre, instead of replacing the phrases as in strict time metres, points or reinforces them, or helps the reader to choose from the alternatives.

Applying all this to Chaucer our task must be—assuming his rhythms not to be too far from ours—to read him as best we can, to note what metre emerges from the reading, and to ask whether and how it improves the reading. The metre must be developed from reading and then contribute to an improved reading: the process is a circular working from poetry to metre and back, if one is conscious of it; and in any case getting to know metre is something within and part of getting to know poetry and not separable

---

[1] E. M. W. Tillyard, *The Muse Unchained*, Cambridge, 1958, p. 96.

from that. Talking about metre is a critical convenience: we may sometimes by looking at poetry in this particular way see better how it lives.

IV

It is impossible to offer 'the beginning student right at the start a clear concept of Chaucer's regular iambic line'.[1] If we ever get such a clear concept (and outside investigations like the present there is no obvious necessity to have one) it will only be by reflection after much experience of reading the poet. In particular it is impossible for the metre to tell us how to pronounce the language of the verse unless we more or less know already. If one knows a metre the metre can be used to determine the stress of a hitherto unknown word (e.g. Byron certainly wants us to accent *Haidee* on the second syllable), but there can be no certainty here greater than the certainty of the metre, and metre arises from speech-rhythm, not *vice versa*. One cannot use metre to give the basis and essentials of speech-rhythm, only some peripheral details.

The weakness of so much metrical theory in Chaucer studies and elsewhere is conceptual, not technical. The main trouble is the application of simple diagrammatic metres to verses which, if it were not for scholarly determination, would never be thought to contain them. The most obviously impermissible thing to do to the medieval poets is to approach them with a nursery-rhyme metre, to force it on them, and to base theories of word-accent (and afterwards speech-rhythm) on the result. This is precisely what the establishment theories of sounded final -e and variable stress have done, as I shall show below in Part 2.

To approach the poet with a determination to impose quaint sounds and strict metres is a mixture of putting the cart before the horse and shutting the stable door after the horse has bolted. But we might hope, if we can be good enough and delicate enough readers, that the language of the fourteenth century is not too far from us to communicate its own rhythms, and that eventually we might develop enough of a sense of them to be able to discuss them as part of seeing how the language of the poets moves and has its life. This can only be done if we bear in mind that metre is functional, that it has no existence separate from the lines where alone it is found, and that the way to talk about it is, therefore, to show what it does.

[1] Cf. E. W. Stone, above, p. 8.

3

History

For a hundred and thirty years after his death Chaucer remained the dominant influence on English courtly poetry. There can be no question of Chaucer's having been forgotten after his death; his 'school' began in his lifetime with his friend Hoccleve and with Lydgate, and it continued unbroken into the sixteenth century.

Afterwards, during the Renascence, when Chaucer was relegated to the status of Ennius, there was still no great divide between Chaucer and Lydgate. Both tended towards barbarity, but the one more interestingly than the other.

So before Tyrwhitt succeeded in making Chaucer's rough places plain there was no rhythmic mystery about the English Chaucerians: they were seen as Chaucer's unrebellious imitators. But one of the results of Tyrwhitt's achievement was the discovery of a mysterious gap between Chaucer and his most admiring imitators and friends, and a gap not of genius, sympathy, taste or the movement of history, but of simple comprehension. For nobody in the nineteenth century undertook the thankless task of showing that Lydgate's lines too are really regular. So the contrast between the good smooth metre of Chaucer and the bad rough one of Lydgate has become one of the commonplaces of the literary history of the period. It is explained by Lydgate's having failed to understand Chaucer's rhythms, or having forgotten how they should go. Lydgate also, it seems, forgot his native tongue, being unable to remember how words were stressed and which had sounded final -e. Despite this handicap he pressed on indefatigably to become one of the most prolific versifiers in the language. The writing of iambic pentameters, however, became a lost art which was not again discovered until Wyatt's labours; but Wyatt often forget it again himself.

Lest I be suspected of inventing this literary history for the diversion of my readers I supply a few of the many available authoritative statements of it.

For even with Chaucer's verses before them as a model, the work of these poets is void of metrical pleasure. There is a prosodic incompetence about it which is well nigh omnipresent. A few writers show some feeling for verse...but for such writers as Lydgate, Hawes and Barclay we can only regret that they were misguided enough to think that they could use Chaucer's verse form. A reader who tries to reach them aloud halts and stumbles as he endeavours to make the lines scan or run with any ease. The incompetence of these poets cannot be entirely explained in terms of the elimination of the final *e* and other changes in syntax and pronunciation which were in process at the time. Hoccleve and Lydgate were both men of thirty and over when Chaucer died, and were both admitted followers of Chaucer, yet their verses are halting and rhythmically insensitive to a degree. In common with their contemporaries and successors, Hoccleve and Lydgate failed to understand what constitutes easy-moving verse.[1]

The phrase 'prosodic incompetence' is a reminiscence of Saintsbury: 'To these defects he [Lydgate] added two faults...The one is prosodic incompetence, the other is long-winded prolixity.'[2] Saintsbury again:

As we have seen, not one single known poet of real poetical value took up the work of Chaucer, for a hundred years and more, among Chaucer's own immediate countrymen. But this was nothing. You cannot bottle up the winds of the spirit in bags for use when they are wanted, nor is there any law of entail in the land of poesy. But, and this is surprising, what is, to some extent at least, the most learnable and mechanical of the constituents of poetry fared as badly as the most ethereal and elusive. Here is Lydgate—a man of vast industry, endowed with nearly all the older culture of his time, a man of wits and wit, educated at the most famous universities abroad as well as at home, nay, a man who has some faint flashes of actual poetry now and then—and he cannot be trusted to write three decent lines running, and people have to invent a morbid growth of verse in order to get some method into his muddle.[3]

Lesser men might have allowed their astonishment to sap their confidence in the history that led to it. 'It is not always realized,' says Professor Harding, 'what an extraordinary psychological problem is suggested by the conviction of literary historians that the English post-Chaucerians lost the art of metrical writing.'[4] But

---

[1] H. S. Bennett, *Chaucer and the Fifteenth Century*, Oxford, 1947, p. 129.
[2] *The Cambridge History of English Literature*, vol. I, p. 200.
[3] G. Saintsbury, *A History of English Prosody*, 3 vols., 1906–10, vol. I, p. 290.
[4] D. W. Harding, 'The Rhythmical Intention in Wyatt's Poetry', *Scrutiny*, vol. XIV, p. 90.

these scholars, accepting their theory as truth, stranger than fiction, just revel in their surprise. 'He [Lydgate] wrote in all of Chaucer's three chief metres...in the decasyllabic couplet, even if allowance be made for the defects of the sixteenth-century texts, with an absolute failure to grasp the elementary principles of its music.'[1] Or, as Emile Legouis puts it in the most widely used one-volume history of English literature, 'With Lydgate decomposition overtook English verse'.[2] Or, even more firmly and simply, 'Lydgate and Occleve wrote bad shambling heroics'.[3] The other Chaucerians are vulnerable to similar treatment:

In Hawes and Barclay, too, there is no unifying pattern. If you read one line in a certain way, you will probably find that the next or the next bu one cannot be read in that way; and in fact that the only way to read these people's verses is to gabble them breathlessly with the hopeful intention of lighting on four [sic] main accents in a line.[4]

These writers are all making the same mistake we have seen so much of in the Chaucer scholars: they approach the Chaucerians armed with a very stiff ideal pentameter, and when the Chaucerians fail to co-operate they are pronounced incompetent. The result is, of course, as Tillyard says, gabbling; for which it seems a little unfair to blame Lydgate, Hawes or Barclay. The alternative is to begin by recognizing that something is wrong with the 'unifying pattern' Tillyard has brought ready-made. We would be able to recognize a better one if it saved us from having to gabble breathlessly.

But so long as we retain Tyrwhitt's notion of pentameter Lydgate is bound to be unmetrical. And while this history of national amnesia after Chaucer's death was being enforced as above by the appeal of the proven regularity of Chaucer's metre, the editors of Lydgate for the Early English Text Society (those intrepid men) were boring from the opposite direction to a similar position, saying similar things about Chaucer's relation to Lydgate by describing the kinds of line they found in Lydgate. The famous five types of Lydgate line[5] was a noteworthy German attempt (whose inspiration was Sievers's five types of Old English hemi-

---

[1] *Chambers's Cyclopædia of English Literature*, 1926, vol. i, p. 79.
[2] *A History of English Literature*, 1953, p. 157.
[3] Enid Hamer, *The Metres of English Poetry*, 4th edition, 1951, p. 46.
[4] E. M. W. Tillyard, *The Poetry of Sir Thomas Wyatt*, 1929, p. 18.
[5] These are described in J. Schipper's *Englische Metrik*, Bonn, 1881–8, and elaborated in J. Schick's E.E.T.S. edition of *The Temple of Glas*, 1891, pp. lvi ff.

stich) to classify the unclassifiable, which left quite untouched the questions whether Lydgate wrote unmetrically by accident or design, and how he should be read. After describing the five types Schick writes, 'In many cases it is, however, impossible to classify a line as belonging incontestably to any particular one of the above-named types'.[1] This seems to remove any point the exercise might have had. Saintsbury very fairly commented, '*Classificatum est*, and apparently nothing more is thought necessary: though we find to our surprise that, after all, Lydgate is a "doggerel poet" who has not "a sensitive ear for rhythm".'[2] The general effect of all the 'work on' Lydgate and the others is to reinforce the establishment theory that there is a great chasm between Chaucer and his disciples who failed to understand him.

But the way language is spoken and the ways in which verse moves cannot suddenly be forgotten without an unimaginable human mutation. The history of English verse rhythms between Chaucer and Wyatt which emerges from the established readings of Chaucer and Lydgate, and which I have shown firmly enshrined in the standard authorities, is not, strictly speaking, credible—even though so many reputable scholars have managed to convince themselves that they believe it. At best it is an academic history: it can only be believed so long as people are not taking it seriously; one natural outcome is the frivolousness of Saintsbury, who is amusing himself at the expense of the subject. It is not credible that a whole generation should suddenly forget the metre of an elder and much admired contemporary: it would be as if our generation (overwhelmed perhaps by linguistic change and the fear of nuclear war) awoke one morning to find we had quite forgotten how to read T. S. Eliot. This simply cannot be believed.

One of the criteria of convincingness for any view of Chaucer's rhythms is that it should not lead to an incredible literary history. The minimum truism, at which the Tyrwhitt–Saintsbury line fails, is that the literary history of England in the fourteenth and fifteenth centuries must be able to make some sort of sense of its material. We must be able if we give the matter enough thought to see the coherent movements of the time, in the poets' attitude to Chaucer as elsewhere. This is not to demand that the period should be easy to understand. The fifteenth century is notoriously

[1] *The Temple of Glas*, p. lix.
[2] *History of English Prosody*, vol. I, p. 223.

queer—the most gothical century, the century that saw a decline in the national population, and those barely credible dynastic wars. My demand is that the literary history of the period should make it seem not less strange but, at least, a human possibility. It is possible that Lydgate might have had a very unintelligent concern with Chaucer; he may have read him badly and taken as the centre things that don't matter much. But any failure of Lydgate's (even more than of ours) must have been one of criticism and taste, not factual knowledge: it is not possible that Lydgate should have forgotten how to read Chaucer in the factual way scholars have supposed.

II

I conclude from these preliminary discussions that the case that Chaucer wrote modern iambic pentameter has always been a literary one, even when it has tried to impress itself on the reader with the authority of a scientific conclusion which all fair-minded men must accept. It has always rested on the assumption, stated or not, that good English poets do write smooth iambics. And its justification, which saves me from having to accuse generations of scholars of having wholly wasted their time, is that the metrical investigations of Tyrwhitt and his followers and Nott and his followers have, with whatever limitations, allowed readers to come closer to the poet. The Tyrwhitt rigid pentameter is not a good metre and not, I think, Chaucer's: but it probably does less damage to him than reducing him to prose would. The objection I have elaborated is not to the nature of the argument; I fully agree that any discussion of Chaucer's rhythms belongs to literary criticism. My objection has been to the quality of the literary criticism on which the case rests in such writers as ten Brink and Baum, and to the argument's failure to know itself. Reading poets well is, after all, one of the most difficult things in the world; and my contention is that reading Chaucer well and understanding his rhythms are the same thing. The disastrous misemphasis in the traditional scholars is their belief that good reading is easily achieved by academics and henceforth to be taken for granted; and that the real work concerns external observation of facts.

The present work is an attempt to see what can be done by trusting literary criticism: that is, by recognizing that Middle English lives if at all as an extension of modern English, and by suggesting a reading of the poet and his followers which we might believe to be true because it still makes sense.

To do this it will first be necessary to tackle some of the usual technical problems in reading Chaucer—sounded final -e and so forth—but my case is that even here the way forward is to show how any proposed solutions affect reading. So even when considering final -e and variable stress in French disyllables we shall be wondering how to read Chaucer's poetry, which (in the critic's perpetual dilemma of fearing that whatever he says will be boringly obvious except to those who need it, to whom it will be obscure) I offer as some inducement to the reader to think about such apparently unpoetic matters.

Part Two: Investigations

4

Chaucer's Terminology

Chaucer mentions metres so rarely and vaguely that it is usually supposed nothing of interest can be learnt of his practice from what he himself said. But this is too extreme. It is certainly impossible to solve any of our problems simply by consulting what Chaucer says, or what he might reasonably be expected to have known; but we can at least make some useful distinctions with the help of Chaucer and other medieval poets and scholars.

Chaucer has three main terms to cover the field we divide into 'verse' and 'prose', and uses them consistently, either in pairs or all three at once, when listing the different forms of written language. Where we would have 'verse and prose' he has 'prose, geest and rym'. When the Host interrupts Chaucer he says,

B 2122   Sire, at o word, thou shalt no lenger ryme.
      Lat se wher thou kanst tellen aught in geeste
      Or telle in prose somwhat, at the leeste.

And the Parson, before his prose tale, says,

I 43   I kan nat geeste, 'rum, ram, ruf,' by lettre,
      Ne, God woot, rym holde I but litel bettre;
      And therfore, if yow list—I wol nat glose—
      I wol yow telle a myrie tale in prose.

'Rym or prose' is found at *LGW* F 66 and elsewhere; and though the phrase 'geest and rym' does not occur in Chaucer, the N.E.D. does cite it from the more or less contemporary romance *Sir Beues*, and the M.E.D. cites a variant reading from *Cursor Mundi* where 'rym' replaces 'geest':

I   Men ȝernen iestes [Vsp.: rimes] for to here
      And romaunce rede in dyuerse manere

87   Of suchon shuld ȝe matere take
      Of hir to make boþe geest [Vsp.: rim] and songe.

75

So too the first sentence of Usk's *Testament of Love* includes the phrase 'the deliciousnesse of jestes and of ryme'. *Prose* appears not to have changed its meaning, but *rym* means, I think, 'verse in feet' and *geest* 'alliterative verse'.

The sense of the verb *geesten* seems perfectly clear in the Parson's quoted lines but (since it is a sense not recognized by the new Dictionary) it may be worth a short discussion. The noun *geest* comes, by way of French, from the Latin *gesta*, 'deeds', in which sense it comes into English and is often used by Chaucer. The word's place in literature is firstly as the name of heroic histories (like, in Latin, the *Gesta Romanorum*) and from that 'a poem or song about heroic deeds, a chivalric romance' (M.E.D. 1 (*a*)) as in the French *chanson de geste*. It is not hard to see how Chaucer's sense of 'alliterative verse' might have developed from these uses, since alliteratives represent the English epic tradition and in the Middle English period are a natural vehicle for heroic romances. (Had *Beowulf* been read in Chaucer's day it could have been called a *geest* in all the above senses—so much for the quirkiness of language, since of course the modern descendant of this word is *jest*.) For Chaucer 'to telle in geeste' is the alternative of 'to telle in rym or prose'.

Rym is the other kind of verse, and this is more generally recognized. *Rym* comes via Old French *rime* from Latin *rithmus* (*rhythm* originates as a graphic variant and *rhyme* and *rhythm* are inextricably confused until the seventeenth century) and is well defined by the N.E.D., as 'measured motion, time, proportion... As similarity of the terminal sounds was a common feature of accentual verse, *rithmus* naturally came to have the sense of "rime".' But in medieval Latin *rithmus* means (see below) accentual in contrast to quantitative verse. *Rym* makes very good sense in Chaucer if taken in a similar meaning. Used either as verb or noun, *rym* can be closely linked with *metre*:

B 47   Chaucer, thogh he kan but lewedly
               On metres and on rymyng craftily

and *vers* ('lines') can collectively make *rym*:

BD 463   He made of rym ten vers or twelve

('He wrote ten or twelve lines of verse.')

76

HF 1046 But for the rym ys lyght and lewed
Yit make hit sumwhat agreable
Thogh som vers fayle in a sillable.

Rym is also often found associated more generally with *write* and *endite*.

The N.E.D. says that *rim* may get this sense in teutonic languages 'partly through association with the native *rim*' ('number'). This can be shown, I think, in the case of *The Ormulum*. Orm certainly uses *rim* in its Anglo-Saxon sense: 'þurrh tale & rime off fow-werti3'[1] ('through a tally and number of forty'). But is not the following a line which goes very well if *rim* means 'numbers' in a specifically metrical sense?

D 41 Icc hafe sett her o þiss boc amang Goddspelless wordess
All þurrh me sellfenn mani3 word þe ríme swa to fillenn

White glosses the word here as 'metre, measures'. *The Bestiary* indisputably uses *rim* for Latin *rithmus*:

In boke is ðe turtres lif. writen o rime[2]

The 'boke' is the Latin original; some is quantitative and some accentual; the passage about the dove is *rithmus*.

The one place in Chaucer where *rym* might have its modern meaning is from the end of *The Complaint of Venus*:

76 For elde, that in my spirit dulleth me,
Hath of endyting al the subtilte
Wel nygh bereft out of my remembraunce;
And eke to me it ys a gret penaunce,
Syth rym in Englissh hath such skarsete,
To folowe word by word the curiosite
Of Graunson, flour of hem that make in Fraunce.

But even here the word could well be interpreted as 'verse in feet'. ('Since verse in feet is so unusual in English [its un-familiarity makes it] a great trouble to me...') This perhaps is not very full of meaning, but it makes no more sense to complain that there aren't many rhymes in English. And in all the other examples in Chaucer 'regularly metrical verse in feet' seems to

---

[1] H 11248; *The Ormulum*, ed. R. Holt, Oxford, 1878, vol. II, p. 36.
[2] *The Bestiary*, line 572; in *Selections from Early Middle English*, ed. J. Hall, Oxford, 1920, p. 194.

make the best sense of the word *rym*. *To rym* is to write such verse. Gower uses it in the same way:

C.A. v 1377 Bot al the hole progenie
Of goddes in that ilke time
To long it were forto rime.

But *rym* can have its modern sense in Lydgate.

Cadence, the word to which Professor Southworth attached such great (though changing)[1] importance, is used only once by Chaucer, and then not about a poem of his own. Miss Morgan's essay[2] clarifies the word. *Cadence* is a kind of rhetorical prose full of cursus forms, bits of *rym* and *geest* and other verbal delights in a diverting mixture. It is particularly practised by the fourteenth-century mystics for their rhapsodic praises of love. A passage from the opening of *A Talkyng of þe Loue of God* (partly cited by Miss Morgan) at once exemplifies and defines *cadence*:

Men schal fynden lihtliche þis tretys in Cadence. After the bigynninge. ȝif hit beo riht poynted ꞏ/ & Rymed in sum stude ꞏTo beo more louesum. to hem þat hit reden. God ȝiue vs grace. so for to rede ꞏ/ þat we mowen haue heuene to vre Mede.[3]

('People will easily find this treatise goes in cadence, after the manner of the beginning, if it is properly punctuated—and versified in some places—so as to be more delightful to them that read it...') On the other hand Gavin Douglas, much later and in Scotland, seems to use the word differently; he has 'elaquent fyrme Cadens regulere',[4] and 'my corruppit cadens imperfyte'.[5] But in fourteenth-century England *cadence* seems clearly enough to be the precious literary prose of Rolle and the mystics. The only Canterbury Tale in cadence is *Melibee*; the numerous metrical lines in *Melibee* (which are specially frequent near the beginning,

[1] In his second book Southworth changed his mind about the meaning of *cadence* without being able to apply the word any more convincingly to Chaucer.
[2] M. M. Morgan, 'A Treatise in Cadence', *Modern Language Review*, 1952. See also F. N. Robinson's note on *HF* 624.
[3] *A Talkyng of þe Loue of God*, ed. M. S. Westra, The Hague, 1950, p. 1. The importance the writer attaches to punctuation for establishing rhythmic phrasing is worth remark: see below, Chapter 7.
[4] *The Palice of Honour*, line 821 [Book II, 51]; *The Shorter Poems of Gavin Douglas*, ed. P. J. Bawcutt, S.T.S. 1967, p. 56.
[5] *Virgil's Aeneid*, I, prologue, 46; ed. D. F. C. Coldwell, S.T.S. 4 vols. 1957–64; vol. II, p. 4.

as if Chaucer tired of writing them) were not so far as I know publicly noticed before Professor Baum's essay.[1]

Now Chaucer always refers to his own poems as *rym*, never as *geest* or *cadence*, and this must surely suggest that he thought of himself as writing in a tradition of regularly metrical accentual verse. What it cannot suggest is the kind of regularity. We should be going far beyond the evidence if we tried to say that *rym* is *the same* in English as *rithmus* in Latin—even if we knew what that assertion meant.

We come to a similar point if we try to argue from what Chaucer could reasonably have been expected to know. He was presumably familiar with descriptions of metre of the kind current in the medieval textbooks of rhetoric, and he certainly knew verse in Latin and Italian which (if anything is recognizable) is written in very regular accentual metre. Descriptions of foot-metres are common enough in the Middle Ages. The earlier works in Mari's collection[2] are not very explicit, and appear to use the terms *spondaici* and *trochaici* interchangeably; but the notion of accentual verse in feet seems plain enough, and becomes even clearer in the *Ars Ritmica* of John of Garland, who introduces the idea of stress or beat (*percussio*):

DE TRESPONDAICIS—Rithmus qui habet tres percussiones clarescit in hoc exemplo sequenti:

> Rose sine nota
> gemma pulchra tota
> lutum peccatorum
> absolve nostrorum[3]

According to Atkins,[4] a reasonably clear differentiation of accentual and quantitative metres (*rithmus* and *metrum*) goes back in Latin at least as far as Bede. But though it is fair to assume that Chaucer knew this terminology it certainly cannot be assumed that he wrote verse in English at all like anything in Latin, or that his equivalent terminology means in English what John of Garland means in Latin. The possible usefulness of being sure that the medieval

---

[1] P. F. Baum, 'Chaucer's Metrical Prose', *The Journal of English and Germanic Philology*, vol. XLV, 1946.

[2] G. Mari, *I Tratti Medievali di Ritmica Latina*, Milan, 1899.

[3] *Ibid.* p. 37. 'SPONDAIC TRIMETER—The metre which has three stresses is made clear in this following example...'

[4] J. W. H. Atkins, *English Literary Criticism: the Medieval Phase*, Cambridge, 1943, pp. 45–6.

poets were not ignorant about metre is when thinking of Lydgate. Lydgate too was an educated man and knew about *rithmi*, so his rhythms cannot be explained by ignorance. His own (traditionally literary) apology for metrical incompetence itself shows that he knew what he was talking about:

> Euer as I can supprise in myn herte
> Alway with feare betwyxt drede and shame
> Leste oute of lose, any worde asterte
> In this metre, to make it seme lame...[1]

Benedict Burgh's continuation of Lydgate's *Secrees of Old Philisoffres* implies similar knowledge under the same mock-humble disguise:

> Yif I shulde talke / in scyencys tryuyal
> Gynnyng at grameer / in signes and figurys
> Or of metrys / the feet to make equal
> be tyme and proporcioun / kepyng my mesurys
> This lady [the Muse] list nat / to parte the tresurys
> Of hire Substance / to myne erys incondigne
> That am nat aquayntid / with the Musys ix.[2]

Further, rhyming Latin hymns of indubitable accentual regularity were familiar both to Chaucer and to Lydgate. Chaucer quotes in *The Prioress's Tale* the line

O alma redemptoris mater

both complete and in bits; and Lydgate translated, among others, *Vexilla Regis Prodeunt, Gaude Virgo Mater Christi, Ave Regina Celorum* and, twice, *Stella Celi Extirpant.*[3] But Lydgate always translates these Latin *rithmi* into his own metres. It would be stretching credulity too far to suppose he did so because he did not understand the metres of the originals.

I apply this argument to the more important case of Italian (see the Appendix, below). Chaucer certainly knew in Italian a regular accentual metre, but there is no evidence that he thought his English *rym* followed the same rules as Dante's or Boccaccio's *rima*.

So although we may be sure that Chaucer was as crafty about

---

[1] *The Floure of Curtesye*, stanza 34. Cited by Spurgeon, *Chaucer Criticism*, part I, p. 15.

[2] *Secrees of Old Philisoffres*, ed. R. Steele, E.E.T.S. 1894, lines 1527–33.

[3] His versions are all to be found in volume I of the *Minor Poems*.

metres as the next man, we cannot learn from his terminology exactly what metrical rules he thought he was following. All we can know for certain from this evidence (if the lesson is necessary) is that the court poets of the fourteenth and fifteenth centuries in England knew what they were doing. A Lydgate who does it on purpose may seem as hard to understand as one who commits his lines by accident; but we must take this first step of allowing him to be responsible for his actions.

5
Final -e

The two linguistic devices used by Tyrwhitt and his followers to make Chaucer's metre regular, and presented by them as forgotten parts of medieval English, were the sounding of some now mute final -e's and the variable stressing of disyllabic words, especially ones of recent French origin; and on these practices to this day Chaucer's status as a writer of iambic pentameter rests. But can it be shown that Chaucer expected these -e's to be pronounced and these words variably accented? And even if he did, need we do the same in our own reading?

It is easy to see that between them these two devices can make a great difference to the number of syllables in a line or the way they are accented, hence, to the rhythms and the metre. If, for example, one could sound -e's and change word-accents in modern English, the sentence you're reading would make a group of nice, though listless, pentameters:

> If, for example, one could sound -e's
>
> And change word-accents in modern English,
>
> The sentence you're reading would make a group
>
> Of nice, though listless, pentameters.

The differences made by sounded -e and variable stress can be striking in Chaucer:

A 954   Hym thoughte that his herte wolde breke
or
         Hym thought that his hert wold break
and
A 3530   Werk al by conseil and thou shalt nat rewe.
         And if thou werken wolt by good conseil...

Moreover, it is usually easy enough to find in the manuscripts any spelling one happens to be looking for, a fact well known to Chaucer editors.

82

But to say that sounded -e's and variable stresses make a difference to reading is not to understand *what* difference; and it has been too easily assumed in the past that any difference is an improvement, and proved to be right, if it renders Chaucer's language metrical or if it reproduces noises made in the fourteenth century. Any convincing argument to make us sound -e's must, however, go as far as showing what that sounding does to the verse. It is only a sufficient justification to say that sounding -e's makes the verse metrical if we go on and explore what that metre is doing; for Chaucer might perhaps retain more of his true life as prose. So I shall try to show that no convincing account of sounded final -e in Chaucer is possible without an explanation of the rhetorical effects of the sound. I would like to make the kind of sense of it that is possible with the disyllabic *-ion* ending optional in Shakespeare's time. In *The Spanish Tragedy* this ending is, so far as I can see, monosyllabic or disyllabic purely to suit Kyd's metrical convenience: you read the one that fills the line. But Kyd is a bad writer. With Shakespeare or Donne you also normally read the form that makes the metre—but which makes, at the same time, some rhetorical point that is the justification for reading metrically (or, perhaps, for reading at all).

> Our two soules, therefore, which are one,
> Though I must goe, endure not yet
> A breach, but an expansion[1]

enacts itself.

But to follow tradition and take first questions of fact—though I concede them no logical priority over questions of taste—we will begin by reviewing the evidence for supposing that Chaucer expected any weak final -e's to be pronounced.

Assuming that Chaucer sounded the same -e's in verse as in speech, it seems reasonable to begin by asking what -e's were sounded in educated London speech of the late fourteenth century. But unfortunately the question cannot be answered at all precisely without one head of evidence that we shall later consider. What we know is that throughout the Anglo-Saxon period many words ended in -a, that the descendants of these words in Middle English were usually spelled to end in -e, and that by the early Tudor period these -e's were all mute. (There were other final -e's, of

---

[1] Donne, 'A Valediction: forbidding Mourning'.

course, but we will confine ourselves to the most important cases.) From these facts a reasonable inference is made that the Anglo-Saxon final -a, whatever sound or sounds it may have represented, changed into a less stressed vowel as, with the disappearance of inflections, it became less functional, and that the resulting -e sound (whatever *that* was) itself died out by the end of the Middle English period. Tyrwhitt says this as well and as vaguely as need be: 'When we find that a great number of those words, which in Chaucer's time ended in *e*, originally ended in *a*, we may reasonably presume, that our ancestors first passed from the broader sound of *a* to the thinner sound of *e* feminine, and not at once from *a* to *e* mute.'[1]

It is even possible to have an opinion about what sound -e represented. All scholars are agreed (with the partial exception of Dr Bond, see below) that it was the unstressed central vowel, the noise one makes by the most unemphasized and unshaped grunt; and this certainly is a sound into which vowels might be expected to subside on their way to oblivion.

Our difficulties begin when we ask *when* the -e's ceased to be pronounced, and become acute if we ask *why* they ceased to be pronounced, or what they did when they were pronounced. We need to know the state of the -e in the London English of the late fourteenth century; but no scholar—in the absence of the one head of evidence we shall consider later—can give accurate enough dates. In any case it could never be possible to give an exact date for the disappearance of any particular -e; they cannot have been here today and gone tomorrow. If the sounding of -e's had ever become unfashionable, they might have died out fairly quickly, but there is no evidence for such a development, so one assumes the dying out was very gradual. And if one says that such and such an -e died out 'about 1400' that must surely imply that some people stopped sounding them ten or twenty years before and others went on sounding them ten or twenty years afterwards. It is because questions about the dying out of -e's do not admit of precise answers that even the most scrupulous philologists resort to metaphor when describing the process:

What really seems to have happened was that at first certain specific viruses attacked certain specific -e's...then other viruses later attacked other -e's...and so on, through four or five quite distinct epidemics. But

[1] Tyrwhitt, 'Language and Versification', pp. 58–9.

just as certain individuals and certain localities frequently escape diseases prevalent on all sides of them, so certain spheres of English...seem not to have been affected equally by all the blights suffered by -e...Finally, during the thirteenth century in the north and during the fourteenth and early fifteenth centuries in the south, there became virulent the epidemic which ultimately obliterated all surviving final -e's.[1]

So Southworth is mistaken when he argues that recent scholarship has achieved 'the setting of the terminal date for the pronunciation of final -e in speech at about 1350'.[2] This cannot be said unless 'about' is so elastic as to make the contention meaningless.

But it would be useful to know whether *any* -e's were sounded uneccentrically in the London speech of Richard II's time. Perhaps there are ways of finding out apart from the broad certainties of historical phonology. Some seem obvious.

The most ready and easy ways that have been attempted in showing that -e's really were pronounced are two arguments from rhyme. Firstly: Chaucer never appears to rhyme words with a possibly sounded -e with words without -e, except in *Sir Thopas*. For instance *chivalrye*, a word with a weak -e, rhymes with *murily*, a word without -e, and *grace* with *was*, only in *Sir Thopas*. Scholars infer that these rhymes were comic for Chaucer because the -e was sounded, and that if -e were not sounded in rhyme these rhymes would not be comic and Chaucer would use them ordinarily. Therefore, the argument runs, all weak -e's in rhyme are to be pronounced—and if they can be pronounced at the line-end they should presumably be pronounced internally as well, unless elided. Hence Chaucer sounded a great many final -e's in speech. This argument is not as finally convincing as it is sometimes taken to be (as in Mr F. W. Bateson's *Guide to English Literature*). There is nothing inevitable about this explanation of the fact that words in -e do not rhyme with words without -e. There might be a variety of other reasons. It would surely be rash to assert, for example, that in Chaucer's day there was no phonemic difference between the vowel sounds in words without -e and vowel sounds in apparently rhyming words that had recently lost an -e. Perhaps the -y of *chivalrye* might have been more of a back vowel or higher than the -y of *murily*, or perhaps it might have been longer. Perhaps *grace* failed to rhyme with *was* for Chaucer (as for us)

---

[1] E. T. Donaldson, 'Chaucer's Final -E', *PMLA*, vol. LXIII, 1948, p. 1110.

[2] J. G. Southworth, 'Chaucer: A Plea for a Reliable Text', *College English*, 1964, p. 175.

both in its vowel and consonant. Or again, even if these rhymes were as phonetically perfect as rhymes can be, the memory that a word had recently had a sounded -e could conceivably have affected its behaviour in rhyme: the rhymes might have sounded wrong to Chaucer even if nothing wrong could be measured. Hopkins in fact makes almost this objection to certain of Dixon's rhymes:

By the by there is one thing Keats's authority can never excuse, and that is rhyming open vowels to silent *rs*, as *higher* to *Thalia*: as long as the *r* is pronounced by anybody, and it is by a good many yet, the feeling that it is there makes this rhyme most offensive, not indeed to the ear, but to the mind.[1]

And even if we opt for sounding the -e's as the simplest way of accounting for the phenomena, we are here making inferences from such very incomplete data that we shouldn't have very much confidence of being right; no opinion based on such facts ought to be held very strongly.

But the explanation of these rhymes which I believe most likely to be true is the exact opposite of the usual one. Chaucer separates words with a possible -e from words without -e not because he insists on -e's being sounded but precisely because he wishes to leave the question of sounding open. Had he rhymed words with and without -e he would have settled the question and forced those who wished to sound to spoil the rhyme. This inference that Chaucer did not wish to tell the reader whether or not to sound -e in rhyme can be drawn from the evidence as naturally as the opposite, that he wished to insist on the sounding; and I choose the former as the more likely, and offer it as an opinion capable of being held (though I would not wish to retreat with it into the last ditch) both because I shall below relate it to a view of the behaviour of -e within the line and because, as I hope to show, it fits into a better reading of Chaucer.

The other argument from rhyme, first elaborated by A. J. Ellis, and used in recent years by both Baum and Donaldson, may be stated thus: Some words that end the line in Chaucer have without doubt a final -e that is sounded; they rhyme with words where the final -e would otherwise be in doubt; therefore the doubtful words have a sounded -e in these places and presumably in their other

[1] *The Correspondence of Gerard Manley Hopkins and Richard Watson Dixon*, ed. C. C. Abbott, second edition, Oxford, 1955, p. 37.

occurrences too. Professor Borroff applies it also to *Sir Gawain and the Green Knight*: 'There are at least two cases in which -*e* is unquestionably sounded in rhyme in *Gawain*, once when *forsoþe* "forsooth" (O E *for sōþe*, with inflectional -*e* preserved in a "petrified dative") rhymes with *to þe* "to thee" (413, 415), and once where *waþe* "danger" (O N *vaði*) rhymes with *ta þe* "take thee", imper. sg. (2355, 2357).'[1] This argument is weaker than the other from rhyme and cannot stand.

Firstly, the rhymes in question are between words which end in strong -e (*me, thee, ye*, etc.), and words in weak -e (*Rome, youthe, Troye*, etc.). This means either that strong -e and weak -e were like enough to rhyme, which no scholar argues, or that the -e's, if pronounced, did not rhyme. But the argument depends on the assumption that they did rhyme.

There is, however, another possible interpretation of these rhymes, not mentioned by any work I know, namely that these apparently strong -e's were really weak and that the words rhymed like any others in weak -e. This may look a wild suggestion but seems at least as probable as that strong -e's and weak -e's were pronounced and rhymed.

The favourite example, used by Donaldson, is the rhyme *Rome | to me*:

A 671   That streight was comen fro the court of Rome.
          Ful loude he soong 'Com hider, love, to me!'

The alternatives here are a rhyme *Rȯmé | tȯ mé* (strong -e's), a non-rhyme *Rómĕ | tŏ mé* or *Rom | to me*, or a rhyme *Rómĕ | tȯ mé* or *Rom | tom* (weak -e's sounded or silent). We may eliminate *Rŏmé* as obviously impossible. So if Chaucer is rhyming, as he usually seems to, we are left (apart from Southworth's odd suggestion that the rhyme is a joke) with the alternative of weak final -e's, sounded or silent, in both rhyme-words.

This is quite possible. The assimilation of *me* into a preceding word can easily be shown from the medieval poets. In *The Owl and the Nightingale*[2] are found the rhymes *dome |tome* (= *to me*)

---

[1] Borroff, *Sir Gawain and the Green Knight*, p. 155.
[2] *The Owl and the Nightingale*, ed. J. H. G. Grattan and G. F. H. Sykes, E.E.T.S. 1935, Cotton manuscript, lines 545–6, 1671–2 (in the latter example the Jesus manuscript has 'come | to me').

and *come* | *tome*; and the rhyme *untome* | *Rome* occurs in Gower.[1] Gower also uses the word *tome* within the line, where it can even, apparently, elide the -e:

> Tho spak he tome in such a wise...
> It were tome a gret desire.[2]

If *me* can become part of a word *tome* accented on the first syllable, it would not be strange if the -e descended from a secondarily stressed syllable to an unstressed one, became an ordinary weak -e, and followed the usual rules for the pronunciation of weak -e— whatever they are. In the case of Chaucer's rhyme *Rome* | *tome* many of the best manuscripts spell *tome* as one word, and the rest display a variety of alternatives which may well mean that some of the scribes were as puzzled as us. Among the manuscripts which spell *tome* are Hengwrt, B.M. Additional 5140, and Corpus (there are seven others). Variants include:

> Ful loude he songe / come heder loue come to me
> > (Manchester *et al.*)
> Ful loude he song com hider loue come
> > (Devonshire)
> Wel loved he song / come hedyr loue to me
> > (Egerton 2864)
> fful lowde he songe come heder love to me bone
> > (Bodley 686)
> fful lowde he song / come hidir / leue grome
> > (Northumberland *et al.*)

Perhaps especially informative is Hatton, whose scribe may have read or heard *tome* as a proper name and wrote:

> fful loude he sange come hither loue Thome

Manuscripts recognize other examples of this kind of assimilation, though less readily. For example at F 675–6 Manly & Rickert's text reads

> Quod the frankeleyn considerynge thy youthe
> So feelyngly thow spekest sire I allowthe

Hengwrt and some dozen others have 'allowthe'; some others read 'I thee alouthe'. The example at the second and fourth lines of

---

[1] *Conf. Am.* III, 99–100.
[2] *Conf. Am.* I, 294; II, 3160; see also I, 232; VIII, 2386. A similar form *byme* ('by me') is found at *Conf. Am.* III, 892; II, 2016 and IV, 1182 (all in rhyme). Skeat's note on the line of Chaucer we are considering quotes another *byme*.

Troilus and Criseyde, the rhyme *Troye | fro ye*, appears with the spelling *froye* in at least four manuscripts (but not in the texts of Robinson or Root). (But only Cambridge Gg. 4. 27 has 'seyye' at D 1456.) Conversely no manuscript spells 'tome' at F 542, where *me* has its usual strong -e and rhymes with *fre*.

The rhymes in *The Miller's Tale* on *blame, ba me* and *pa me* confused many scribes as much as *Rome | tome*. But this is one of the places where (to anticipate a main argument) one might perceive the rhetorical effect of this particular weak -e. Here Absalon's speech is ridiculously soft and Alison, by repeating his rhyme derisively, parodies his softness. The form may perhaps have had a special informality or intimacy which fits it both to Absalon's squeamish dandyism and to Alison's robust burlesque, as well as the more sinister sexuality of the Pardoner and Summoner.

In any case it seems that the monosyllable in strong -e becomes attached to the preceding word, the strong -e becomes weak—and the problem of whether to sound the weak -e is unsolved. These words no doubt obey the same rules as the others in weak -e but we cannot use them to discover the rules.

The other apparently easy ways of discovering whether -e's were sounded by Chaucer turn out equally elusive. As Professor T. J. Morgan pointed out to me, modern Welsh gives evidence for the medieval pronunciation of some English final -e's because words borrowed by Welsh from English in the medieval period sometimes retain the sounded -e in Welsh pronunciation: but the borrowings can never be dated as accurately as our purpose demands. On the face of it it would also seem that we can solve the problem by an appeal to music: all one would have to do is find settings of the words in question then read the music to see if it required the -e's to be pronounced. But the material is scarce (surprisingly enough no contemporary setting of Chaucer has survived) and inconclusive. Part of Dr John Stevens's reply to my request for help reads, '...the whole conception of the relationship between words and music is too casual and imprecise ever to tell us much...Anyway the composer expected the singer to *know* what to do with the detail of the underlay.' Again, progress might be made on the problem by a variety of statistical investigations, but all would have needed computers, years, money and mathematics not available to the present researcher.

So, having run through ideas such as these, scholars are still left, unless mistakenly convinced by some of them, with the question whether Chaucer expected any final -e's to be pronounced. To settle, finally and to their complete satisfaction, this question which is so necessary for the establishing of Chaucer's metres, scholars appeal to the head of evidence I have mentioned— which is none other than the metre itself and its consistency with grammar.[1] This position as traditionally held may be stated thus: The metre is regular because final -e's are sounded in accordance with historical grammar; final -e's are sounded in accordance with historical grammar because the metre is regular; therefore the metre is regular and final -e's are pronounced in accordance with historical grammar. Mrs McJimsey has an authoritative statement of the argument:

The scansion of a word in the interior of the line has, in the whole course of scientific investigation, been the chief key to Chaucer's pronunciation... In almost every line of Chaucerian [i e. Chaucer's] verse this assumption has served, and has allowed scholars to deduce such a regularity of grammar and meter in Chaucer's poems that the assumption may be accepted implicitly as a rule.[2]

Professor Donaldson too writes, 'within the verse the test of meter is a far better indication of whether a poet wished an -e pronounced than the spelling of the scribes',[3] and Dr Bond relies on metre in just the same way: '...the work of these scholars [Urry, Tyrwhitt, Ellis et al.] has provided a tool for determining when residual -e is syllabic and nonsyllabic—the method of scansion, which has been used and found adequate.'[4]

If the facts were as Mrs McJimsey stated them, her argument that the agreement of metre and grammar tells us which -e's to sound would be, within its limits, perfectly convincing. It would need refinement to make its notion of 'metre' less mechanical and more to do with the way poetry moves, but it would not be mistaken. But the grammar, which is the safeguard against a simple dependence on an unproven metre, is not regular, if by 'regular' is meant that these words obey comprehensible rules. Mrs

---

[1] 'The reasons for sounding the final -e...are grammatical.'—Skeat's one-volume edition of Chaucer, p. xviii. 'The philologist believes that the use of -e in Chaucer is in the main grammatical.'—E. T. Donaldson, op. cit. p. 1102.

[2] R. B. McJimsey, Chaucer's Irregular -E, New York, 1942, p. 5.

[3] Donaldson, op. cit. p. 1123.

[4] G. Bond, The Factors Governing the Pronunciation of Chaucer's Final -E, University of Michigan Ph.D. dissertation, 1946, p. 9.

McJimsey's statement about her assumption's right to be a rule comes at the beginning of a medium-sized book whose function is to provide a list of the exceptions, in the most heavily edited text, to the grammar, hence to the rule which can be a rule only if the exceptions are insignificant. The point of Donaldson's essay is similarly the consistency between metre and grammar; but consistency is achieved only by recognizing alternative forms of *all* words with a possibly sounded -e, that is, by saying that there is no grammatical rule about when to pronounce any of the possible -e's. With so widely permissive a 'rule' it might well be that any longish line of fourteenth-century verse could be read as pentameter; at any rate, a statistical investigation of some subtlety (and quite beyond the scope of the present work) would be needed before the grammatical argument for sounding -e could be shown to have any weight.

The simplest grammar would be to say that the -e's which do not occur in places where they elide should be sounded; but if so, Miss Babcock showed, the verse is even more unmetrical than if none of the -e's is pronounced.[1]

If we remove grammar, this argument for sounding -e is seen to depend nakedly on metre. As Kittredge—surely the best of the elder Chaucer critics—put it, 'apocope of -*e* cannot be brought under any rules but those of metrical exigency'.[2] Dr Bond too makes the observation with clarity and force:

Pronunciation of Chaucer's final -*e*, though it was a major concern of Chaucerian scholarship from 1721 to 1900, still remains a puzzle. The -*e* of a very large number of words is sometimes pronounced as a syllable, more frequently not. No reason is known for this unpredictable behaviour, and it has accordingly been concluded that the -*e* is pronounced or not pronounced 'at the pleasure of the writer', or in response to 'metrical exigency', that is, the demands of meter.[3]

The obvious retort to this line of argument (not made by Dr Bond, who is more interested in the absurdities of the grammar of alternative forms of words with and without -e) is that it depends on a certainty about metre which we simply do not possess. I have tried

---

[1] C. F. Babcock, 'A Study of the Metrical Use of the Inflectional -E in Middle English', *PMLA*, vol. XXIX, 1914. Writing before the appearance of the Chaucer Concordance, Miss Babcock thought that no word in Chaucer always retained its sounded -e; but in fact in the Concordance text read as modern pentameters a few words always have sounded -e.

[2] Cited by Bond, *op. cit.* p. 8.   [3] *Ibid.* p. 1.

to show that metre is not some indisputable demonstrable fact: the standard iambic pentameter, unlike the standard yard, cannot be stored in the Palace of Westminster; and metre cannot be used like this to tell us how to pronounce words unless also we are confident enough about our pronunciation to be able to read metrically. For all its obvious weaknesses, however, this argument might have a certain kind of convincingness, and we must continue by exploring what kind. But it perhaps begins to be clearer why, if metre and -e's establish each other, that can be only the first step in the argument: we shall have to go on and ask what these sounds and metres *do* in the verse, and replace grammar by reading as the nearest we can come to guarantees of the argument's validity.

Yet this traditional proof of the sounding of -e in Chaucer's verse is not wholly false. As they stand the arguments are inconsistently circular and the effects unexplored; but I think it possible to refine the old circularity to bring out, at least, some probabilities that some -e's are to be pronounced and, more important, to give some real evidence that these -e's should be sounded because such sounding has effects in the verse that a modern reader can appreciate.

It is possible to uncover certain statistics about the sounded -e's demanded by a regular metre which may to some extent take the place of grammar in the circular argument. The state of Chaucer's text introduces a degree of doubt into any such observations, but the following are true if the text of the Concordance[1] is reasonably close to Chaucer's and if we read his long lines as modern iambic pentameter.

1. Statistical investigations have shown that Chaucer's final -e is not sounded in accordance with any very simple grammar. But there is an important negative coherence. Words that cannot take -e obey grammar and never or hardly ever do so in a metrical reading, although the manuscripts frequently *spell* such words with an -e: so a metrical reading of the Concordance text demands that words should lose -e's arbitrarily but hardly ever that they should gain an ungrammatical -e. Perhaps this is only to say that there are *some* real rules in this game.

2. The problem whether or not to sound -e's occurs preponderantly at certain places in the line: at the third, fifth, seventh, ninth

---

[1] J. S. P. Tatlock and A. G. Kennedy, *A Concordance to the Complete Works of Geoffrey Chaucer*, Washington, 1927.

and possibly eleventh syllables of the line beginning with an un-stressed syllable, and at the fourth, sixth, eighth and tenth of the 'headless' line. That is to say that if -e's are sounded so as to produce regular pentameters the -e's are never metrically stressed,[1] and are not used as the unstressed part of a trochee. This can hardly be accidental and would alone show that the Concordance text places the -e's carefully, whether or not they are to be sounded. The strong suggestion here is that since the -e's occur in places where they can be thought of as filling the arsis of an iambic foot, there is point in seeing the line as metrical in the way traditionally supposed, i.e. a succession of feet.

3. A by-product of the Southworth–Donaldson controversy[2] of which neither scholar seems to have been aware is a set of figures that seems to show that Chaucer was often, perhaps normally, careful *not* to sound the final -e's. Southworth counted the silent -e's from some passages without distinguishing apocopated and elided -e. Donaldson then counted the silent -e's from the same passages, making the distinction. By subtracting the elided -e's from Southworth's total Donaldson reduced Southworth's number of unsounded -e's by over two-thirds. Dr Bond observed this too: 'examples of nonsyllabic -e occurring before words beginning with a vowel greatly outnumber the examples occurring before words beginning with a consonant'.[3]

Further: within Chaucer's lines words ending in a possibly

---

[1] There are a few exceptions even to this rule.

A 4020 John knew the wey hem nedede no gyde

A 4161 Ther nas na moore hem nedede no dwale

B 3943 And Phebus with his towaille so clene

Sounded final -e as part of a trochaic substitution is rather more common, though still very scarce.

A 219 As seyde hymself moore than a curat

A 320 His purchasyng myghte nat been infect

Cf. also A 1948, A 2304, A 2854, A 3484, A 3557, A 4112, B 163, B 3769, D 517, D 1609.

[2] *PMLA* 1947–9; see bibliography. Southworth began with an almost wholly orthodox essay on -e; only when attacked by the even more orthodox Donaldson did he inspect his arguments with the attention that led him to abandon them and write his heretical books.

[3] Bond, *op. cit.* p. 49. Bond is writing only about one passage of *Troilus and Criseyde*.

sounded -e are, I believe, followed by a vowel or h- much more often than words without -e.

Not counting dubious examples, *lord*, a word without -e, occurs within the lines of *The Canterbury Tales* 162 times. (Those inclined to make recounts will probably alter this and other figures by a few per cent, but not enough to affect the general picture.) In 101 cases *lord* is followed by a consonant and in 61 by a vowel or h-. This I believe to be a very ordinary set of figures for a word without -e, though there are no doubt exceptions. So too *god* in its first hundred internal verse listings in the Concordance is followed by a vowel or h- 40 times, by a consonant 60 times. The comparable figures for *man* (specimens only in the Concordance) are 20 and 35 and for the first 30 instances of *death* 10 and 20.

Words with a possible -e fall into two groups, both of which can be seen to contrast with words without -e. Most words with -e that I have counted (well over three-quarters) are followed far more often by a vowel or h- than is normal for words without -e, as:

Internal verse occurrences

	Before vowel or h-	Before consonant
cause	94	62
turne	33	12
trouthe	88	42
visage	11	2

There are also many words like *chide*, which looks as if it could have a sounded final -e but for which one cannot use the metrical test because *all* its internal occurrences are followed by a vowel or h-.

This seems to suggest that Chaucer's habit, conscious or not, was often to avoid the question of whether or not to sound an -e, by eliding it. The exceptional group of words strongly retaining their sounded -e provide some confirmation—words such as those giving modern words in *er*, *-en*, *-el*, and *-ow* were rarely given the chance to drop the -e in Chaucer. *Bettre*, for instance, which appears to be able to elide its -e, is followed by vowel or h- in thirteen internal verse occurrences but by a consonant in thirty-seven.

Unfortunately for this neat picture there is also a small group of words whose -e is now mute which in a great majority of cases Chaucer follows by a consonant. *Deere* (adjective) has only eight occurrences before vowel or h- within the lines of *The Canterbury Tales* as against thirty-nine before consonants; *church, sweete* and *leeve* (adjective) are all similar. The explanation of this group could be that in a few cases Chaucer felt that the ordinary pronunciation of a word was with sounded -e (*deere* for instance frequently appears to break the elision rule and have its -e sounded before a vowel or h-, especially in the phrase *deere herte*), though in most cases the -e is only to be sounded on special occasions, and on others left unambiguously silent through elision. This *could* all also link with my earlier contention that Chaucer leaves optional the sounding of -e at the line-ends: in all these cases he tends to avoid unnecessary problems whether by leaving the reader discretion at a place where some readers might otherwise damage the verse, or by preventing the problem arising at all when he elides the -e.

But a competent statistical enquiry into all the words in the Concordance would be necessary before one could be sure of the significance of these figures. It would be very difficult to be sure of what variation between numbers of occurrences is significant; moreover, any such investigation is full of difficulties about quantifying variables like the collocability of different words. (For example my attempts to compare verse occurrences with prose occurrences, an obvious line of enquiry, were hampered by the way phrases are often repeated in the prose works: *cause* was useless to count because in prose a majority of its occurrences are in the phrases *cause of* or *cause that*.) There would also be a set of problems connected with the possibly various tenacity of different words' hold on their -e's. There is a useful piece of work to be done by somebody who can command at once the necessary statistical competence and linguistic subtlety (not to mention the use of a computer). And since in one of its aspects this is a problem in statistics someone will certainly tackle it quite soon. Meanwhile these difficulties prevent me from making any great claims about my information: all I can say is that it *might* suggest that Chaucer differentiated words with -e from words without -e and that if so an obvious explanation would be that he wanted a few -e's to be sounded.

If the Concordance text were reliable these three sets of observations, taken together, could suggest fairly strongly a metrical value for -e pretty much in accordance with the established

95

theory, though that could only be our starting point, not the finished product the scholars suppose. The Concordance text is not reliable, however. There are over eighty manuscripts of *The Canterbury Tales*, and the Victorian editors, even Skeat, were strongly inclined to pick the most smooth-looking reading they could find. It may be that we have only so far shown that Chaucer's lines were rather like our iambic pentameters, not that they were the same.

4. It is possible to argue to Chaucer from metrical history. It is not difficult to find poets before, contemporary with and after Chaucer, whose verse, in almost any conceivable reading, is metrically regular in a sense Skeat could recognize. To show this by quotation is, of course, not a scientific proof, but would bring us as close to certainty as we can reasonably hope to come. Almost every reader will agree that *The Ormulum* has to be read in an extremely regular accentual metre which may be represented

$$\cup \text{ / } \cup \text{ / } \cup \text{ / } \cup \text{ / } \text{ | } \cup \text{ / } \cup \text{ / } \cup \text{ / } \cup$$

where ' / ' is a caesura or line-break. It is possible to offer this model in Orm's case, despite my objections in Chapter 2, above, to metrical models, precisely because Orm is a notoriously bad and mechanical writer: it fits one's sense of his work to think of him striving to imitate this model in every long line. Gower also appears, almost[1] incontrovertibly, to write in a very regular accentual metre both in *Confessio Amantis* and in his long-line poem *In Praise of Peace*. The anonymous fifteenth-century translation *Palladius on Housbondrie* has long been an exception made by the scholars to their belief that English courtly verse of that age is unmetrical. (Barton Lodge's E.E.T.S. edition of this work has many metrically irregular readings that are obviously corruptions of the smoother Wentworth Wodehouse manuscript.)[2]

If these three writers, Orm, Gower and the Palladius translator, are not writers of verse which ten Brink could have recognized as metrically regular, nothing can be known of Middle English verse. No hard questions about poetry are raised by this proposition, since all three are in their different ways hacks (and it seems right

---

[1] The 'almosts' in this paragraph are necessary because Professor Southworth dissents; but I have not been able to see the force of his objection.

[2] This manuscript seems to be lost, but fortunately there is a good photographic copy in the Bodleian.

that this sort of argument should lead us to pay more attention to hacks than to Chaucer). So it seems fair to base a sketch of the history of the verse use of sounded -e on their practice. And this, not surprisingly, is just what scholars have always supposed. (I forbear to quote the evidence for this statement: it would in any case only be an invitation to others to repeat my year's grubbing among the manuscripts which, of course, anyone who wishes is quite at liberty to do.) Orm has that consistency of metre and grammar which scholars would like to find in Chaucer. The sounded -e's permitted by grammar are usually, though with some exceptions, the ones demanded by his metre. At the other end of the history I only found three apparently sounded -e's in the first book ('January') of the Wentworth Wodehouse manuscript of the Palladius Translation. Gower is midway: he frequently uses words which lose their -e's before a consonant (less frequently, I believe, than Chaucer; though this is an impression which until the appearance of a Gower concordance cannot be demonstrated statistically) but also has many words that retain sounded -e. And where a good Gower manuscript has an -e we can say that the -e is normally to be pronounced or elided or taken as lengthening the preceding vowel: there is no haphazard scattering of -e's as in many good Chaucer manuscripts both early and late.[1] Therefore in Gower grammar is no longer much of a guide to the sounding of -e's, some of which have, nevertheless, to be pronounced.

So Chaucer, as a contemporary of Gower, is exactly where we might expect to find him, at the critical point where -e is in process of disappearance but sometimes still seems to be sounded.

Chaucer may well, then, have sounded some of the grammatically possible final -e's to give his long lines normally ten syllables and an iambic metre. This cannot be shown to be more than probable, and there are other tenable interpretations of the data. We might, with Skeat,[2] suppose that far more -e's are lightly sounded than the metre demands, which would be to abandon ten syllables per line in favour of a simpler grammar; or again we could follow the Nott tradition, sound no -e's, and settle for a line that has something in common with iambic pentameter but which is not quite iambic pentameter. The sounding of some -e's may be somewhat more probable than these other alternatives, but not so

---

[1] For some discussion of the Gower manuscripts see below, Chapter 7.
[2] See his remarks on 'Versification', *Chaucer's Works*, vol. VI.

much so that it would force us to rule out other alternatives if they made better poetry.

Any real argument in favour of sounding -e's so as to produce iambic pentameters must show how that improves the poetry. Tyrwhitt and his school have always taken this, the most difficult and important part of their argument, quite for granted: regularity is of itself preferable, they feel. But if there is a way forward it must be to link the questions of why Chaucer seems to sound some -e's and not others and of what effect a sounded -e might have on the movement of the verse.

Dr Bond is alone amongst the scholars whose work I know in asking any of these questions about why some -e's and not others are sounded. This being so, it is necessary that I should also show why his work as a whole is made completely unconvincing by one decisive fallacy in its central thesis. Bond begins by realizing that 'metrical exigency' is not in itself a good reason for believing that -e's should be sounded, and tries to find other explanations, coming up in the end with three rules of 'accentual context' which determine which -e's to pronounce. For these rules he claims triumphantly:

All 1,539 examples—words with inflectional -e, words with analogical -e, words with stems ending in -e; the words that rarely appear with syllabic -e, the ones that frequently appear with syllabic -e, the ones that are said 'never' to appear with syllabic -e—behave exactly the same. Weak adjectives, subjunctives, nouns, pronouns, adverbs, exhibit syllabic and non-syllabic -e in mechanical conformity with their accentual environment.[1]

These rules are:

A. Final -e belonging to an unaccented word or following an unaccented syllable does not in any instance constitute a syllable required by the meter.
B. Final -e following an accented syllable does not constitute a syllable required by the meter if the following word is an unaccented monosyllable or begins with an unaccented syllable.
C. Final -e following an accented syllable constitutes a syllable required by the meter if the next word is an accented monosyllable or begins with an accented syllable.[2]

This certainly looks very striking and simple; but it will not rescue the argument from dependence on metrical exigency, for unfortunately Dr Bond does not distinguish accent from metrical

---

[1] Bond, *op. cit.* p. 44.   [2] *Ibid.* pp. 33, 36, 40.

stress. So his three rules can be stated more simply as: -e is only pronounced if it occurs between two metrically stressed syllables. Moreover, Bond nowhere asks how we know which syllables are metrically stressed, and his scansions are in fact rather rigid. (For example

$$\smile \; \prime \;\; \smile \; \prime \;\; \smile \;\; \prime \; \smile \; \prime \; \smile \; \prime$$
My purpos is, er that I parte fro ye)[1]

Bond does not escape from the old metrical argument; his work is on the contrary only a restatement of it, without demonstration, in different terms. (But there are in the restatement certain points of interest we shall use below.) The worst result is that though Bond thinks he has solved the question of why some -e's are pronounced and not others he has really left it quite untouched: if the only reason is 'accentual environment' we can ask again the first question, 'Why does accentual environment demand that the same word shall sometimes appear with its -e and sometimes without?' And on this, except for a few paragraphs about why some consonants seem to retain a following -e more strongly than others, Bond has nothing to say. So the book disappointingly fails to advance very far with the questions it has interested the reader by formulating.

The question of what sounded -e could do in verse is, however, though not usually asked, capable of being answered.

In the first place, the old argument to -e from metre will not leave the metre untouched. This way of establishing that Chaucer wrote pentameters can only work if it modifies our idea of the pentameters he wrote; we can only have pentameters with -e's if we are willing for them to sound unfamiliar and at first odd. This is so whether or not one thinks of iambic pentameter as a time-metre. For if an -e occupies the arsis of an iambic foot it is the smallest sound that could possibly do so. If such a small sound has to occupy the time between two theses or, alternatively, if it has to maintain itself as the smaller partner of the stressed syllable in its foot, the movement of the language must be slowed, or else the metrical pattern will not be perceptible. The stresses on each side of the -e will have to be pronounced rather deliberately, so as to make it apparent that the -e is the whole of the unstressed part of the foot; and this in turn must create a peculiar sort of rhythmic

---

[1] Bond's investigation is confined to Book I of *Troilus and Criseyde*, in which he recognizes hardly any trochees.

phrase, which may well have some rhetorical point in the verse. For instance, in the Tercel Eagle's line

PF 427   My deere herte, have on my wo som routhe

the sounded -e on *deere* throws back a stress on to that word and makes the stresses on both *deere* and *herte* slow and deliberate. The result is an obviously effective way of speaking the phrase 'My deere herte'.

Secondly, let us imagine situations in which -e may have survived longest in spoken English. It is usual to say that final -e is sounded in Chaucer except when it is apocopated or elided. But since a great majority of final -e's are apocopated or elided it would be a fairer statement to say that in the comparatively unusual conditions created by the absence of elision or apocopation, -e may sometimes be pronounced. This distinction is not frivolous if it helps towards understanding how -e might have survived in common speech at the end of the fourteenth century, what sort of sound it might have been and what it might have done. Perhaps -e was sometimes called into being in certain circumstances, which is very different from saying that it was sometimes dropped.

Indeed the line between existence and non-existence of this sound need not be easy to draw. A phoneme must, one might suppose, either exist or not; but I have myself read Chaucer to an audience of academics in such a way that some thought they heard sounded final -e's which others thought were silent: the rhetorical effect was not, though, as far as I could discover, in any doubt. Ten Brink's position, that -e can occupy the arsis of an iambic foot without creating any special effect, is as misleading as the opposition belief that -e is not a syllable; for the effect of the ten Brink reading is to turn -e into -er, that is, to give the sound more prominence than we can believe it to have had in speech. In the *Parliament* line just quoted it would be only an extreme of my scansion to read with silent -e, lengthen and stress *deer* in the same way, and treat it as a monosyllabic foot: the rhetorical effect on the verse movement is similar in either case because -e is the smallest possible syllable. Dr Bond is right here: he is puzzled about what sound -e might represent and imagines it as even less than the small central vowel all other scholars wish to make it:

The variable behavior of residual -e points inevitably to the fact that the sound was no longer really vocalic. Instead, what had once been a weakened vowel had been gradually shortened and reduced until it had become merely a *conditioning factor in the pronunciation of whatever consonant preceded it*. In effect, Chaucer's -e constitutes a phonetic notation for a modified consonant. The combined sound represented by consonant plus residual -e is the sound of the consonant modified to some degree (not definitely determinable) by the vocalic remnant.[1]

If so it would be possible to see the consonant preceding the -e, rather than the -e itself, as syllabic, and that might explain why some scribes spelled words without syllabic -e, a fact to which Southworth attaches great importance. They might just have been taking it for granted that the last consonant would be given the required quantity, which final -e would only be another way of indicating.

Now if the -e was this tiny vestigial sound, called into being on some occasions, the situations where it would be pronounced would be, it is reasonable to guess, formal ones. Words would be pronounced less slowly and deliberately in gossip, any quick speech, or trivialities, and there the formal pronunciation of the last consonant, or the pronunciation of final -e, would be lost. But it might be retained for *sentences*, deliberate or formal speech of any sort, or proverbial phrases. This suggestion would replace a grammatical criterion for the sounding of possible -e's with a stylistic one.

It does seem true that if one pronounces the -e's in Chaucer to produce a sort of pentameter, the -e's one has to pronounce usually occur at such formal 'high' places, and the effect of the slowed rhythmic phrase produced by an -e in a pentameter is to emphasize the formality (with, of course, the particular fine variation that is the point of each line, and which must make such critical generalities as these seem crude). If this can be shown it will be an account of final -e that can make sense of the history of the language by showing the language at work in a convincing reading of Chaucer.

To take an extreme: two or more final -e's sounded in the same line almost always give a slowing and formalization which is used by the poet for grand or pathetic effects. Here for example are all the lines of *The Canterbury Tales* to include two or more sounded -e's one of which is on the word *herte*. (We are still reading the Concordance text as near as we can go to modern iambic pentameter.)

---

[1] Bond, *op. cit.* pp. 48–9.

A 954   Hym thoughte that his herte wolde breke

This is Theseus pitying the group of courtly ladies at the beginning of *The Knight's Tale*. The effect of the sounded -e's is to throw back stresses on 'thoughte', 'herte' and 'wolde' and, by making us create the metre so deliberately, to give an effective phrase-movement.

A 2649   His hardy herte myghte hym helpe naught

Again, the stress is thrown back before the -e's, with the result that the most important words in the line are most emphasized.

Oonly the intellect...

A 2805   Gan faillen when the herte felte deeth

The slowing of the movement in the second half of this line, with its culminating stress on 'deeth', is surely not hard to see and admire.

B 4578   They ronne so hem thoughte hir herte breke

Again, the slowing makes for a more forceful expression. One can see a comparable point in all the other examples.

D 1103   So wolde God myn herte wolde breste

E 142   Made the markys herte han pitee[1]

E 753   I deeme that hire herte was ful wo

The next five are all from *The Merchant's Tale* and have the force of that tale's malign denigration of all fineness of life. It is fitting that the only heartless tale should so overstress *herte*.

E 1341   Ther may no tonge telle or herte thynke

E 1980   That from hire herte she ne dryve kan

E 2075   So brente his herte that he wolde fayn

E 2096   She wayteth whan hire herte wolde breste

E 2306   Or elles swelle til myn herte breke

F 566   Me thoughte I felte deeth myn herte twiste

---

[1] This seems to be the very rare -e as the arsis of a trochee: but Chaucer may have written 'Maden'.

Examples from *Troilus and Criseyde* are also convincing. I quote
only one, from the Letter of Troilus:

v 1401   Ywis myne owne dere herte trewe

Almost all these lines justify their sounded -e's by rhetorical
effectiveness, whether of the simple dignity of the Knight's slowed
movement (A 954 and A 2805) or the Nun's Priest's increased
emphasis (B 4578, where one might have expected the narrator to
be in too much of a hurry to sound the -e) or the ironic effects of
The Merchant's Tale. The expressiveness is convincing, also, in
many lines where *herte* is the only word with sounded -e:

c 655   This daggere shal thurghout thyn herte go

B 4079   She was agast and seyde O herte deere

B 879   The Constable gan about his herte colde

Conversely the loss of -e from *herte* often sounds right, giving a
more ordinary and unemphasized run to the verse:

D 572   I holde a mouses herte nat worth a leek

This is the Wife of Bath, too much in a hurry to pause. Similarly
the Squire's immature haste makes him drop -e's his father would
have retained:

F 212   Myn herte quod oon is evermoore in drede

F 541–2   And yeven hym my trewe herte as fre
          As he swoor he yaf his herte to me[1]

But the Franklin who immediately follows sounds his -e's as
befits his mature seniority:

F 860   For verray feere so wolde hire herte quake

F 893   Thise rokkes sleen myn herte for the feere

F 1023   Hym semed that he felte his herte colde

Perhaps *herte* is a loaded word: you expect it to occur in places
of high sentence or grief, and so the correlation between such
places and sounded -e might be coincidental. But similar principles

[1] This line may be headless; alternatively it may have a monosyllabic second
foot.

seem to determine whether or not the -e on *face* is sounded. *Face* is one of the words which normally drop -e by elision or occurrence at the line-end. The places where its -e is sounded are nearly all solemn or formal or sad. The *Canterbury Tales* instances are:

A 1403   That sith his facĕ was so disfigured

A 1578   As he were wood, with facĕ deed and pale

B 3956   And covere hir brightĕ facĕ with a clowde

(the Monk's high style)

B 4213   With a ful pitous facĕ pale of hewe

C 209   And with a facĕ deed as asshen colde

E 1399   With facĕ sad his tale he hath hem toold

E 2269   With facĕ boold they shulle hemself excuse

(*sententia*)

F 1340   In al hire facĕ nas a drope of blood

B 1779   With facĕ pale of drede and bisy thoght

F 1353   With facĕ pale and with ful sorweful cheere

H 276   Now listow deed with facĕ pale of hewe

(It is also true of course that most of these faces with sounded -e are in the dative case, which might help the -e to survive.) Jolly faces tend to elide the -e; and there are two *Canterbury Tales* instances of *face* with apocopated -e which fit the scheme reasonably well:

B 649   Men myghte knowe his face that was bistad

and (the Wife again):

D 540   That made his face ful often reed and hoot

There is one sounded -e in *Troilus and Criseyde* which I would have expected to be silent:

II 110   Do wey your barbe and shewe your facĕ bare

but otherwise the picture is coherent.

Hooste tends to have a sounded -e when Chaucer is introducing some new activity of Harry Bailly which justifies the stressing of his title.

The only example of a sounded -e on *nose* is:

D 2264   Ful sadly leye his nosĕ shal a frere

which, as the solution of the problem set in *The Summoner's Tale*, is mock-heroic.

The -e's on *hye* are rather different. The -e seems ordinarily to have disappeared from this word but to survive firstly in a few rhetorically justifiable places like

A 2075   This goddesse on an hert ful hyĕ seet

A 2463   Myn is the ruine of the hyĕ halles

(this is said by Saturn, *infortuna major*)

B 3766   To telle his hyĕ roial magestee,

    His hyĕ pride, his werkes venymus.[1]

Secondly the -e on *hye* is usually found sounded in the proverbial phrase 'hye God' for which the explanation is itself obviously rhetorical.

Once one begins to develop a sense of why -e might be sounded, some soundings can look irresistibly right. When May in *The Merchant's Tale* advances from cuckolding January to cozening him, she speaks a line whose slow movement, made above all by a repeated sounded -e, expresses the exact hypocrisy of her explanation that up the tree with Damian she was only 'struggling':

E 2387   Ye maze, maze, goode sire, quod she

---

[1] Where *hye* drops its -e in high places we very often find instead a trochaic fifth foot which, as will be explained in the next chapter, has a rhetorical effect rather like that of sounded -e. For example:

A 306   And short and quyk and ful of hy sentence

A 1798   Now looketh, is nat that an heigh folye

A 2487   And spenten it in Venus heigh servyse

105

So too the Reeve's Miller (on being told by the 'clerk' that he has swyved his, the Miller's, daughter 'bolt upright' three times) gets the feeling of his reply into a line whose movement is controlled by two final -e's:

Hast?

A 4269 　　　　A! false traitour, false clerk, quod he

The heavily lagging emphasis on the repeated *false* is made by its sounded -e's.

Leeve is a word that cries out for emotional treatment and receives it in the mad sermon of the Pardoner:

C 731 　　　　And seye 'Leeve mooder, leet me in'

The Wife of Bath on the other hand has no time for such fine language when she is remembering how she dealt with her husbands:

D 365 　　　　O leeve sire shrewe, Jhesu shorte thy lyf!

Of the four possible -e's she only sounds one: I think it is the one I mark (though we can take our pick) because that gives the contemptuous emphasis on *shrew* that fits the line without slowing down the tirade too much. But the Wife is quite capable of slowing down, and sounding her -e's, when that helps her onslaught on her husbands. She emphasises the right word here with an easily perceptible tone of offensiveness:

D 332 　　　　Ye shul have queynte right ynogh at eve

Similarly when bringing off her finest and most insincere effect she relies on two beautifully sounded -e's to convince Jankin:

D 800 　　　　'O hastow slayn me false theef?' I seyde

　　　　　　　'And for my land thus hastow mordred me?

　　　　　　　Er I be deed yet wol I kisse thee.'

Finally, the second stanza of the Palinode to *Troilus and Criseyde* could, with apocopated -e's, start with a very catchy little tetrameter:

V 1835 　　　　O yong fressh folkes he or she

106

It is the sounding of the -e's which puts a very solemn stress on the adjectives and at the same time makes the line go at a more fittingly slow and decorous pace:

O yongĕ fresshĕ folkes, he or she

I do not say that I can make sense of *all* the sounded -e's in Chaucer. Sometimes the stress and movement resulting from a sounding seem inappropriate: I don't know what to do with 'Stratford attĕ Bowe', and there are several instances of sounded -e on *hadde* which I don't see the point of. (See for instance A 310, A 386, A 3969.) But this is only to observe firstly that even Homer nods; not all Chaucer's lines are good—and secondly that critics nod too and I must be missing many of Chaucer's felicities.

Sounding a final -e in Chaucer is always very like reading a monosyllabic foot. If an unstressed syllable is missing in an iambic line the monosyllabic foot, receiving a stress which has to be perceived as a stress without the unstressed syllable one usually has to compare it with, must also be a phrase-stress or 'beat'. Because of the missing syllable the beat will come next to another metrically stressed syllable, resulting in a phrase with two stresses. But phrases with two stresses are, we have seen, the units of alliterative verse: a phrase with two stresses is the same as a half-line. So the very corner-stone of the iambic theory must itself support the creation in Chaucer's lines of phrases that move in ways that have something in common with those of *Piers Plowman*. It is at least possible that such phrases may be part of the metre that leads to them; they may form part of our expectation, and the exploration of this idea will be a central part of this work. At any rate, in the examples above, the sounded -e's are effective because of the phrase-rhythms they control. The reason for sounding some -e's is that to do so helps the expressiveness of Chaucer's poetry.

Unless this kind of reason can be adduced it cannot matter whether or not we sound -e's in our own reading—or whether Chaucer did in his. I apply this, finally, to the vexed question of the final -e in rhyme. In showing that there can be nothing like a final demonstration that Chaucer expected these to be sounded, I have been willing to concede that such probabilities as we can find suggest that he may well have sounded them. But we are not here in a scientific context where such a weighing of probability could commit us to believing the most probable conclusion. The

-e in rhyme is one of those inessential sounds we can if need be ignore without doing disastrous damage to the poetry. And there is a very good reason for not sounding the -e's in rhyme: they make Chaucer's poetry sound second-rate, bad in an uncharacteristic way: they make him sound stilted, sing-song and artificial.

A 1251   Allas why pleynen folk so in commune
             On purveiaunce of God or of Fortune?

There the sounded -e's are the push from simplicity over into childishness.

All our metrical arguments are based on the way we read and are successful only if they lead back to an improved reading. If the opposite occurs the argument is wrong. So: do not sound the -e's in rhyme (or anywhere else) unless you can make them sound *right*. That is the best advice I can offer: if the metre seems to demand an -e sound it, but if the resulting reading damages the poetry, suspect the metre that led to it.

6

Variable Stress

Many of Chaucer's lines are made unmetrical to the modern ear if words of two syllables are accented in the modern way. To read

$$\text{And bathed every veyne in swich li}\overset{/}{\text{co}}\overset{\smile}{\text{ur}}$$
$$\text{Of which v}\overset{/}{\text{er}}\overset{\smile}{\text{tu}} \text{ engendred is the flour}$$

offends orthodox iambic expectations because it causes trochaic substitutions in the fifth and second feet. So Chaucer's couplet is usually read:

$$\text{And bathed every veyne in swich li}\overset{\smile}{\text{co}}\overset{/}{\text{ur}}$$
$$\text{Of which v}\overset{\smile}{\text{er}}\overset{/}{\text{tu}} \text{ engendred is the flour}$$

But since *licour*, *vertu* and many similar words are elsewhere stressed in the modern way to make pentameters it follows that if Chaucer's lines obey the editorial rules for pentameter these words must be able to be stressed either way, that is, must be of 'variable stress' or, as it is sometimes called, 'alternative accentuation'. For instance, at all its other occurrences in Chaucer's verse *vertu* appears to be stressed *vértu*.

The usual explanation of variable stress is that the majority of the words concerned had in Chaucer's day been only recently borrowed from French and that their accentuation in English had not yet settled down, so that they could be equally well stressed either way. The situation is said to persist into the seventeenth century:

A second important feature of sixteenth- and seventeenth-century accentuation is that there was considerable uncertainty in many words where to place the chief stress. The causes are various. . . In disyllables of French and Latin origin there is conflict between the English system of stress on the first syllable and the original stressing on the second; in recent adoptions the foreign stressing is apt to prevail.[1]

[1] Dobson, *English Pronunciation 1500–1700*, 2nd edition, vol. II, pp. 446–7. An essay which I did not see until after this work went to press (M. Halle and S. J. Keyser, 'Chaucer and the Study of Prosody', *College English*, vol. XXVIII,

But in Chaucer the question of variable stress only arises at all because we are reading metrically. The reason for stressing these words variably takes the form of a circular argument very like the one traditionally used to justify the sounding of some final -e's: the metre is regular therefore some words are of variable stress; some words are of variable stress therefore the metre is regular: therefore the metre is regular and some words are of variable stress. But if there is no evidence for variable stress except the metre, the strength of the argument for variable stress depends wholly on how well we know the metre. And since 'knowing the metre' is being able to use it to make sense of the poetry, we shall only be convinced by this circular argument if the metre it appeals to and at the same time offers to establish is one that leads to poetry good enough to attribute to Chaucer. But before proceeding to this essential and neglected question it will first be necessary to show that the usual argument about variable stress is as circular as I have asserted it to be.

This circularity of argument is in fact clear in all the standard scholarly treatments of the question, including those by Luick, Learned and Danielsson (see the Bibliography), and it is so well established that Professor Gimson treats its conclusions as mere fact: 'Finally, the metre of verse reveals the stress accent of words. It is for this reason that we know that French words, in Chaucer's verse, generally retained their original accentual pattern.'[1] Unfortunately the problem is that if one relies on verse-stress these words (which, by the way, are all English) don't 'generally' do one thing or the other; their stress seems to vary at the poet's whim.

Danielsson's book, the painstakingly thorough standard work, accepts verse-stress as evidence of speech-stress only after

1966, pp. 187–219) offers an alternative theory, that the words of alternative stress are really alternative forms produced by the regular operation of a predominant 'Romance stress rule'. I cannot now discuss this view, but I am not convinced by it. I regard it as a relevant objection that the metrical theory of the essay generates scansions such as

A 2128   Ther maistow seen cominge with Palamon   (p. 195)

but regards

A 122   Ful weel she soong the service dyvyne

as unmetrical. These are unlikely to find acceptance.

[1] Gimson, *Pronunciation*, p. 15.

exhausting all the other heads of evidence. Danielsson realizes the trickiness of this evidence but is driven to it in the end.

> Since there are no primary sources—i.e. accented dictionaries—prior to 1570, my account of accentual conditions before that time has been mainly based on inferences from verse-stress. . . In this connection it ought to be pointed out that, in the absence of definite evidence, we have no right to assume that the accentuation of loan-words in Middle English was fundamentally different from the historically demonstrable accentuation, i.e. the accentuation indicated in Modern English dictionaries, by modern English lexicographers, orthoepists, etc.[1] . . .
>
> But from *verse-stress* certain conclusions can be drawn as to *word accent*, for an all-pervading characteristic of English verse is what Scripture. . . terms the Prose Principle, expressed by Young. . . in the following way: 'Within a foot stress must not contravene accent.'[2]

The difficulty in this line of argument is, of course, that one can only be as sure of the word stresses as of the metre that produces them. Danielsson knows this:

> Now if we want to decide the stressing of words in a poetical work, we must first and foremost find out the criteria for ascertaining a correct scansion in the spirit of the author. . . Thus in many cases a final decision on the scansion of a metrical line can only be arrived at by a careful study of the metrical habits of a poet.[3]

and:

> I have therefore had to investigate the prosodical habits of every individual poet from whom I have quoted, and to consider whether prosodical irregularities are due to variation of word accent or to variations in verse-stress.[4]

But Danielsson felt no need to make such careful studies and investigations of Chaucer, because it had already been done by ten Brink—whose authority, rather than any authority possibly to be gained from experience of reading Chaucer, is used to establish the crucially controversial point on which Danielsson's argument rests: 'For both the four-stress and the five-stress line the last stress of the line must fall on the syllable within the rime carrying a principal or secondary accent. Cf. ten Brink. . .'[5] And since 'final

---

[1] Bror Danielsson, *Studies on the Accentuation of Polysyllabic Latin, Greek and Romance Loan-words in English*, Stockholm, 1948, p. 2.
[2] *Ibid.* p. 440. Scripture is a man's name.
[3] *Ibid.* p. 442.
[4] *Ibid.* p. 2.   [5] *Ibid.* p. 492.

stress-shift does not occur'[1] it is very easy by following these rules to deduce word-accents. But I know of no reason for believing ten Brink's contention that trochaic substitution is impossible in the fifth foot of Chaucer's pentameter, and neither he nor Danielsson presents any. It is important to realize that this firm belief in the impossibility of 'final stress-shift' is really just the kind of controversial matter that needs to be thought about before the scholar can read the verse 'in the spirit of the author', and that by failing to make any investigation here Danielsson invalidates his conclusions. It is only true that final stress-shift does not occur if there are words of variable stress; so we cannot know whether there are words of variable stress until we know whether final stress-shift occurs. The argument is perfectly circular.

H. D. Learned's formulation was even more straightforward: 'The usage of the Middle English poets as to the accentuation of French words seems to be based solely on metrical convenience. From *The Owl and the Nightingale* to Chaucer and even later, literally countless examples occur.'[2] What this really means is, 'Our reading of the medieval poets is based solely on metrical convenience: we want to read with what we take to be modern metre, and that causes literally countless examples of variable stress.' But whether our metrical convenience is the same as Chaucer's is the essential question that is never asked. 'Metrical convenience' *is* all that we are offered as an explanation of variable stress in Chaucer. Professor Baum (who as shown below, p. 116, confuses variable stress with trochaic inversion) writes, 'Inversion serves for emphasis and for variety, but in Chaucer's practice it seems often a mere convenience.'[3] Professor Borroff, who assumes with all other scholars that in four- or five-foot English iambic lines the last foot is always an iamb, says that variable stress at the line-end must often 'represent an artificial mode of accentuation used solely for purposes of rhyme'.[4]

This traditional position is almost the worst possible one, because by attributing variable stress solely to metrical convenience, scholars deny it any expressive function.

But perhaps it will be objected that all this is cavilling about a

[1] *Ibid.* p. 491.
[2] H. D. Learned, 'The Accentuation of Old French Loanwords in English', *PMLA*, vol. XXXVII, 1922, p. 710.
[3] *Chaucer's Verse*, p. 16.
[4] Borroff, *Sir Gawain and the Green Knight*, p. 151.

perfectly ordinary part of English, whether of the fourteenth century or the present day. Are there not plenty of words of variable stress in modern English? Why make such a fuss about their existence in the fourteenth century?

Genuine variable stress in modern English disyllables is most common as an aspect of what Dobson calls 'fluctuating stress',[1] which he thinks a modern development from disyllables of level stress, two monosyllables of more or less equal stress which join into one word, as *churchyard*. It is true that in modern English there are some disyllables which can have either of two accent-patterns at the whim of the speaker: *dispute*, for instance, or *finance*, or *week-end*, or *Doreen*. When these words occur in verse, metre does take the place of individual inclination and choose from the alternatives:

> The mighty queen
> Was called Doreen

but

> Hot and panting from the town
> Doreen dashed the pudding down

But words whose stress is genuinely variable according to individual choice are not common in modern English. It is more usual with words that can have different stress-patterns for only one to be correct in any particular place, and correctness would not then be determined by metre. We say *sixtéen* or *síxteen* in different contexts. 'She was sixtéen.' 'Séventeen did you say?' 'No, síxteen.' In counting, *sixteen* would be stressed on the first syllable: 'Thírteen, foúrteen, fífteen, síxteen...' 'Thírteen, foúrteen, fífteen, sixtéen' would be wrong except in special cases (as when a man was trying to reach a total of sixteen, counting shillings perhaps, and succeeded). So when Professor Borroff, following Jespersen, uses as examples of words of variable stress *uphill* and *unmade* one must object that they belong with *sixteen* more than with *Doreen* where we really can choose the accent scheme. We say

---

[1] E. J. Dobson, *op. cit.* vol. II, p. 449. I neglect the question of secondary stress often introduced by writers on variable stress, since it cannot affect the metrical problems. If the last foot of an iambic pentameter consists of a word stressed ′ ﹨, the foot is still trochaic and our problems remain, unaltered.

'an úphill walk' but 'a walk uphíll' and 'to leave a bed unmáde'
but 'to leave an únmade bed'. If a poet altered these stress-patterns
for the sake of metre the effect would be as odd as any other
wrenched accent:

> He liked the downs of turf and chalk;
> He went away for an uphill walk,

but not

> The wind was north, the weather chill,
> He contemplated an uphill
> Walk.

We could say 'an úndone duty' but Beaumont and Fletcher make
a joke of the incorrectness of 'custom úndone':

> And let it ne'er be said for shame that we the youths of London
> Lay thrumming of our caps at home, and left our custom undone.[1]

Now it is happily assumed by those who argue for words of
variable stress in the medieval poets that all the disyllabic words in
question were like *Doreen*, and that their right accentuation depends only on metre. But the step from a rather scarce pheno-
menon (the words like *Doreen*) to a class so large and powerful that
it can influence by analogy words not apparently of variable stress,
is an enormous one.[2]

The opposite objection, that it is normal for English poets to
wrench stress, and that therefore the question of 'variable stress'
in Chaucer need not arise, is less substantial. It is true that
Cowper, Wordsworth and (more frequently) Shelley do sometimes
wrench word-stress for the sake of metre. But here too difference
of frequency matters: if there were as many wrenched stresses in
Shelley as words of apparently variable stress in Chaucer, Shelley's
verse would read very differently. And in any case the practice of
a later age cannot without difficult and subtle argument be applied

---

[1] *The Knight of the Burning Pestle*, IV, v.

[2] An admirable recent dissertation has shown how the same jump from a few
examples to a large mass used to be made in Wyatt's case. Miss Endicott, after
listing the reasons why some words in Wyatt may have been of variable stress
adds, 'But the great majority of words for which..."Romance accent" is
suggested fall into none of these categories.'—Annabel M. Endicott, *A Critical
Study of Metrical Effects in the Poetry of Sir Thomas Wyatt*, London M.A.
dissertation, 1963, p. 37.

to Chaucer. It might be more persuasive to remark that the age when metre was so strong that it could affect word-accent was the same one that decreed variable stresses in Chaucer.

This belief in large numbers of words of variable stress seems to fly in the face not only of the deep-rooted habits of Germanic languages but also of the great traditions of British snobbery. It seems unlikely that a society that could sneer at the French of Stratford atte Bowe would not establish one stress-pattern as more proper and civilized for a word than another. And since in the great majority of the occurrences of these words in Chaucer they seem already to have their modern accent-pattern, why should we not believe that any other was already incorrect? The only official answer to this question is metrical: the words must have been of variable stress because the metre demands it.

The alternative is to change our ideas about the metre. Let us put side by side the following observations.

Although 'variable stress' is found predominantly at the line-end it does occur quite often elsewhere. *All* the places where it occurs are those where it is possibly to be seen instead as the trochaic inversion of an iambic foot, what Danielsson calls 'stress-shift'. Almost all the words concerned are accented on the first syllable, if they survive in modern English, like *labour* and *honour*.[1] When such words are found occupying the second syllable of one foot and the first of the next no problem arises, because it has never occurred to anybody not to accent them as in modern speech. It is only when a word of this class occupies a foot that we have to decide between variable stress, wrenched stress and trochaic inversion. But we need infer from this nothing more than the existence of the two-syllable unit, the foot; which suggests that we are considering something to do with feet, a metrical problem, rather than something to do with speech-accent.

---

[1] The other possible sort of variable stress, where a word ordinarily accented ᵕ ´ appears in verse ´ ᵕ, has never received much attention, for two reasons: one, it is comparatively scarce; two, it can almost always be taken instead as a weak iamb followed by a strong iamb, and so accommodated within an iambic metre, as in Pope's line

And without sneering, teach the rest to sneer

(*Epistle to Dr Arbuthnot*, 203)

An example from Chaucer is:

A povre person dwellynge upon lond.

A 702

Next, the problem of 'variable stress' is confined almost exclusively to disyllabic words. Words of three syllables are hardly ever, if they are to fit an iambic metre, of variable stress in Chaucer. I have found only about a dozen cases of trisyllables where the stress apparently varies, most of them being proper names. In *Troilus and Criseyde Apollo* seems sometimes to be stressed in our modern way, sometimes as *Ápollò*; but such cases are exceptions not numerous enough to invalidate the general rule. If one reads Chaucer metrically there are plenty of examples both of *conseíl* and *cónseil* but none of *conseillour*. Both *hónour* and *honóur* are frequent but *honoúrable* never occurs.[1] All but a handful of Chaucer's trisyllables seem to have a stress-pattern ′ ◡ ′ even if they are now pronounced differently, as *Decémbér*.

Thirdly, Professor Baum, the most recent authority, seems more or less to recognize that trochaic substitution is possible in any foot of Chaucer's long iambic line, even if the recognition is made somewhat confusedly with regard to the fifth: 'Inversion of the fifth foot is rare at all periods. It occurs in Chaucer only when he forces the stress, for rime, on an ordinarily unaccented syllable: *rédy, lády, wórthi,* etc.'[2] If these stresses are forced the feet are not inverted. This is not one of Baum's clearest pages (he goes on next paragraph to the choicely mixed metaphor 'from the very beginning...the elemental structure of Chaucer's five-stress iambic line is that which remained his staple. He learned at once to play the instrument.') but he does seem to be contemplating the possibility of fifth-foot trochees, which will save us from long arguments to prove their existence.

Fourthly, 'variable stress' is not confined to romance loan-words. There is no reason to believe that *lady* was ever accented *ladý* in English speech, but Chaucer can put it in the final foot.

BD 1152   For wostow why? She was lady

So if this is an iambic line this good Anglo-Saxon word is of variable stress, in Chaucer's verse.

[1] *Honourable* counts as a trisyllable because -e is neglected.
[2] *Chaucer's Verse*, p. 17.

Fader appears in Chaucer occupying the first, second, third and fourth feet, places where *honour* would be supposed to have its alternative accentuation *honoúr*:

first foot

B 274   'Fader,' she seyde, 'thy wrecched child Custance,'

B 1105   'Fader,' quod she, 'youre yonge child Custance...'

second foot

B 1109   It am I, fader, that in the salte see

(taking the first foot as trisyllabic)

third foot

B 3622   Unto hym seyde, 'Fader, why do ye wepe?'

fourth foot

B 3945   Thou shalt anhanged be, fader, certeyn.

It will perhaps be conceded that it is better to take these as trochaic substitutions than to wrench the stress and pronounce *fadér*, though I have met the explanation that 'variable stress in words of French origin encouraged similar variations (for metrical purposes) in many native words', which is like saying that the examples of *garage* and *chauffeur* in the early years of this century spread to affect native words so that persons of a literary turn could write poems in which they address him as *fathér*. *Fader* is not an untypical case. In the same way *after* can appear as a trochee at any place except the fifth foot:

A 125   After the scole of Stratford atte Bowe

A 176   And heeld after the newe world the space

A 136   Ful semely after hir mete she raughte

A 731   Whoso shal telle a tale after a man.

Body appears presumably as a trochee at several of Chaucer's line-ends and is also found as the first and second foot of lines. But the overwhelming majority of the occurrences of these words are in places where the metre regularly stresses them as they are now accented.

Other verse in Middle English and later allows Anglo-Saxon

disyllables to occupy feet. *Lady* and *body* frequently appear as the last foot of a line of folk-songs and ballads. When they are sung the stress is wrenched; but we do not know that in the Middle Ages they were not trochees. *Pénknife* is found in Britten's setting of 'Little Sir William'; *bréakfast* occurs in several ballads. The examples of 'variable stress' in Middle English verse are indeed, as Learned remarked, countless.

He might have added that if one insists on an iambic line-end the effect is often very odd indeed.

> ABELL: Caym leife this vayn carpy̆ng
>
> ffor god giffys the all thĭ lĭfyng
>
> CAYM: Yit boroed I neuer a farthy̆ng[1]

Would it occur to anybody meeting the first phrase in prose not to take advantage of the alliteration and stress it 'Cáym léife this váyn cárpyng'? Only a hypothetical metre could make us alter the usual stress on *carpyng*. Similarly,

> Veniance, veniance, lord I cry
>
> for I am slayn and not gĭlty.[2]

and

> ffor thay may the avay̆ll / when al this thyng is wroght
>
> Stuf thi ship with vitay̆ll / ffor hungre that ye perish noght
>
> Of beestis, foull and catay̆lle / ffor thaym haue thou in thoght
>
> ffor thaym is my counsay̆ll / that som socour be soght.[3]

The alternative is to allow trochaic substitutions.

But if in some cases when a word normally of stress-pattern / ᵕ occupies a foot of an iambic line we read the foot as a trochee, why not all? There are some difficulties in seeing all the supposed variable stresses as really trochaic substitutions, but at least it is as reasonable to do so as either to wrench the stresses or to postulate

---

[1] *The Towneley Plays*, ed. G. England, E.E.T.S. 1897, p. 12, lines 97–100.
[2] *Ibid.* p. 18, lines 328–9.   [3] *Ibid.* p. 27, lines 154–7.

the existence of a large class of English words of variable speech-stress, like *Doreen*, for which there is no other evidence but our insistence on an unproven metre.[1]

Moreover, the above examples of words of Anglo-Saxon origin all seem to be making expressive use of trochaic substitution. The various breaks of the simpler iambic flow to accommodate the word *fader* all produce a sort of emotional catch in the rhythmic movement appropriate to the different situations. Trochaic substitutions later than the first foot juxtapose two metrical stresses; and the resulting phrases often seem only a variety of the movement brought about by a sounded final -e. With a trochaic substitution there is always a distinctive phrase-movement as well as a distinctive foot-pattern, and characteristically, in Chaucer as elsewhere, one finds a trochaic substitution where some particular meaning is helped by it. 'Not guilty' is a phrase of some power in English, and the Towneley Play, just quoted, emphasises the power of the ordinary speech-phrase by making a trochaic substitution in the verse.

This will need more exemplification, and it will be interesting to see what happens to Chaucer's verse (the real test) if one denies the existence of words of variable stress and reads the resulting trochees; but it will first be convenient to clear a few awkward questions.

If disyllables in Chaucer are not of variable stress how are we to decide how to stress them? There is room here for research of the kind Professor Borroff has usefully undertaken for *Sir Gawain and the Green Knight*. Every word would have to be individually considered and the following heads of evidence taken into account:

1. The standard and dialect stressings of the modern descendants of the word, and of cognate words in other languages. This is the most important evidence and it would need something very weighty to overset it.

---

[1] If variable stress is really trochaic substitution a consequence is that Chaucer, like many sixteenth-century writers, could rhyme a stressed with an unstressed syllable. Cf. P. Simpson, 'The Rhyming of Stressed and Unstressed Syllables in the Sixteenth Century', *The Modern Language Review*, vol. xxxviii, 1943. There is at least one such rhyme in Chaucer which does not involve a disyllable:

T & C IV 1009 'I mene as though I laboured me in thís
　　　　　To enqueren which thyng cause of which thyng be
　　　　　As wheither that the prescience of God is
　　　　　The certeyn cause...'

2. Any metrical evidence there may be from alliterative poetry. This seems less tricky than the evidence from *rym*. It is reasonable to suppose that in alliterative verse the alliterating syllables generally bore the main stresses and that words were not stressed otherwise than in speech. There are difficulties about finding Chaucer's word-stresses from alliterative verse: the stressed words in alliterative verse are preponderantly those of that tradition's poetic diction, which Chaucer did not share. But, for example, *manere, comfort, comune*, all notoriously words of 'variable stress' in Chaucer, all alliterate consistently on the first syllable in *Piers Plowman*.

3. Any evidence that can be extracted from the Chaucer Concordance. But this would be a delicate matter: it would not do to count the different accentuations of a word and declare the one with a majority duly elected.

This is not the place for the large volume such an investigation would need: I am afraid that there is work here for several Ph.D.'s. But I am confident from some years' observation that most of Chaucer's disyllables are stressed as they would be in modern English, and that almost all his trisyllables are pronounced with the stress-pattern $/ \cup /$ or $/ \cup \setminus$.[1]

Unfortunately this reclassification of all apparent variable stresses as really trochaic substitutions will not without further enquiry answer all the main objections. Although examples of 'variable stress' on words of Anglo-Saxon origin have been given, and though many more could be given, it is true that they are comparatively scarce, whereas 'variable stress' of some disyllables of recent French origin is very common. This needs to be explained. May not variable stress after all be the likeliest explanation for the behaviour of words like *honour* and *labour* which can and do appear anywhere in a line including frequently at the end, where the Anglo-Saxon words are hardly ever found? (*Fader* is never rhymed in Chaucer, perhaps because it would be difficult to rhyme on. *Brother* appears often in rhyme, but never as a trochaic substitution.) I think not, though this is certainly a question that demands a difficult balancing of different senses of what lines are

---

[1] Among the commoner words in Chaucer which seem to be accented differently from our practice are *ánswére* (but cf. D 1025 and D 1029), *convéy*, *consúme, geómetríe, requést, revérse*.

like to read. But the trochaic alternative still seems to me more likely even in the cases of words like *honour*.

One can uncover some rules about Chaucer's trochees which may suggest why he used some words but not other apparently possible ones as trochaic fifth feet. Some disyllables are hardly ever permitted to occupy a foot, the most obvious class being monosyllables with sounded final -e. *Deere* (adjective) and *take*, which are words with very commonly sounded final -e's, are never found with sounded -e at the beginning of the line, where the -e would have to be the unaccented syllable of the trochaic foot. One of the scarce examples of -e as the arsis of a trochee is

LGW F 562   Make the metres of hem as the lest

—which seems to joke about the metrical rule by breaking it, with an obvious appropriateness to the sense. See above, p. 93, for other examples. So too Chaucer rarely inverts feet ending in -ing, -eth, -es, and other such weak sounds, but Bond has a list of exceptions. The most natural explanation of this rule about final -e's only being sounded in an iamb is that for Chaucer -e is not powerful enough to occupy the arsis of a trochee, though it can be the less glaring arsis of an iamb. I suggest that when shifting the stress in a trochee Chaucer felt the need for a sound in some way fairly substantial to follow the accented part of the foot: perhaps this would make it easier to re-establish later the simpler iambic pattern. And the ways in which the words that can be trochees most often seem substantial in their second syllable are in either that syllable's secondary stress or in its length. (I regret to have to add quantity to Chaucer's other metrical complications, but he does seem to pay this attention to it.) Most of the words of French origin and 'variable stress' seem to have a long, perhaps secondarily stressed, second syllable. These are words with endings like *-aunce, -our, -eere, -aille*.

Next: the fact that trochaic substitution or 'variable stress' occurs most commonly in the fifth foot corresponds to the existence of what I shall call 'endwords'. Chaucer has a class of words that appear only or predominantly at the line-end, which cannot easily be accounted for by the ordinary habits of the language in placing certain words at the ends of phrases, or by the demands of rhyme. (The statistics of this statement may be problematic, but the class does seem to exist.)

Number of occurrences

	In Chaucer's verse	At the line-end
adversite	33	28
affraye	7	5
appetite	13	10
between	16	12
bone	18	13
brimstone	5	4
dure	26	26

There is another group of words never or rarely found at the line-end even if rhymes are available and there are no obvious syntactic reasons why they should not go there. Some of these are words of Anglo-Saxon origin and stress-pattern ′ ᵕ, as

almost	36	3

Some have apparently awkward final -e's like

bettre	59	7
evere	(several hundred)	10

Between these two extremes there are many words that occur at the line-end with more or less the frequency they occur anywhere else:

mankynde	21	10
bataille	24	12

The thing which many but not all endwords have in common is a long last syllable. This applies to monosyllables like *bone* and *dure* and trisyllables like *appetite* as well as to most of the disyllables. The words of apparent 'variable stress' also commonly have a long second syllable. I conclude that Chaucer liked to end his lines with a long or secondarily stressed syllable in a trochaic foot. *Why* he liked to do so is a question about the movement of the lines in question.

So the alternative to 'variable stress' is trochaic substitution—but trochaic substitution of a peculiar sort, with a long second syllable to the foot. The test of either alternative can only be in reading. For, whatever we are discussing, it was certainly a favourite device of Chaucer and the other medieval poets, especially at the line-end.

My contention is that the fifth-foot trochee (and to a lesser extent trochees earlier in the line) can often be shown to make good expressive sense, by creating a movement comparable with the one caused by sounded final -e.

All trochaic substitutions tend towards the creation of two-beat phrases. Even when there is no long second syllable one can often see why an inverted foot works:

A 1773

$$\text{Upon a lord that wol have } \overset{\prime}{\text{no}} \overset{\prime}{\text{mercy}} \overset{\text{Fy}}{\underset{\smile}{}}$$

—the phrase 'no mercy', coming as it does at the culmination of a run of stresses, has an expressive power rather like the Towneley Play's 'not gilty' quoted above. So with the 'wrenched stress' on present participles, fairly common in Chaucer: try reading these lines of *Troilus* with iambic fifth feet:

II 1014

$$\text{And thow shalt fynde us, if I may, } \overset{\smile}{\text{sit}}\overset{\prime}{\text{tynge}}$$

$$\text{At som wyndow, into the strete } \overset{\smile}{\text{lo}}\overset{\prime}{\text{kynge}}$$

The second is surely ludicrous if as well as *lokynge* we insist on *wyndow* and *into*; but if these feet can be inverted we get a pleasantly and rightly chatty effect from the resulting phrase-balance:

And thow shalt fynde us   if I may   síttynge

At som wýndow   ínto the strete lókynge

Similarly

I 269

On this lády   and now on that lókynge

The Magician in *The Franklin's Tale* has an interest in food which we may well find amusing: but I do not believe that the amusement should be at his ridiculous mispronunciation of the word *supper*:

F 1209

To hym this maister called his squier
And seyde hym thus: 'Is redy oure soper?'

Surely that goes better as a pair of fifth-foot trochees.

The famous line about the Knight,

A 45

he loved chivalrie
Trouthe and honour, fredom and curteisie

goes far better if we wrench no stresses and allow the rhythmically parallel phrases

Tróuthe and hónour   frédom and cúrteisie.

Speaking to the royal widows at the beginning of *The Knight's Tale*, Theseus makes a speech which sounds strange indeed if we insist on variable stress:

A 905   'What folk been ye that at myn hom comÿnge

Perturben so my feste with criÿnge?'

Quod Theseus 'Have ye so greet envye

Of myn honoúr that thus compleyne and crye?'

Does he not sound more like a king if we allow him to invert those three feet? At the end of the tale Theseus says, rebuking those who cry out against the necessary conditions of life,

A 3045   And whoso grucceth ought he dooth folye
             And rebel is to hym that al may gye.

The difference made to this couplet by the choice of stress-pattern for 'folye' seems to me important. Is Theseus a pedantic old fool or is he a ruler of real wisdom and dignity? The tone created by the trot of a line ending 'folye' fits the former. But there is a grave force in the line if the word retains its usual stress, so constructing a phrase with three successive speech-stresses: 'hé dóoth fólye'.

    Another couplet of *The Knight's Tale* which a refusal to invert the fifth foot can make merely silly is the beginning of Arcite's meditation, already cited for its final -e's:

A 1251   Allas why pleynen folk so in commúne
             On purveiaunce of God or of Fortúne

That metre—even if without sounded -e's in rhyme—encourages a reading in which Arcite is like a schoolboy repeating a sing-song lesson; but the tone is more like that of a real meditation if we invert the last feet and form the resulting phrases:

Allas why pleynen folk so   in commúne

On purveiaunce of God   or of Fórtune

With *comune* and *Fortune* we have come to the real test of any theory of the words of 'variable stress', the line that ends with a disyllable of recent French origin and a long second syllable. We may hope to understand the lingering movement created by treating these as trochaic fifth feet if we dwell on such examples as

ABC 1   Almighty and al merciable queene

                       /   ⌣   / ⌣
To whom that al this world fleeth for socour...

The power of the second line comes from the phrase made by its two concluding trochees; the movement is made beautiful by the

                       /
drawing out of the last syllable. (*Socour* is well-established as the normal accentuation in the rest of Chaucer and in Langland it always alliterates on s- not c-.) Or, from the same stanza,

                                    / ⌣
ABC 7   Have mercy on my perilous langour

There it is surely not difficult to see the trochee enacting the languor in its lingering final sound. *Socour* works equally well in its other occurrences at the line-end.

A 918   But we biseken mercy and socour

(the ladies to Theseus, making a strong phrase of the second half-line, with a fittingly dignified beauty). So too Dorigen in *The Franklin's Tale*:

                ⌣   /   ⌣ / ⌣ /   ⌣ / / ⌣
F 1357   Fro which tescape woot I no socour

And

LGW 2440   Unto the court to seken for socour.

Socour as an internal trochee later in the *ABC* is also good in a way that needs no analysis:

                     ⌣   /   ⌣ /   / ⌣ ⌣ /   ⌣ /
ABC 168   This thanke I yow   socour of al mankynde.

It may be objected that *socour* and *langour* would be expected to occur at places where some sense could be made of a lingering trochaic movement, and it is true that most of the romance disyllables are words for high style which might be expected to linger well. But I can make good sense of the trochees caused by a word from another end of the stylistic scale, *vitaille*, which becomes Dickens's *wittles* and is listed politely by the Concordance under *victual*. I quote all the occurrences of this word in *The Canterbury Tales*. This peculiar rhythmic movement used of the avaricious squeamishness of the Friar is plainly ironic:

A 243   For unto swich a worthy man as he

      Acorded nat, as by his facultee,

      To have with sike lazars aqueyntaunce.

      It is nat honest, it may nat avaunce

      For to deelen with no swich poraille,

      But al with riche and selleres of vitaille.

Vitaille is the let-down into material considerations whose impact is increased by the normally grand and lingering trochee. I can make no special sense of the *vitaille* in the description of the Manciple:

A 568   achatours myghte take exemple
       For to be wise in byynge of vitaille

The next three, all iambic, could well be *wittles*:

           [oure Hoost]
A 746   He served us with vitaille at the beste

A 3568   And hast oure vitaille faire in hem yleyd

(Nicholas giving Alisoun's husband his instructions).

(A 3951   And han therinne vitaille suffisant
       But for a day

is dubious because the -e on *therinne* might be sounded; if so *vitaille* is an iamb.) In those two saints' lives, *The Man of Law's Tale* and *The Clerk's Tale* the word creates beautiful lingering inversions like *langour*—with the effect in the latter case of reminding us that Griselda's sanctity is of the real world:

E 59   A lusty playn habundant of vitaille...

E 265   Ther maystow seen of deyntevous vitaille...

The *Man of Law's Tale* example also brings us towards the real world—perhaps dangerously, for the question it asks is not easy to answer:

B 499   Three yeer and moore? How lasteth hire vitaille?

The same tale has an internal trochee which if taken as an iamb reduces the line to doggerel:

ˇ /   ˇ /   ˇ / ˇ   /   ˇ /
B 443   And sooth to seyn vitaille greet plentee

Try it instead as

/   /   /   /   /
And sooth to seyn   vitaille greet plentee

Then there is

B 1437   Thee lakketh noon array ne no vitaille

(not specially expressive, but neither is *The Shipman's Tale* where it occurs).

E 1713   And ful of instrumentz and of vitaille

—which is part of the Merchant's mock-heroic. An internal trochee in *The Franklin's Tale* puts a rhetorical stress on the word which is justified when we realize it means that the Magician is more interested in his supper than his magic:

F 1186   Hem lakked no vitaille that myghte hem plese.

By contrast when the word would not benefit by prominence, earlier in the tale, it appears as an iamb:

F 902   a gardyn that was ther bisyde
             In which that they hadde maad hir ordinaunce
             Of vitaille and of oother purveiaunce.

At the end of the tale it is again the Magician who gives the word the prominence of a last-foot trochee. For him the word represents beauty:

F 1618   Thou hast ypayed wel for my vitaille.

(The same character of course also inverts *supper*.) The examples from *The Former Age* also fit into this range of uses, sometimes giving the word the lingering beauty which is the simple case of the effect.

Sweetness too makes sense when it comes as a last-foot trochee. Words in -*ness* are, of course, in English before Chaucer and before the Norman conquest, and *sweetness* is a well-established Anglo-Saxon word which there is no good reason to believe was ever pronounced swéetness. As early as the Peterborough Chronicle it could be spelled 'sweetnis'. But, perhaps because like the words of recent French extraction it has a long second syllable, Chaucer uses the word as he uses them. In this case it is hard to believe that the demands of metre could have overcome the usual stress of a word so long in the language; and here too the lines where it appears at the end go better if it is read as a trochee.

Mars 179   Of soun of instrumentes of al swetnesse

and

PF 198   Herde I so pleye a ravyshyng swetnesse

which are perhaps self-explanatory. The three examples from the *Troilus*, coming at high moments, also move well:

I 1043   And of my spede be thyn al that swetnesse

—where the fourth foot is plainly a trochee, and to revert to an iamb for the fifth is to deny the line its beautiful phrase-movement.

III 44   In hielde, and do me shewe of thy swetnesse...

III 179   Your bittre tornen al into swetenesse...

and so on. Nevertheless *sweetness* can be found going well as an iamb, too, in such lines as the Prioress's

B 1745   The swetnesse hath his herte perced so

where 'swetnesse' balances the stresses put by the -e on the phrase 'herte perced'.

Penaunce too is well-established by alliterative verse and its occurrences internally in Chaucer's lines as having its modern stress-pattern. But it is an endword, being found at the line-end more than twice as frequently as within the line. It seems to me that every time it comes at the end there is an effective rhythm if we take it as a trochee:

A 223   He was an esy man to yeve penaunce

A 1315   And yet encresseth this al my penaunce

B 286   Wommen are born to thraldom and penance

E 1649   With tribulacioun and greet penaunce

G 446   That every Cristen wight shal han penaunce

H 12   Do hem come forth he knoweth his penaunce

The most sustained example in Chaucer of long syllables at the line-ends, both trochees and iambs, is that magnificent Envoy of the Clerk's which is a sort of buffer between the superhuman Griselda and the subhuman January. Here Chaucer rhymes for 35 successive lines on *-ence*, *-aille* and *-ynde*. One indication of the poem's success is what he does with these rhymes. Part of the beauty of movement which contrasts so effectively with the extractable advice comes from them, including the ones I think trochaic, like

E 1177   Grisilde is deed and eek hire pacience

      And bothe atones buryed in Ytaille

—where the long-drawn-out 'Ytaille' is the nostalgic recognition that Griselda is a long way off. By the second stanza some of these trochees are rather ironical than simply beautiful:

E 1186   To write of yow a storie of swich mervaille

E 1188   Lest Chichevache yow swelwe in hire entraille.

And by the fourth stanza there can be such an outrageous line as

E 1195   Ye archewyves stondeth at defense

      Syn ye be strong as is a greet camaille

which uses the fifth-foot trochee for the exact opposite of its normal function: the lingering effect is there because it is wholly inappropriate. This, of course, is the only rhyme in Chaucer on *camel*. The interested reader could do worse than ponder the rhymes in that marvellous Envoy further than we have space for.

The foregoing discussion is not an attempt to *define* the function of the trochaic fifth foot. There are, of course, other uses—in one sense, as many as there are instances in Chaucer. There is for example that moment in *The Parliament of Fowls* when the Falcon, having (after the manner of the military mind) exhausted to his own satisfaction other possible ways of settling the dispute, falls back on what is to him the obvious alternative and makes his point snappily with a fifth-foot trochee:

PF 538   I can not se that argumentes avayle

                            / ⏑
Thanne semeth it there moste be batayle.

Nor do I wish to suggest that there is anything automatically expressive, in Chaucer or elsewhere, about trochaic substitution. My contention is that this, like the other aspects of Chaucer's metre, is an opportunity for the poet: we see him making the most of his opportunity when we make sense of his use.

The juxtaposing of stresses caused by trochaic substitution is an extension of the drawing together of stresses caused by sounded final -e; like minimally sounded -e, trochaic substitution must control phrase-rhythms as well as foot-metre. It is a half-line principle to build up phrases of two beats, often next to each other, and trochaic substitution, by creating such phrases, pushes the verse in the direction of a half-line movement, as we shall continue to see.

It is at any rate clear from these investigations of final -e and 'variable stress' that any attempt to read Chaucer's lines as iambic pentameter must itself modify the idea of iambic pentameter. Sounded -e's and fifth-foot trochees both lead to strange halting phrases, which can be very pleasing once they are familiar, which can be believed in because they suit the poetry, but which have no place in established metrics.

The alternative to this view of long trochees is to believe that Chaucer's metre is so strong that it overrides the ordinary accentual habits of spoken English, as nursery-rhyme metres can. This is possible. Perhaps Chaucer boomed out his verse like Tennyson or chanted it like Yeats: if so it wouldn't be altogether surprising to find him wrenching word-stress for the sake of metre. But perhaps he read more naturalistically: the Wife of Bath doesn't *sound* as if she should be read in a Tennysonian way. And what Chaucer's verse ought to sound like is here the crucial consideration.

For the alternatives—to take Chaucer as an intoner, a fourteenth-century bard, or to concentrate on his language as closely related to speech—are essentially stylistic ones. Both the traditional argument that we should vary stresses and my argument that we shouldn't are really contentions about ways of reading. We may work from reading to arguments about word-stress, then back to a modified or confirmed reading, but it is not possible to prove that one reading is best or more consonant with the facts. If one believes Chaucer's rhythms are more delicately expressive than the Tyrwhitt metre allows them to be, one will not read Chaucer in the Tyrwhitt metre. Similarly the way to refute the above argument would be to show that it leads to a bad reading of Chaucer. I can only ask you to agree that Chaucer goes better with fifth-foot trochees than with wrenched or variable stresses. This is so, isn't it?

7

Manuscript Punctuation

Medieval punctuation is generally thought to be mysterious and (whether as a cause or an effect of the mystery) has never been very extensively investigated. Yet some of the functions of the punctuation marks in the manuscripts are quite unmistakable, and these can help us to understand distinctions the scribes made between different kinds of verse and, in turn, to get some idea of what they thought of Chaucer's metres. The scribes may of course be mistaken, but their opinion would be worth having. The main difficulty in considering medieval punctuation is its unfamiliarity; all the editions of Chaucer discard it and it is likely to intimidate the general reader.

The marks . / · ፦ etc., found in many English manuscripts of the fourteenth and fifteenth centuries (similar and other marks are found in other centuries and languages but this enquiry must be limited) derive ultimately from the *neumes* of Gregorian chant. These were a musical notation, but of a kind which divided a text into phrases as well as indicating a tune to which the phrase was to be sung. From this early notation one can see, in a very general way, two developments: modern musical notation and modern punctuation. But what the marks mean in the fifteenth-century verse and prose manuscripts nobody seems to know with any precision. Did they indicate intonation (as Mrs Salter argues of a manuscript of Love's *Mirror*[1]) or are they just stops and, if so, of what kind?

It seems quite clear that one function of the punctuation of Middle English *prose* manuscripts is to divide the longer speech-phrases. Prose is far more often punctuated than verse. I would say (from experience, not statistics) that it is comparatively rare to

---

[1] Elizabeth Salter, 'Punctuation in an Early MS of Love's *Mirror*', *The Review of English Studies*, new series, vol. VII, 1956.

find Middle English prose manuscripts unpunctuated. But the punctuation is always phrasal, not syntactic, and the phrases marked are often the secondary ones, smaller than a breath-length but longer than the one-beat unit, which we have met as the half-lines of *Piers Plowman*.

Modern prose is punctuated syntactically: main clauses are separated by the appropriate heavier stop and, for instance, strings of adjectives by commas, no matter how they are spoken. Speech-rhythms have their own ways of indicating clause-structure, but there is no direct instruction from modern punctuation to the voice. Writing here has precedence over speech: when Henry James writes a sentence in which almost every word is separated by a comma we do not necessarily take each comma as an instruction to pause. (Here we are on the verge of a discussion of the profound differences between the English of, say, Dryden's essays on the one hand and the King James Bible on the other.)

Often enough it is impossible to punctuate Middle English prose in the modern way, because it is simply not written in sentences. The Bodleian manuscript Rawlinson D. 82 (S.C. 12900) has a prose *Siege of Thebes* from which I transcribe the following passage:

The king stonding in a Windowe · seing this case · come sodenly rennyng to the gate · rehercyng this Edippes · whi he didde þat offence within his Castell ⟨ Edippes holding his swerde draweñ in his honde · withoute eny more · smote the king his fader · and þer slowe him · taking his horse al sodenly · and rode fast on his wey · oñespied of eny mañ · holdyng his iournay toward Thebes · where yn his wey · vppon a montayne as he rode · he met with añ horrible beest a monstre · called a Spinx · And was so cruel a beest · that he had ny destroyed þe contre aswel of man as of beest / the which beest · þere · of manhode · slowe And brought þe hede with hym to Thebes ⟨ Of which manfull dede · þe Cite and contre abought merveiled gretly · that hit might be in þe power of mañ to do so mervelouse a dede · And weren so glad and ioyful therof · þat þey helden him as conquerour // And within short tyme...[1]

How many sentences has this passage? Characteristically a main clause relates itself to what has gone before in some way we would have to show by using a colon or semi-colon: by our standards many a medieval prose work consists of one vast sentence. Yet there is no clumsiness here: the passage reads very easily as the sequence of phrases marked by the punctuation. Whether the punctuation

---

[1] MS Rawlinson D. 82 f. 2 r. / is in red.

also does other things I will not conjecture; but this function of dividing phrases is something we can be sure of by our usual criterion of certainty, viz., that it makes good sense of the language.

Of the eighty or so surviving manuscripts of *The Canterbury Tales* that include one or both of the prose tales, all but a handful punctuate the prose in this sort of way. They vary considerably in detail but there is at least a strong central tradition of marking the divisions of longer phrases. For instance a bit of the beginning of *Melibee* appears thus in the Ellesmere manuscript:

> he lyk a mad man rentynge his clothes / gan to wepe and crie ⟦ Prudence his wyf / as ferforth as she dorste / bisoghte hym / of his wepynge for to stynte / but nat for thy / he gan to crie and wepen / euere lenger the moore ⟦ This noble wyf Prudence / remembred hir / vpon the sentence of Ouide / in his book / that cleped is the remedie of loue / wher as he seith / he is a fool / that destourbeth the mooder to wepen in the deeth of hir child / til she haue wepte hir fille / as for a certein tyme ⟦

So far, perhaps, so good; and it is a natural transition here from prose to alliterative verse. A line which consists of two balancing phrases can naturally be punctuated phrasally in the same way as medieval prose. Skeat writes, of *Piers Plowman*,

> I have adopted the system of long lines, as Early English poems in this metre and of this period are invariably written in long lines in the MSS., except when written continuously, as we write prose. Every long line is divided into two short lines or half-lines by a pause, the position of which is marked in the MSS. by a point (sometimes coloured red), or by a mark resembling an inverted semi-colon, or, very rarely, by a mark resembling a paragraph mark (¶) or inverted D (⟦), coloured red and blue alternately. In some MSS., but these are generally inferior ones, the mark is entirely omitted. It is also not infrequently misplaced.[1]

This seems clear enough. But I want to go a stage further and say that this punctuation in *Piers Plowman* manuscripts is best seen as *metrical*, and that punctuation can certainly be metrical elsewhere. As far as alliterative verse is concerned, the distinction between phrase-division and metrical punctuation is not easy to draw, because the division of the line into phrases is the same as a metrical division: for lines that work by the balance of two phrases the indication of the phrases will be at the same time rhythmical and metrical, and I have followed Miss Daunt in the idea that

---

[1] *Piers Plowman*, ed. *cit.* vol. II, p. lix.

with alliteratives there is usually no tension between metre and rhythmic phrases.

But these phrases are still not necessarily the best ones to indicate from a rhetorical point of view; and as an aid to the reader it is not *necessary* to indicate them all. If every line of a *Piers Plowman* manuscript has a stop, that suggests that the stop was as much an ordinary part of writing the verse as the division into lines. In Gower manuscripts (see below) scribes usually only put in stops where to omit one would endanger the sense.

Older manuscripts are sometimes punctuated metrically: 'Old English verse is written out continuously, like prose, but the ends of the half-lines are indicated by some scribes by means of stops. Of the four major poetic codices, the Vercelli and Junius MSS. have these indications of the half-verse end.'[1] Similarly both surviving manuscripts of Laȝamon's *Brut* point the half-line and line; Cotton Otho C xiii does so by using ⫽ fairly consistently for the half-line and . for the line.

So I see a link between *Piers Plowman* punctuation and punctuation that is indisputably metrical: I offer *The Ormulum* as an example of the latter. This manuscript is also written out continuously like prose, but if any further confirmation of its metre were needed beyond what I have offered (above, p. 96), one could use the punctuation. The lines and half-lines are consistently separated by two different punctuation marks, which have no consistent rhetorical function, since the half-lines of *The Ormulum* are by no means always the same as speech-phrases.

Many manuscripts of verse, including the Cotton *Owl and the Nightingale* and Campsall *Troilus and Criseyde* put a stop at the end of every line regardless of whether there is a pause, and if one tries to treat the stop as a pause-mark the effects can be very odd:

II 1737   Fy on the deuel þenk which on he is.
           And in what plyt he lith com of a noon.
           Thenk that al swych taried tyd but lost it nys.
           That wole ye bothe. seyn whan ye ben on.
           Secundelich þer yet deuyneth noon.
           Vp on yow two com of now yf ye konne.
           Whil folk is blent / lo al þe tyme is wonne.

           In titeryng and pursuyte and delayes.
           The folk deuyne at waggynge of a stre.

[1] A. Campbell, *Old English Grammar*, Oxford, 1959, p. 13, section 28.

And þough ye wolden han after merye dayes.
That dar ye nought / and why for she and she.
Spak swych a word þus loked he and he.
Las tyme y lost .I. dar not with yow dele.
Com of þerfore and bryngeth hym to hele.[1]

These stops just mark a metrical unit, the line; and this use is confirmed in many *Canterbury Tales* manuscripts and some of the 'standard' manuscripts of *Confessio Amantis* (the latter are discussed below). All the manuscripts of Chaucer and Gower follow our convention of starting a new line for each line of verse (this is worth noting because not all earlier manuscripts and not all manuscripts of alliterative verse do so) but sometimes the text is squeezed up by the side of an illuminated capital, continuously like prose. When this happens manuscripts almost always separate the verse lines by some sort of stop. For example the Bodley 294 manuscript of *Confessio Amantis* begins like this:

O ff hem þat writen vs
tofore · The bookes
dwelle and we þerfore
Ben taught of þat was
writen þo · ffor þy good
is þat we also /
In oure tyme among vs heere

—after which it goes on in verse without marks at line-ends. The same manuscript does the same thing at the beginnings of books III and VIII. Cambridge University Library Dd.8.19 also begins:

f hem that wri
ten vs to fore ·
The bokes dwelle
and we therfore ·
Ben taught of
that was write
tho · ffor thi good
is

—and so on. (This manuscript was not completed and the illuminated 'O' not supplied.) Similar punctuation is found in many of the other Gower manuscripts and in some *Canterbury Tales* manuscripts, for instance Egerton 2864. Devonshire does the same and also punctuates when beginning a tale in capitals and

---

[1] Campsall manuscript.

spreading the first line over more than one line, as in its beginning
of *Sir Thopas*:

LISTENETH LORDINGES IN
gode entent · & I wol telle verrament ·
Of merthe and of solace ·

This is just the same as our own use of / when quoting verse in
prose. Comparable metrical punctuation is found a hundred years
later in Wyatt's poems. Miss Endicott writes, 'In Wyatt's poulter's
measure, his strokes...appear consistently in the same metrical
positions, after the sixth syllable in the hexameter and after the
fourth and eighth syllables in the fourteener. Moreover, the marks
appear in the same place even when the natural phrasing does not
correspond to the [metrical] pattern.'[1] One of her examples is:

That same quod he that we / the world do call and name[2]

Some verse punctuation is found in most of the early Chaucer
and Gower manuscripts. It is supposed by many scholars including
Professor Southworth that these marks within the line, most
commonly · or /, are rhetorical, instructions to stop, raise the
voice, or pause. This will indeed explain most of the punctuation
marks in the Chaucer manuscripts and perhaps all in Gower. The
biggest group of *Canterbury Tales* manuscripts that punctuate
verse at all do so by an occasional mark quite obviously meant to
stop the reader at places where not to pause would ruin the sense.
Over half the eighty or more *Canterbury Tales* manuscripts fall
into this class; the next most numerous group do not punctuate
verse at all. *Confessio Amantis* manuscripts usually have a similar
infrequent rhetorical stop.

I cannot assert that Gower is never punctuated by a consistent
half-line stop like Skeat's *Piers Plowman*, since I have not seen all
the extant manuscripts.[3] However, unlike Chaucer, Gower had a
careful, not to say fussy, publication policy, and from the Gower
manuscripts I have seen—mainly those in Oxford, Cambridge
and London, perhaps half the total—I will say with some confidence

---

[1] Endicott, *Metrical Effects*, p. 28.
[2] 'Jopas' Song', line 5.
[3] Duke University has a collection of photostatic copies of Gower manuscripts
which I was not able to use; but I can speak of 'all' the *Canterbury Tales*
manuscripts because I was able to use the complete collection of photostats
presented to the British Museum by Manly and Rickert. These are not always
good enough to allow one to distinguish a virgule (/) from a hair or a mistake—
the mark is a fine hairline stroke—but were sufficient for most of my purposes.

that there is a standard type of *Confessio Amantis* manuscript, some of the features of which are bookhand, illuminations, and folio size. (Gower was catering for a class of rich book-buyers.) G. C. Macaulay's task in editing Gower was comparatively easy (no less honour to him for having done it so well) and his remarks on the punctuation of the Bodleian manuscript Fairfax 3 would apply to all the ones I have seen of the 'standard type':[1] 'The frequent stops at the ends of lines are for the most part meaningless, but those elsewhere are of importance and usually may be taken as a guide to the sense...There is usually a stop wherever a marked pause comes in the line, and this punctuation occurs on an average about once in ten lines.'[2] Macaulay also makes remarks about some of the Gower manuscripts I have not seen (Keswick Hall, for instance) which confirm my impressions of the ones I know.

It appears then that punctuation in Gower and most of the Chaucer manuscripts is not metrical but rhetorical. The metre is indicated if at all by the lines of verse and by the dots at the ends of lines in some manuscripts, whereas alliterative verse is usually punctuated by a half-line metrical stop.

But there are about a dozen manuscripts of *The Canterbury Tales* which are punctuated, wholly or in spasms, in just the same way as Skeat's Langland, with a point in nearly every line over and above the occasional rhetorical stop. These manuscripts, though a minority, are not an eccentric one; they include not only all the ones on which the editors say the text is based (which has not prevented all editors including Manly and Rickert from removing the punctuation) but the most carefully written manuscripts throughout the fifteenth century.

The *Canterbury Tales* manuscripts present a cross-section of fifteenth-century English manuscripts in general; there is nothing like a standard type. They come from every decade of the century and almost every part of England; from every section of the book-selling trade and beyond. They vary from the magnificently illuminated like Ellesmere and Devonshire through the cheap-and-nasty to the amateur—the Fitzwilliam manuscript, for example, is a do-it-yourself Chaucer in which the scribe arbitrarily rejected

---

[1] A list of the 'standard' *Confessio Amantis* manuscripts would include: B.M. Egerton 1991, Additional 22139, Harleian 7184, Harleian 6291; Bodley 294, Fairfax 3, Bodley 693, Hatton 51, Arch. Selden B. 11, Laud 609, Bodley 902; Cambridge Dd. 8.19 and Mm. 2.21.

[2] *Gower's English Works*, vol. 1, p. clix.

lines and passages he didn't like, and had bursts of grandeur in which he attempted bookhand. Some are on paper, some on vellum, some on both; there are traces of many styles of binding and some including Hengwrt seem not to have been bound in the fifteenth century at all. *Canterbury Tales* manuscripts were owned, as Manly and Rickert show,[1] by a very wide social range of people, from the rival royal families down as far as woolmerchants, provincial lawyers and Privy Seal clerks. Some are carefully and beautifully written, some carelessly and beautifully, some in ugly cursive hands but with care. Some are glossed as learnedly as the scholarly works of the period (it is not generally known that many of the most helpful Chaucer notes go back to the fifteenth century); some are not glossed at all. Some are simply manuscripts of *The Canterbury Tales*, some select tales, some include the whole or parts in different pious or courtly collections. The size varies from the medieval equivalent of a pocket volume to large and unwieldy tomes. And some manuscripts use careful metrical punctuation, some less frequent rhetorical stops, others no verse punctuation.

Out of all this variety I did observe some connections and disconnections. There is no connection between the expensiveness of a manuscript on the one hand and its carefulness or use of punctuation on the other. There is no connection between date and care of writing. There is, however, a strong connection between care in copying and spelling, and the use of metrical punctuation. I think it fair to call the punctuating manuscripts a central tradition. The manuscripts in this tradition would not consist of the ones the editors have made most use of (though it would include them) for some of them are far from the origins of the text. But these manuscripts present a text with similar features, the most important of which from our point of view are spelling to indicate, apparently, ten syllables per long line[2] and punctuation to indicate half-lines. My list of these careful, punctuating manuscripts is:

---

[1] Their account of the manuscripts in the first volume of their monumental *Text of the 'Canterbury Tales'* is the best and fullest—much better than McCormick's (Sir William McCormick, *The Manuscripts of Chaucer's 'Canterbury Tales'*, Oxford, 1935); and if their edition had only recorded manuscript punctuation and use of -e the present work would have been much easier to prepare.

[2] Emendations in good manuscripts usually preserve the decasyllable. As to spelling: final -e is not a very reliable guide to a manuscript's care (above, p. 101), but, for example, the manuscripts of my 'central tradition' are usually better than the rest at distinguishing the forms *paraventure* and *paraunter* and

B.M. Additional 5140. Late, cheap, unimportant to the editors.

Cambridge Dd.4.24. Early, important to editors. (Unfortunately much of this highly intelligent manuscript is missing.)

Christ Church 152. Late, cheap, unimportant to editors.

Egerton 2864. Late, cheap, unimportant to editors.

Ellesmere. Very early, very expensive, one of the foundations of the text.

Hengwrt. Very early, not very expensive, the most important manuscript. (Better punctuated than Ellesmere, which I suspect of using the virgule as symmetrically as possible to improve the look of the page.)

Lichfield 2. Mid-century, expensive, unimportant to the editors.

Manchester 113. Late, cheap, editorially unimportant. (Metrical punctuation in patches.)

Morgan. Mid-century, expensive (but cursive hand), editorially unimportant.

Royal College of Physicians. Mid-century, cheap, not important to editors.

Royal 17.D.XV. Late, not expensive, unimportant to editors. (Two hands, the *second* only punctuates.)

Selden Arch. B. 14. Late, expensive, editorially unimportant.

Sloane 1686. Early, expensive, editorially unimportant.

In these circumstances the really careful manuscripts without metrical punctuation (above all Corpus, Oxford, 198 and Harleian 7334[1]) become an insignificant minority.

Further, the punctuating *Canterbury Tales* manuscripts often distinguish different kinds of verse within the collection. *Sir Thopas* is obviously in a metre not found elsewhere in Chaucer, and most of the manuscripts on the list recognize this by writing it differently (usually marking its rhyme scheme in a sort of diagram) and not supplying half-line marks. (But the Hengwrt manuscript does, perversely, punctuate *Thopas*.) Conversely, the spurious tale of *Gamelyn*, which obviously goes best in half-lines, is left unpunctuated by many of the manuscripts that do not punctuate Chaucer.

---

using the one correct for a decasyllabic line. (But hardly any distinguish *benedicitee* from its shortened form and no manuscript writes a monosyllabic *certes* where that seems required.)

[1] On this manuscript see J. S. P. Tatlock, *The Harleian Manuscript 7334 and Revision of the 'Canterbury Tales'*, 1909, which decisively shows the manuscript's eccentricity.

Confessio Amantis in the best manuscripts is punctuated differently from *The Canterbury Tales* in the best manuscripts because the scribes were distinguishing different kinds of verse. The way Chaucer is punctuated suggests strongly that the half-line phrases were thought to be important for the metre, like those of *Piers Plowman*.[1] And it *certainly* shows at least that the scribes worried over Chaucer's phrases more than Gower's. I do not think one can escape the conclusion that Chaucer's lines were thought in his own day and later to move in half-lines as well as feet.

Nothing similar is suggested by the manuscripts of Gower (whose only long-line poem *In Praise of Peace* is not punctuated in the excellent Trentham manuscript) or of those fifteenth-century writers of unphrasal pentameter, Charles of Orleans and the Palladius Translator. But Hoccleve, the best of whose manuscripts are thought to be in his own hand,[2] is punctuated metrically in them like Chaucer in Ellesmere and Hengwrt; and later in the century metrical punctuation of the verse of the English Chaucerians is common enough to be taken as normal. Were these scribes and poets right about Chaucer? Is a half-line movement part of his metre? We can try to answer the questions in our usual way by seeing the effect of half-line movement on reading.

II

Before you start to read a page you have expectations about the way to read it, and they can be very strong. The expectations that concern us here are those produced by the *look* of a page. Chaucer without half-line punctuation looks, and perhaps is, very different from with it. The wrong expectations here may damage reading.

Whether a passage is prose or verse can depend wholly on how it

---

[1] But all the Chaucer manuscripts come from the fifteenth century, the age of Lydgate. Could not Chaucer have been rewritten in half-lines to suit the taste of the age?—in the way *Tottel's Miscellany* gave a rewritten text of Wyatt to suit a different taste? This large question cannot be properly answered in a footnote, and a whole chapter would be very boring. I will merely say I think it highly improbable that Chaucer was rewritten: if he had been, there would have been many visible loose ends. Alternatively, since the Chaucer we have is so good the hypothetical rewriting could be seen as an improvement. . . There *are* one or two half-hearted attempts to alter Chaucer's lines to make them shorter and more Gower-like (manuscripts Delamere and Harl. 7333 sometimes do this) but these leave unchanged much more than they alter.

[2] See H. C. Schulz, 'Thomas Hoccleve, Scribe', *Speculum*, vol. XII, 1937.

is printed. Few would deny that Dickens's novels are works of English prose; but who could object to finding the following passage like this?—

> 'I don't know what great aid may come to me.
> When Richard turns his eyes upon me then,
> There may be something lying on my breast
> More eloquent than I have been, with greater
> Power than mine to show him his true course,
> And win him back.'
> Her hand stopped now. She clasped
> Me in her arms, and I clasped her in mine.[1]

Nevertheless, one reads this very differently if it is printed as prose.

Everybody opens *The Canterbury Tales* and sees, except in *Sir Thopas* and the two prose tales, pages of iambic pentameters. That is what we see, so that is what we read. It was a chastening experience when collecting final -e's from the Chaucer Concordance to read any of the longer entries and notice, or fail to notice, that the quotations from *Melibee*, between large blocks of verse, quite often went as iambic pentameter just as well as the verse on either side. Try the experiment and see how long you can go before the verse expectation defeats the prose fact.

Of course pentameters are very various, and F. N. Robinson's text merely presents pentameters, allowing us to take them as any sort we like. But if Chaucer is not writing any of the kinds of pentameter to be found in the modern English poets the instruction given by the book of the page to read as pentameter would be misleading. There is nothing in the editions of Chaucer to prevent our taking his lines just like those of Marlowe, or of George Eliot. Her blank verse has, as far as I can see, no caesura. She varies phrase-length, rather mechanically, but my sense is that these phrases are not part of the metre and create no expectations; there is no element of metre usefully recognizable between the line and the foot:

> O may I join the choir invisible
> Of those immortal dead who live again
> In minds made better by their presence: live
> In pulses stirred to generosity,
> In deeds of daring rectitude, in scorn

[1] *Bleak House*, Chapter LX.

> For miserable aims that end with self,
> In thoughts sublime that pierce the night like stars,
> And with their mild persistence urge man's search
> To vaster issues.

The metre of these lines is sufficiently indicated by printing them *as* lines. Perhaps it will be objected that I have prejudiced this argument by using as an example of modern pentameter verse I think second-rate. But I could quote Wordsworth with equal aptness. The wonderful fluidity of the verse of *The Prelude* owes nothing to phrase-length prescribed by metre: its phrases are as various as those of modern prose, and (*qua* phrases) work in the same way: 'With a heart joyous / nor scared at its own liberty / I look about / and should the chosen guide / be nothing better / than a wandering cloud / I cannot miss my way.'[1] (The poet who decisively moved English verse away from phrases towards the periodic sentence was Milton; but that is another story.) It is just the same over two hundred years before Wordsworth with the blank verse of Marlowe (or perhaps all English blank verse before Shakespeare):

> why then I hope my ships
> I sent for Egypt and the bordering isles
> Are gotten up by Nilus' winding banks;
> Mine argosy from Alexandria,
> Loaden with spice and silks, now under sail,
> Are smoothly gliding down by Candy-shore
> To Malta, through our Mediterranean sea.[2]

Only one of these lines has, coincidentally, a half-line movement. The last quoted line is also divided by a comma, but in my reading the onrush of the words overrides any pause and makes us take the line as one unit.

But some long lines of English verse have a prescription about phrases as an important part of the metre. This passage can be read without extreme rhythmic difficulty:

> And þanne gan a Wastoure to wrath hym and wolde haue yfouȝte
> And to Pieres þe plowman he profered his gloue
> A Brytonere a braggere abosted Pieres als
> 'Wiltow or neltow we wil haue owre wille

---

[1] *The Prelude* I, 14–18, barbarously transcribed as prose.
[2] *The Jew of Malta*, I, i.

143

Of þi flowre and of þi flessche fecche whan vs liketh
And make vs myrie þermyde maugré þi chekes'[1]

But it goes more easily if the half-line division is indicated as in Skeat's text:

B VI 154   And thanne gan a wastoure to wrath hym · and wolde haue
        yfouȝte
    And to Pieres the plowman · he profered his gloue
    A Brytonere a braggere · abosted Pieres als
    And bad hym go pissen with his plow · forpyned schrewe
    'Wiltow or neltow · we wil haue owre wille
    Of thi flowre and of thi flessche · fecche whan vs liketh
    And make vs murie thermyde · maugre thi chekes'

The good Chaucer manuscripts with their half-line stops look quite different from the editions. They create the different expectation that Chaucer's lines are to go in half-line phrases as well as lines. And once one considers the suggestion that half-lines are more important in Chaucer than George Eliot it is easy to find passages where a half-line movement is irresistibly right.

It is well known that when describing battles Chaucer can 'fall into the "tune" appropriate to the subject'[2] by simulating an alliterative manner.

A 2597   Tho were the gates shet, and cried was loude:
    'Do now youre devoir, yonge knyghtes proude!'
        The heraudes lefte hir prikyng up and doun;
    Now ryngen trompes loude and clarioun.
    Ther is namoore to seyn, but west and est
    In goon the speres ful sadly in arrest;
    In gooth the sharpe spore into the syde.
    Ther seen men who kan juste and who kan ryde;
    Ther shyveren shaftes upon sheeldes thikke;
    He feeleth thurgh the herte-spoon the prikke.
    Up spryngen speres twenty foot on highte;
    Out goon the swerdes as the silver brighte;
    The helmes they tohewen and toshrede;
    Out brest the blood with stierne stremes rede;

---

[1] *Fourteenth Century Verse and Prose*, ed. K. Sisam, 2nd edn. Oxford, 1937, p. 83.

[2] D. Everett, 'Chaucer's Good Ear', *Essays on Middle English Literature*, Oxford, 1959, p. 142. Miss Everett also remarks of Chaucer's line

B 460   Flemere of feendes out of hym and here

'If this line were met with out of its context, one's first thought would probably be that it came from some M.E. poem in alliterative verse.' *Ibid.* p. 139.

With myghty maces the bones they tobreste.
He thurgh the thikkeste of the throng gan threste;
Ther stomblen steedes stronge, and doun gooth al;
He rolleth under foot as dooth a bal...

But with the punctuation of the Ellesmere manuscript before one, it is easy to see that Chaucer follows the alliterative 'tune' here because his verse is organized in half-lines in the alliterative manner:

Tho were the gates shet / and cried was loude
Do now youre deuoir / yonge knyghtes proude
❡ The heraudes / lefte hir prikyng vp and doun
Now ryngen trompes loude and clarioun
Ther is namoore to seyn / but west and Est
In goon the speres / ful sadly in Arrest /
In gooth the sharpe spore / in to the syde
Ther seen men / who kan Juste & who kan ryde
Ther shyueren shaftes / vpon sheeldes thikke
He feeleth / thurgh the herte Spoon the prikke
Vp springen speres / twenty foot on highte
Out gooth the swerdes / as the siluer brighte
The helmes they tohewen / and toshrede
Out brest the blood / with stierne stremes rede
With myghty maces / the bones they to breste
He thurgh the thikkeste / of the throng gan threste
Ther semblen [*sic*] steedes stronge / and doun gooth al
He rolleth vnder foot / as dooth a bal

If our insistence on modern regular metre is strong enough we might read

$$\breve{} \quad / \quad \breve{} \quad / \breve{} \quad \breve{} \; / \breve{} \quad / \quad \breve{} \; /$$
With myghty maces the bones they tobreste

in strict iambic time, getting a kind of Celtic or Tennysonian lilt. The reading indicated by Ellesmere's punctuation does not destroy the metre, but it does make that version impossible: one truth about the line is that it consists of two balancing phrases, each built on two main stresses:

$$\quad / \qquad / \qquad\qquad / \qquad\qquad /$$
With myghty maces   the bones they tobreste

So the phrase-balancing which is so central to the alliterative tradition is as much a part of the structure of this verse as the iambic metre. If so, if this is consistently so in Chaucer, we may well develop an expectation of such balances—which will then be as much a part of the metre as they are in *Piers Plowman*. This is the suggestion made by the manuscript punctuation and which, it seems to me, often makes good sense in reading. It is not merely that Chaucer, like anyone else, goes in phrases: the phrases are enough part of the expectation to be metrical. Sometimes the half-line phrasing will control the lexis or syntax.

E 996   Ay undiscreet and chaungynge / as a fane

would be wrong because 'undiscreet' does not qualify 'fane': the half-lines, always the same as the syntactic phrases, are

Ay undiscreet / and chaungynge as a fane

So too, because sloes are black but not bent, the line about Alison's brows goes

A 3246   And tho were bent / and blake as any sloo

(Some of the older editions got this wrong by putting a comma after 'black'.) But generally the point of the half-line phrasing is more subtle: if one sees it, the poetry is more powerful, though it consists of the same words in the same sense.

Does not part of the life of the superb chase that brings *The Nun's Priest's Tale* to its climax come from a half-line movement? I punctuate F. N. Robinson's text:

B 4580   The dokes cryden · as men wolde hem quelle
                The gees for feere · flowen over the trees
                Out of the hyve · cam the swarm of bees
                So hydous was the noyse · a *benedicitee*
                Certes he Jakke Straw · and his meynee
                Ne made nevere · shoutes half so shrille
                Whan that they wolden · any Flemyng kille
                As thilke day · was maad upon the fox

The Pardoner's sermon too goes naturally in half-lines:

C 549   A lecherous thyng is wyn · and dronkenesse
                Is ful of stryvyng · and of wrecchednesse
                O dronke man · disfigured is thy face
                Sour is thy breeth · foul artow to embrace
                And thurgh thy dronke nose · semeth the soun
                As though thou seydest ay · Sampsoun Sampsoun
                And yet God woot · Sampsoun drank nevere no wyn

The Wife of Bath's lively tirade is composed of half-lines as well as of feet—'pieces of language' that may be part of the metre:

146

D 371
        Thou liknest eek · wommenes love to helle
        To bareyne lond · ther water may nat dwelle
        Thou liknest it also · to wilde fyr
        The moore it brenneth · the moore it hath desir
        To consume every thyng · that brent wole be
        Thou seyest · right as wormes shende a tree
        Right so a wyf · destroyeth hire housbonde
        This knowe they · that been to wyves bonde

It is possible also to imagine George Eliot's verse printed with half-line stops:

        O may I join · the choir invisible
        Of those immortal dead · who live again
        In minds made better by their presence · live
        In pulses stirred · to generosity
        In deeds of daring rectitude · in scorn
        For miserable aims · that end with self
        In thoughts sublime · that pierce the night like stars
        And with their mild persistence · urge man's search
        To vaster issues.

This is possible but perverse, working against the most natural metrical reading and adding nothing to it. But if reading Chaucer with a half-line movement improves his verse and builds a metrical expectation endorsed by the manuscripts, that may be the best way to read—and to modify our notion of his metre.

At any rate Chaucer cannot be punctuated in the modern way. F. N. Robinson's attempts add colons and semi-colons to the text quite arbitrarily; this peppering of punctuation does nothing whatever for reading. The really helpful punctuation is the medieval sort, the phrase-division. And it is surely more than accidental that the phrase-divisions the scribes indicate are also the half-lines that in alliterative verse are the metre. The phrases of which Chaucer's verse is built make us treat his long lines as two balancing halves; this completes one's sense of the movement of his verse to which the earlier discussions of sounded -e and trochaic substitution have contributed. All make Chaucer's lines balance in two halves. It is time to draw these ideas more closely together and try them out more extensively in reading.

Part Three: Readings

8

The Rhythms of
'The Canterbury Tales'

I

Joining the results of the investigations in previous chapters, I offer the following as the best description I can attain of the metre of the long lines of *The Canterbury Tales*, which I shall call 'balanced pentameter'.

This line is a variety of iambic pentameter; though it has certain differences from modern iambic pentameter it is sufficiently like to allow us to extend the term to include it. The evidence for this statement is simply that very many of Chaucer's lines in the good manuscripts go in ways that remind us of the pentameters we know in other English poets. In anybody's reading

A 12   Thanne longen folk to goon on pilgrimages

will be some sort of iambic pentameter. By saying so I offer no definition of iambic pentameter (to *define* Chaucer's pentameter I would reprint his works) nor do I say that his lines are the same as Shakespeare's or Pope's; I assert only that the range covered by the term needs extension to include Chaucer's lines, but not such a large extension as to make it more useful to coin a new term.

Ordinarily Chaucer's long line has five feet and they are most frequently iambs, though the line with five iambs is perhaps not even in a majority. Common variations include:

1. The trochaic inversion of any one or more of the five feet, including, commonly, the last. Inversions are most commonly embodied in words of two syllables, but I will quote examples of trochaic inversions formed of monosyllables since they are less likely to be challenged:

foot 1

the yonge sonne

A 8   Hath in the Ram his halve cours yronne

A 3031   Som in his bed, som in the depe see

foot 2

A 564   A whit cote and a blew hood wered he

(Cf. *T & C* I, 122   [al th'onour...]

Ye shul have, and youre body shal men save)

foot 3

B 3400   And seyde 'King, God to thy fader lente'

E 1134   Til that the soule out of his body crepeth

A 3031   Som in his bed, som in the depe see

foot 4

C 533   Of whiche the ende is deeth, wombe is hir god

(Cf. *ABC* 2   To whom that al this world fleeth for socour)

foot 5

B 878   And asketh where his wyf and his child is

B 3571   Where as he with his owene hand slow thee

D 2114   For who kan teche and werchen as we konne?

2. The headless line beginning with a stress, as

A 1   Whan that Aprill with his shoures soote

3. Feet of three syllables. How common one thinks these will depend on how many final -e's one pronounces, but there are plenty of examples of trisyllabic feet where no question of pronouncing -e arises:

A 364   Of a solempne and a greet fraternitee

A 764   I saugh nat this yeer so myrie a compaignye

(For further examples see Baum, *Chaucer's Verse*, pp. 20 ff.)

4. Monosyllabic feet. The frequency of these too depends on the number of sounded -e's, but there are some plain cases:

C 534

      O wombe O bely O stynkyng cod

(this line is discussed below)

A 2367

      The nexte houre of Mars folwynge this

A 3183

      So was the Reve eek and othere mo

B 621

      But nathelees ther was greet moornyng

D 104

      Som this, som that, as hym liketh shifte

B 3116

      Loo Rouchestre stant heer faste by

A 384

      Maken mortreux and wel bake a pye

(Cf. *Chaucer's Verse*, p. 25.)

With all this, it is more ordinary for a foot in *The Canterbury Tales* to be iambic than anything else. We develop from the verse the expectation of a recognizably iambic movement. But the line whose flow of iambs constitutes its complete metre is a not too common variant, usually with some fairly obvious expressive point:

F 1503

      As she was bown to goon the wey forth right

Though there are other possible ways of taking this line, it makes good sense to exaggerate the repetition of iambs which express Dorigen's plodding walk towards her meeting with Aurelius. Cf. A 3748. These lines with five iambs are generally the tiny minority left unpunctuated by the manuscripts that punctuate the rest.

But though I call Chaucer's long lines 'pentameter' I have to add another term to complete the description of his metre and register the difference of his lines from Wordsworth's. For Chaucer's pentameter is usually also *balanced*, that is, works in half-lines as well as feet. These half-lines appear consistently enough to be expected and so to form part of the metre. They are not definably restricted in length or number of stresses,[1] and not every line has two halves. Some—the ones left unpunctuated by

---

[1] But the half-lines of *Piers Plowman* also vary greatly in length, which has led some scholars to think many of Langland's lines irregular, i.e. that they know more about alliteratives than the foremost Middle English practitioner.

the best manuscripts—have only one group; some have more than two groups:

T & C v 1319   With herte / body / lif / lust / thought / and al[1]

Moreover, lines with the usual two groups need not have even approximately the same number of syllables per group. In the line

A 4268   'Ye, false harlot' quod the Millere / 'hast?'

the last word balances the whole of the rest of the line, and is shouted to give it the requisite force, which is also the way of making the best sense of that indecorous moment of *The Reeve's Tale*.

But normally, in more than three-quarters of the lines of *The Canterbury Tales*, there are two rhythmic groups of approximately equal length which balance each other after the manner of alliterative lines. The ordinary number of stresses or beats per half-line is two and this is, again, ordinary enough to create an expectation and make us read with two stresses per half-line where we have a choice. Each half-line is one phrase, one 'piece of speech' in the same way as the half-lines of *Piers Plowman*, most commonly having one main and one subsidiary stress and up to seven unstressed syllables. The half-line is the same as the syntactic phrase: the sense of the phrase dictates the shape of the phrase as well as *vice versa*, and so there can (as also in almost all the lines of *Piers Plowman*) be no tension between this part of the metre and speech-rhythms. Two or more (but most often two) phrases make a line, which is usually the same as the larger speech unit, the breath-length.

After the half / half division, the next most common phrasal grouping in Chaucer's lines is the three-group line, often with a weak iambic second foot giving phrases:

$$\cup \; \prime \; \cup \; / \; \cup \; \cup \; \prime \; \cup \; / \; \cup \; \cup \; \prime$$

Lines with three phrases form perhaps a tenth of the verse of *The Canterbury Tales*. For example:

A 431   Olde Ypocras Haly and Galyen
         Serapion Razis and Avycen

---

[1] I neglect the opportunity for a disquisition here upon *brachylogia*: the line has in any case several rhythmic groups, not just two.

Averrois Damascien and Constantyn

Bernard and Gatesden and Gilbertyn

B 4157   Pekke hem up right as they growe and ete hem yn

Other divisions are scarcer.

Just as one extreme of Chaucer's metre is the line formed simply by its succession of iambs without half-lines, the other extreme is the line that depends wholly on half-line organization without any perceptible foot organization. The mistakes of the establishment proceed from taking as typical the first of these extremes: Southworth sometimes seems to want to make a model of the second (whose existence is, of course, hotly denied by contemporary traditionalists and not suspected by ten Brink). Both types are rather unusual. I do not wish to say there are no lines in Chaucer which just go as two halves without feet, though this is certain to be disputable in the case of a poet who usually writes metrically and in lines of approximately the same length, for any ten syllables in English can, given sufficient scholarly perseverance and ingenuity, be seen as some sort of pentameter. It seems true that the best way of taking quite a number of effective lines in Chaucer is to follow the half-line rhythms and forget any possible feet altogether.

G 856   Oilles, ablucions, and metal fusible

can be iambic if read

Oilles ablucions and metal fusible

(with two trochees and trisyllabic fourth foot) but, in the middle of the Canon's Yeoman's outburst, it surely goes better just as two balancing phrases:

Oilles ablucions / and metal fusible

(Baum has a long list of such lines from the tale, which cause him some perplexity.) Most of these lines are tidied up in the editions, but Manly and Rickert have to print them, albeit with disapproval: they say of that expressive line

A 3810   And Nicholas in the ers he smoot

155

'The reading "amid the", which seems necessary for the metre of the line, is found only' in bad manuscripts.[1] But the line goes well, at the climax of that improper passage, as two balancing halves:

> And Nicholas   in the ers he smoot

To see these lines as more objectionable than the other extreme, the full-line pentameters, is metrical prejudice. And they were certainly used by Chaucer's disciples. But I do not wish to press them on an unwilling reader; they are only a rather unusual extreme of the range of my term 'balanced pentameter'. The great central body of Chaucer's verse consists of lines where the metre as traditionally understood co-operates with the half-line phrases: these two together shape the rhythms, the way we read the lines.

Chaucer developed and used this complex metre for the reason behind all metres, that it helped him to say what he had to say, to write his poetry. And though it is a complex metre and, especially, looks complex in description, it has the central metrical function, once one is used to it, of making language less ambiguous, *easier* to read. The half-line element has in particular the function of permitting within metre the freedom of phrase-making we have in speech or those 'pieces of speech' with which the alliterative poets composed. Hence its use is, by shaping what is still speech, the precise invocation and control of tone and mood. The iambic and half-line elements join in a metre that conveys a precision and power of language one cannot get from traditional readings of Chaucer: that, at least, is the claim by which the metre must be tested.

II

The whole great range of Chaucer's styles in his long line go better if he is read as balanced pentameter. High style is made wooden by suppressing the half-line movement, and comes alive if it is permitted; conversely Southworth's uniambic reading loses a certain grandeur: the verse needs both half-lines and feet. Take Duke Theseus's majestic speech at the end of *The Knight's Tale*, with the half-line punctuation of the Hengwrt manuscript:

> That same Prince / and that moeuere quod he
> Hath stabliced / in this wrecched world adoun
> Certeine dayes / and duracioun

[1] Manly and Rickert, *ed. cit.* vol. III, p. 442.

To al that is engendred in this place
Ouer the which day / they may nat pace
Al mowe they yet / tho dayes abregge
Ther needeth noon auctoritee to allegge
ffor it is proued / by experience
But þat me list / declaren my sentence
Thanne may men wel / by this ordre discerne
That thilke moeuere / stable is and eterne
Wel may men knowe / but it be a fool
That euery part · is diryued from his hool
ffor nature / hath nat taken his bigynnyng
Of no partie / or of cantel of a thyng
But of a thyng · that parfit is and stable
Descendynge so / til it be corrumpable
And ther fore / for his wise purueiaunce
He hath so wel biset his ordinaunce
That specis of thynges / and progressions
Shullen enduren / by successions
And noght eterne / with outen any lye
This maistow vnderstonde / and seen at Iye
    ⟨ Loo the ook / that hath so long a norisshynge
     ffro the tyme / that it first gynneth sprynge
And hath so long a lyf / as ye may see
yet at the laste / wasted is the tree
    ⟨ Considreth eek / how þat the harde stoon
Vnder oure foot / on which we ryde and goon
It wasteth / as it lyth by the weye
The brode Ryuer / som tyme wexeth dreye
The grete townes / se we wane and wende
Thanne se ye / þat al this thyng hath ende
Of man and womman / se we wel also
That nedeth in oon of thise termes two
This is to seyn / in youthe · or ellis age
He moot be deed / the kyng as shal a page
Som in his bed / som in the depe see
Som in the large feeld / as ye may se
Ther helpeth noght / al gooth that ilke weye
Thanne may I seyn / þat al this thyng moot deye

In F. N. Robinson's second edition the passage appears thus:

A 2994   'That same Prince and that Moevere,' quod he,
'Hath stablissed in this wrecched world adoun
Certeyne dayes and duracioun
To al that is engendred in this place,
Over the whiche day they may nat pace,
Al mowe they yet tho dayes wel abregge.
Ther nedeth noght noon auctoritee t'allegge ,

For it is preeved by experience,
But that me list declaren my sentence.
Thanne may men by this ordre wel discerne
That thilke Moevere stable is and eterne.
Wel may men knowe, but it be a fool,
That every part dirryveth from his hool;
For nature hath nat taken his bigynnyng
Of no partie or cantel of a thyng,
But of a thyng that parfit is and stable,
Descendynge so til it be corrumpable.
And therfore, of his wise purveiaunce,
He hath so wel biset his ordinaunce,
That speces of thynges and progressiouns
Shullen enduren by successiouns,
And nat eterne, withouten any lye.
This maystow understonde and seen at ye.
   Loo the ook, that hath so long a norisshynge
From tyme that it first bigynneth to sprynge,
And hath so long a lif, as we may see,
Yet at the laste wasted is the tree.
   Considereth eek how that the harde stoon
Under oure feet, on which we trede and goon,
Yet wasteth it as it lyth by the weye.
The brode ryver somtyme wexeth dreye;
The grete tounes se we wane and wende.
Thanne may ye se that al this thyng hath ende.
   Of man and womman seen we wel also
That nedes, in oon of thise termes two,
This is to seyn, in youthe or elles age,
He moot be deed, the kyng as shal a page;
Som in his bed, som in the depe see,
Som in the large feeld, as men may see;
Ther helpeth noght, al goth that ilke weye.
Thanne may I seyn that al this thyng moot deye.'

In some places, though not many, the manuscript is plainly wrong. But it is so much better than the edition because the editor, by removing the punctuation that indicates the half-line, has pushed the verse away from the vividness it owes to the half-line movement. Often the result is a woodenness I am unwilling to attribute to Chaucer. In

That same Prince   and that Moevere quod he

it is surely better to follow the three-stress first phrase (a strong iamb followed by a foot with final -e) by a rhythmic echo, 'and that móver' than to alter the stress on *Moevere* and continue a simple iambic flow throughout the line:

That same Prince and that Moevere quod he

is not merely dull, it loses all the particular grandeur of the tone of Duke Theseus. The third line of the passage also makes its way much better if the feet are allowed to point the half-lines than if they are strongly emphasized and the half-lines ignored:

Certeyne dayes and duracioun

—it is the weak third iamb that steers us into the expressive half-lines; which is as much as to say that the line's success comes from the interaction of both these elements to express its convincing rhythms. Hengwrt drops the -e from *whiche* in 'Ouer the which day' but preserves the halting movement by so doing. Put the -e back if you like, but retain the movement, so appropriate to the magisterial Theseus: 'Óver the whíche dáy...' In the next line Hengwrt omits the 'wel' of the editions. This may just be a mistake, but the manuscript reading does not harm the line, as a too heavily metrical or completely unmetrical reading would. As it stands in Hengwrt I take the half-lines to be emphasized by the missing syllable in the third foot together with the trochaic fourth:

Al mowe they yet / tho dayes abregge

Line A 3003 puts 'wel' in a different place from Robinson's text, and seems superior to it; the resulting trochaic inversion of the fourth foot creates an effectively stern tone. The next line is a regular enough iambic pentameter in anyone's reading, but its life comes from the emphasis given by the half-lines:

That thilke moeuere / stable is and eterne

—the strong stress on 'stable' comes from the half-line rhythms more than the foot-metre.

It would be exasperating to extend this commentary throughout that very great passage, which expresses itself well enough to those who allow it its own movement, but it is worth pointing to a few more instances of wonderfully good half-lines.

Yet at the laste / wasted is the tree

—here the powerful sadness of 'wasted' comes from its position as main stress-bearer in the second half-line, to which the final -e at the end of the first contributes. And the genuineness of the invitation in the next line to 'consider' is expressed by its occupation of one complete phrase, followed by the very effective stress on 'harde', caused partly by its being the first stress of its half-line, partly by the usual rhythmic effect of a sounded final -e. The parallel phrases 'the brode ryver' and 'the grete tounes' both create similar half-line movements from their sounded -e. But best of all are the lines almost at the end of the passage, where the repeated *som* introduces lines the dignity of whose tragic emotion can only be expressed through their half-line phrases. 'Som in the large feeld' is a rhythmic echo of 'som in the depe see', both phrases concentrating stress towards their close by having a sounded final -e as the penultimate syllable.

The rather different high style of the beginning of *The Clerk's Tale* comes delicately alive in a comparable way if one follows the half-line balances as well as the feet. This passage could be used as a last bastion of iambic pentameter if it were seriously argued that the metre is wholly uniambic: but it is only by adding the half-line principle that we save its lines from monotony and allow them their own life. This is how the passage appears in Robinson's second edition:

E 57   Ther is, right at the west syde of Ytaille,
        Doun at the roote of Vesulus the colde,
        A lusty playn, habundant of vitaille,
        Where many a tour and toun thou mayst biholde,
        That founded were in tyme of fadres olde,
        And many another delitable sighte,
        And Saluces this noble contree highte.

        A markys whilom lord was of that lond,
        As were his worthy eldres hym bifore;
        And obeisant, ay redy to his hond,
        Were alle his liges, bothe lasse and moore.
        Thus in delit he lyveth, and hath doon yoore,
        Biloved and drad, thurgh favour of Fortune,
        Bothe of his lordes and of his commune.

Here is the same passage as it appears in the Cambridge Dd.4.24 manuscript:

THere is right at the west side of ytaille
Doun at the rote / of Vesulus the colde
A lusty playn / habundaunt of vytaille
Wher many a Toūn & Tour / þou mayst byholde
That founded were / in tyme of fadres olde
And many a nother / delitable syght
And Saluces this noble countree hyght
(A Markys whylom / lord was of that londe
As were his worthy elderes / him byfore
And obeissaunt / ay redy to his honde
Were alle his lieges / bothe lasse and more
Thus in delyt he lyueth / and hath doon ʒore
Byloued and dred / thurgh fauour of Fortune
Bothe of his lordes / & of his comune

The distinction of this passage's rhythm appears in what it shares with the alliterative tradition; and it shows with peculiar clarity how the normal variations of the medieval five-foot line can create the balances of the half-line movement. The trochaic inversions at 'Ytaille', 'vitaille' and 'fortune' do more than save the passage from dull stiffness; together with the groupings indicated by the manuscript punctuation they gently divide the lines into peculiar, slightly pedantic speech-rhythms such as we could believe Chaucer's Clerk to have used. The two last quoted lines would be scanned thus by ten Brink:

Biloved and drad, thurgh favour of Fortune,

Bothe of his lordes and of his commune.

Really they would only need alliteration to appear quite at home in *Piers Plowman*:

Biloved and drad / thurgh favour of Fortune

Bothe of his lordes / and of his commune

The way feet and half-lines co-operate to create rhythms could be hinted at by an analysis which marks the two rhythmic systems separately, though such deliberate and separate marking is necessarily crude compared with what really happens as we read: I mark the half-line rhythms above the feet:

Ther is   right at the west syde   of Ytaille

Doun at the roote   of Vesulus the colde

A lusty playn   habundant of vitaille

Where many a tour and toun   thou mayst biholde

That founded were   in tyme of fadres olde

And many another   delitable sighte

And Saluces   this noble contree   highte

A markys whilom   lord was of that lond

As were his worthy eldres   hym bifore

And obeisant   ay redy to his hond

Were alle his liges   bothe lasse and moore

Thus in delit he lyveth   and hath doon yoore

Biloved and drad   thurgh favour of Fortune

Bothe of his lordes   and of his commune

Many good things come from the coincidence of half-lines and feet.

Coming down to a less respectable kind of rhetoric, we find the elements of balanced pentameter just as indispensable to the insane vigour of the Pardoner's sermon. In Skeat's text, quoted first, the determined reader might notice nothing very unusual about the metre by the standards of Skeat's own day:

C 531   I seye it now weping with pitous voys,
         That they been enemys of Cristes croys,
         Of which the ende is deeth, wombe is her god!
         O wombe! O bely! O stinking cod,

Fulfild of donge and of corrupcioun!
At either ende of thee foul is the soun.
How greet labour and cost is thee to finde!
These cokes, how they stampe, and streyne, and grinde,
And turnen substaunce in-to accident,
To fulfille al thy likerous talent!
Out of the harde bones knokke they
The mary, for they caste noght a-wey
That may go thurgh the golet softe and swote.

This is how the passage appears in the Hengwrt manuscript:

I seye it now wepyng / with pitous voys
Ther been enemys / of Cristes croys
Of whiche the ende is deth / wombe is hir god
O wombe / o bely / o stynkyng cod
ffulfilled of dong / and of corrupcioun
At either end of thee / foul is the soun
How greet labour / and cost / is thee to fynde
Thise Cokes / how they stampe / & streyne / & grynde
And turnen substance / in to accident
To fulfillen al / the likerous talent
Out of the harde bones / knokke they
The mary / for they caste nat awey
That may go thurgh the golet / softe and soote

In conventional terms Skeat's text is quite close to the manuscript, but Hengwrt's punctuation makes a great difference and, it seems to me, an improvement. It helps us to speak the lines; without it the metre is more difficult. For here Chaucer both includes extra syllables and omits syllables we should normally suppose to be necessary in iambic pentameter. In

$$\breve{\text{O}}\ \text{wombe}\ \acute{\text{O}}\ \text{bely}\ \breve{\text{O}}\ \text{stinking}\ \acute{\text{cod}}$$

we seem to have a regular iambic tetrameter, whose jaunty rhythm contrasts strangely with the Pardoner's declamatory intention. But if we allow the punctuation to guide us into the phrases we get also a sight of the line as a pentameter with a monosyllabic foot:

$$\breve{\text{O}}\ \text{wombe}\ \acute{\text{O}}\ \text{bely}\ \acute{\text{o}}\ \text{stinking}\ \acute{\text{cod}}$$

The unusual foot- and phrase-patterns justify themselves by the very striking rhetorical force they give. So too 'the end' often appears in manuscripts as *thend* and was probably pronounced as a monosyllable. To do so would give another powerful line with one monosyllabic foot:

> Of which thend is deeth wombe is hir god

> To fulfille al thy likerous talent

is a variant Skeat found in the Corpus group of manuscripts. It is a dull line compared with the Hengwrt version, where the -en and the punctuation give the clue to the most expressive rhythmic grouping:

> To fulfillen al   thy likerous talent

The final push of the line into the commonplace is surely given by the treatment of *talent* as a word of variable stress:

> To fulfille al thy likerous talent

What could be prettier or further from the Pardoner?

Below the high style but above the low come things like the descriptions in the *General Prologue*, for instance the Manciple. I quote some lines of the Ellesmere manuscript:

(A 567)
> A gentil Maunciple / was ther of a temple
> Of which Achatours / myghte take exemple
> ffor to be wise / in byynge of vitaille
> ffor wheither that he payde / or took by taille
> Algate / he wayted so / in his Achaat
> That he was ay biforn / and in good staat
> Now is nat that of god a ful fair grace
> That swich a lewed mannes wit shal pace
> The wisdom / of an heep / of lerned men
> Of maistres hadde he / mo than thries ten
> That weren of lawe / expert and curious
> Of whiche / þer weren a dusȝeyne in that hous
> Worthy to been stywardes / of rente and lond /
> Of any lord / that is in Engelond /
> To maken hym lyue / by his propre good
> In honour dettelees / but if he were wood
> Or lyue as scarsly / as hym list desire

Chaucer is here frequently writing feet with more than the two syllables permitted by ten Brink—but if we can put it like that it means that he is still writing in feet. The phrase-rhythms, however, seem more important than the feet here. In the first quoted line the iambic flow is weak compared with the unambiguous phrase-divisions:

A gentle Maunciple was ther of a temple

A phrase-break occurs between the two unstressed syllables and the stressed syllable of the third foot; and the pattern of the fourth foot is made less marked by its moving over the second phrase-break.

Worthy to been stywardes of rente and lond

has trochaic substitution of the first and third feet (or, if you prefer, dactyllic substitution of the third) which make the feet rather weakly marked. The three consecutive syllables which are unstressed in both foot-metre and half-line phrasing divide the line by arranging themselves round the distant stresses.

Finally we must look at the Chaucer of vivid conversation and lively narrative, the side of Chaucer to which, in places like the *fabliaux* and *The Wife of Bath's Prologue*, his work owes its survival of six centuries and the development of courses in Eng. Lit. Chaucer's verse is here liberated from a mechanical metre if we allow the pentameters their full metrical freedom and their half-line movements.

The Wife of Bath speaks hardly any lines to whose indubitable vigour the traditional metre gives any clue. Here is a bit of her diatribe in the version of Southworth's favourite manuscript, B.M. Additional 5140:

(D 236)   Whi is my neyhbors wyf / so gay
                    She is honoured oviral / wher she goth
                    I sit at home / I haue no thryfty cloth
                    What dost thou / at my neyhbours hous
                    Is she so fair / art thou so amerous
                    What rowne ye wyth oure maide / benedicite
                    Sire olde lecchour / lat your iapes be
                    And yif I haue a gossip / or a frend
                    Wythouten gylt / thou chidest as a frend [*sic*]
                    If that y walke and pley unto hir hous
                    Thou comyst homc / as dronkyn as a mous

This verse would be equally far from Tyrwhitt's regularity if the careful but late manuscript had put in the -e-'s in *neyhebores*, for the passage goes into balanced phrases not by the contradiction of metre so much as by the concentration of heavy stresses in places that naturally make lines divide: 'Í sit at home, Í have...', 'Whát dóst thou at my neýhbours...', 'Sire óld lécchour lát...' and so on.

That magnificent passage in which Chaucer transcends in his description of Alison the usual limits of the fabliau also depends for its life on rhythms not recognized by the traditional metre. I print it, experimentally, in F. N. Robinson's text but with the half-lines marked (as in many editions of Anglo-Saxon poetry) by spaces: this is perhaps the least offensive way of showing the half-line movement to the modern reader:

A 3233   Fair was this yonge wyf   and therwithal
As any wezele   hir body gent and smal
A ceynt she werede   barred al of silk

A barmclooth eek   as whit as morne milk
Upon hir lendes   ful of many a goore
Whit was hir smok   and broyden al bifoore
And eek bihynde   on hir coler aboute
Of col-blak silk   withinne and eek withoute

The tapes   of hir white voluper

Were of the same suyte   of hir coler
Hir filet brood of silk   and set ful hye
And sikerly   she hadde a likerous ye
Ful smale ypulled   were hire browes two
And tho were bent   and blake as any sloo

She was ful moore blisful   on to se

Than is the newe   pere-jonette tree
And softer   than the wolle is   of a wether
And by hir girdel   heeng a purs of lether

Tasseled with silk   and perled with látoun
In al this world   to seken up and doun

Ther nys no man so wys   that koude thence
So gay a popelote   or swich a wenche
Ful brighter   was the shynyng of hir hewe
Than in the Tour   the noble yforged newe
But of hir song   it was as loude and yerne

As any swalwe   sittynge on a berne

Therto she koude skippe   and make game
As any kyde or calf   folwynge his dame

Hir mouth   was sweete as bragot   or the meeth
Or hoord of apples   leyd in hey or heeth
Wynsynge she was   as is a joly colt
Long as a mast   and upright as a bolt
A brooch she baar   upon hire lowe cóler
As brood as is the boos   of a bókeler
Hir shoes were laced   on hir legges hye
She was a prymerole   a piggesnye
For any lord   to leggen in his bedde
Or yet   for any good yeman   to wedde

Chaucer's racy conversations almost anywhere in the endlinks
give the modern reader the illusion of hearing what fourteenth-
century speech was really like, so freshly and naturally do they
cross the barriers of time and language-change: perhaps there is
some truth in the illusion. Here Chaucer is in an obvious way
working with the pieces of speech of the alliterative tradition and
here, above all, the function of the metre is to point the speech and
suggest its shades of tone without turning it into something that is
not speech. These 'pieces of speech' are, just as in *Sir Gawain* or
Piers Plowman, the half-line phrases. This can be shown by further
quotation from the Hengwrt manuscript, whose punctuation so
well indicates the half-lines:

(B 2113)   'Myne erys aken / of thy drasty speche
            Now swich a rym / the deuel I biteche
            This may wel be / rym dogerel' quod he
        ['Why so' quod I / 'why wiltow lette me
            Moore of my tale / than another man
            Syn that it is / the beste rym I kan'
        ['By god' quod he / 'for pleynly at o word
            Thy drasty rymyng / is nat worth a tord
            Thow dost noght ellis / but despendest tyme
            Sire at o word / thow shalt no lenger ryme
            Lat se / wher thow kanst tellen aught in geste
            Or tel in prose / somwhat at the leeste
            In which ther be som myrthe / or som doctrine'[1]

The punctuation in the last quoted line is especially useful: it
prevents our forming the inferior division

In which ther be / som myrthe or som doctrine

[1] B 2113 ff. I supply quotation marks.

—the host is even willing to listen to 'doctrine' in preference to *Sir Thopas*; and his perfectly unruffled sureness of his own opinions surely also comes out in the contempt for *prose* expressed by the stress given by its place at the end of its phrase and by its sounded final -e. So also the Wife of Bath in full reminiscence of how she dealt with her husbands is even more formidable if we follow manuscripts' hints about the half-line phrasing: this is from Ellesmere:

(D 348)

     ❲ Thou seydest this / that I was lyk a Cat
        ffor who so wolde / senge a Cattes skyn
        Thanne wolde the Cat / wel dwellen in his In
        And if the Cattes skyn / be slyk and gay
        She wol nat dwelle in house / half a day
        But forth she wole / er any day be dawed
        To shewe hir skyn / and goon a Cat*er*wawed
        This is to seye / if I be gay sir shrewe
        I wol renne out / my borel for to shewe
     ❲ Sire olde fool / what eyleth thee to spyen
        Thogh thou preye Argus / *with* hise hundred eyen
        To be my wardecors / as he kan best
        In feith / he shal nat kepe me but lest [*sic*]
        Yet koude I make his berd / so moot I thee

The half-line 'Sire olde fool' is particularly expressive, the accumulation of stress coming as usual from the sounded -e on *olde*.

Professor Baum sees *The Canon's Yeoman's Tale* as containing an unusually large number of unmetrical lines,[1] though it seems to me not less smooth than many passages elsewhere in Chaucer. But the Canon's Yeoman certainly expresses more of his frustration if he is allowed to do so in half-lines as well as feet: this conversation with the Host (which I also quote from the Ellesmere manuscript) needs both the elements of the metre to shape its speech-phrases to their best effect:

(G 652)

     ❲ Ther of no fors / good yeman / quod oure hoost
        Syn of the konnyng / of thy lord thow woost
        Telle how he dooth / I pray thee hertely
        Syn that he is / so crafty and so sly
        Where dwelle ye / if it to telle be ⋮
     ❲ In the suburbes / of a toun quod he

[1] Cf. *Chaucer's Verse*, Appendix 2.

> Lurkynge in hernes / and in lanes blynde
> Where as thise robb*e*res / and thise theues by kynde
> Holden / hir pryuee fereful residence
> As they / that dar nat shewen hir p*r*esence
> So faren we / if I shal seye the sothe
> ⸿ Now quod oure hoost / · lat me telle tothe
> Why artow / so discoloured of thy face ⸝
> ⸿ Peter quod he / god yeue it harde grace
> I am so vsed / in the fyr to blowe
> That it hath chaunged my colour I trowe

Or, similarly, the last conversation in the Tales, from Hengwrt:

(H 22)

> Sire preest quod he / artow a vicary
> Or arte a p*e*rson / sey sooth by thy fey
> Be what thow be / ne breke thow nat oure pley
> ffor euery man saue thow / hath toold his tale
> Vnbokele / and shewe vs / what is in thy Male
> ffor trewely / me thynketh by thy cheere
> Thow sholdest / knette vp wel a greet matere
> Telle vs a fable anon / for Cokkes bones

Does not the half-line phrasing make very well the point of Harry Bailly's sudden descent into the very unfitting oath?

Since this work began with a skirmish against H. C. Wyld's reading of the most famous lines of Chaucer it would be perhaps appropriate to end this section with a better version, in so far as that can be done without recordings; we will for the occasion revert to the full paraphernalia of half-line and foot marking which I have been gradually dropping through the earlier parts of this chapter in the hope that an increasingly familiar metre would no longer need them. But the reader is invited for the last time to see how these different elements co-operate to express the life of the poetry.

> Whan that Aprill   with his shoures soote
>
> The droghte of March   hath perced to the roote
>
> And bathed every veyne   in swich licour
>
> Of which vertu   engendred is the flour
>
> Whan Zephirus eek   with his sweete breeth

169

Inspired hath   in every holt and heeth

The tendre croppes   and the yonge sonne

Hath in the Ram   his halve cours yronne

And smale foweles   maken melodye

That slepen al the nyght   with open ye

So priketh hem nature   in hir corages   (?)

Thanne longen folk   to goon on pilgrimages

And palmeres   for to seken straunge strondes

To ferne halwes   kowthe in sondry londes

And specially   from every shires ende

Of Engelond   to Caunterbury they wende

The hooly blisful martir   for to seke

That hem hath holpen   whan that they were seeke

Bifil that   in that seson   on a day

In Southwerk   at the Tabard   as I lay

Redy   to wenden on my pilgrymage

To Caunterbury   with ful devout corage   (?)

At nyght was come   into that hostelrye

Wel nyne and twenty   in a compaignye

Of sondry folk   by aventure yfalle

In felaweshipe   and pilgrimes were they alle

That toward Caunterbury   wolden ryde

The chambres and the stables   weren wyde

And wel we weren esed   atte beste

And shortly   whan the sonne was to reste

So hadde I spoken with hem   everichon

That I was   of hir felaweshipe anon

And made forward   erly for to ryse

To take oure wey   ther as I yow devyse

But nathelees   whil I have tyme and space

Er that I ferther   in this tale pace

Me thynketh it   acordaunt to resoun

To telle yow   al the condicioun

Of ech of hem   so as it semed me

And whiche they weren   and of what degree

And eek in what array   that they were inne

And at a knyght than   wol I first bigynne

In fact of course one is not conscious of these two parts of metre, and especially not of them separately, but of being pulled by Chaucer towards this natural way of joining his words in the best rhythms.

Now if by reading Chaucer in the way I have been illustrating we find so many wonderful things invisible to Tyrwhitt and ten Brink; if we maintain the feeling that Chaucer is speaking to us in these rhythms, I submit that the feeling is likely to be more than an illusion. It will not, either, be a final unalterable truth. But if we improve the reading we are coming closer to Chaucer. And I offer this process of familiarization, working back and forwards from the poetry to thought about it, getting to know its rhythms, as the way in which the modern reader really can commune with the English of the fourteenth century—a way, moreover, which makes traditional phonological considerations seem rather trivial.

III

Few readers would want to deny that Chaucer's verse conveys more of a sense of the speaking voice (and speaking voices) than Gower's; and the basic reason is that he works like the alliterative poets with 'pieces of language'. Yet Chaucer's verse is, to bring in a different quotation, 'speech heightened', very unlike the naturalistic prose by which a modern novelist might attain some comparable end. One heightening agent is the metre, the compound of pentameter with half-line movement. This compound of balanced pentameter is evidence of an accomplished technique; but the intention triumphantly fulfilled in the best of Chaucer is the concealment of technique—the simulation of speech by a heightening of speech which can yet seem fresh and natural. If Chaucer had wanted real speech he could have taken his tablets out into the street and written it out in prose; but for the lively simulation of speech he needed verse and that complex metre. The metre justifies itself by a concentration of expressiveness, a significance not found so consistently in real conversation. The life of Chaucer's verse is that of the spoken language, but it is a life quite unlike chunks of liveliness.

If Chaucer's poetry is speech heightened, it is speech in its basic rhythmic shaping. The half-line movement is the final sign that the metre in Chaucer cannot be at war with speech-rhythm, on which it is built and with which it co-operates.

An undue concentration on one or other element of Chaucer's metre has led to most of the unsatisfactoriness of all the authorities. The presence of the pentameter element made historically possible the position developed by Urry, Tyrwhitt, Child, ten Brink and Baum; the presence of the half-line metre has given Nott and Southworth in their different centuries their chance to state their admirable but incomplete opposition to the establishment. The validity of my contention that neither establishment nor opposition has even as much of the whole truth as might be possible to mortals can only be tested in reading Chaucer. It is my minimal claim that the metre I have described is not, at least, quickly contradicted by a reading of Chaucer. And any further enforcement would have to be a critical essay, an argument of the form 'Chaucer's rhythms go like this because his poetry is like this', for which this is not the place.

But I can point to a general agreement about Chaucer's poetry which supports the paradox of the naturalness of Chaucer's rhythms which results from thoroughgoing technique. For critics are always remarking, truly enough, on the paradox of Chaucer's learned spontaneity. Sometimes one half of the paradox predominates, sometimes the other. Chaucer the wayward genius unaffected by his time is an obviously incomplete picture, but when Blake says in the Prospectus for his engraving of the Canterbury Pilgrims, 'Let the Philosopher always be the Servant and Scholar of Inspiration and all will be happy', he is certainly stating one side of the truth about Chaucer's greatness. Nowadays, of course, we have come full circle to Lydgate's view, and it is more fashionable to emphasize the other side of the paradox, Chaucer's professional expertise—which is equally incomplete. Chaucer is learned and spontaneous: the Wife of Bath is a mixture of quotations from anti-feminist literature; she is also an uncomfortably convincing real person. It does seem to me that the metre I have outlined fits the paradox better than the metrical models of Baum or Southworth. Chaucer's rhythms too are learned, skilled, artificial, spontaneous and fresh—which is part of what I mean by Hopkins's phrase 'speech heightened'.

What has been said of The Canterbury Tales applies generally to Chaucer's later poems. The Moral Ballades make similar use of half-line rhythms in their balanced pentameters:

> Trouthe is put doun   resoun is holden fable
> Vertu hath now   no dominacioun
> (Lak of Stedfastnesse, 15–16)

and if any stylistic evidence is needed for the attribution to Chaucer
of *Merciles Beaute* it can surely be found in the rhythms:

3 So woundeth hit   thourghout my herte kene

—this has just the kind of effective stress on the important places
which has been discussed many times above. But these remarks
about balanced pentameter do not fit the earlier poems so well.
The Second Nun's Tale (but not *The Knight's Tale* which in the
form we have it there is no reason to believe an early work) seems
to depend more on feet than half-lines; and perhaps Puttenham is
right about *Troilus and Criseyde* itself: he distinguishes its metre
as 'very graue and stately, keeping the staffe of seuen, and the
verse of ten', from that of *The Canterbury Tales*, which 'be but
riding ryme, neuerthelesse very well becomming the matter of
that pleasaunt pilgrimage'.[1] If there is a perceptible metrical
development in Chaucer it is almost certainly away from pentameter as usually understood towards an increased dependence on
half-line movement.

Moreover, we have not yet touched the short-line poems, which
can be no more than mentioned in the next chapter. But if it has
been shown that balanced pentameter fits one's idea of the Chaucer
of *The Canterbury Tales*, I shall consider the aim of this work
accomplished and will gladly leave completeness to those who think
it important.

IV

What ought the common reader to do to surmount the obstacles
placed in his way by the editions of Chaucer? My advice will
sound impossibly idealistic: I would recommend him to read
Chaucer in a good manuscript. Most big libraries have the
magnificent facsimile of the Ellesmere manuscript;[2] the hand is
easy to read and the advantages make it worth mastering. The
Hengwrt manuscript can be had in photostatic copy (but Hengwrt,
though the best complete text of *The Canterbury Tales*, was
unfortunately gnawed by rats and suffered accidents at the hands
of the binder which make it not very beautiful or convenient).
Failing a real manuscript or facsimile, try for one of the good ones

[1] Cited by Spurgeon, *Chaucer Criticism*, vol. I, p. 126.
[2] *The Ellesmere Chaucer Reproduced in Facsimile*, 2 vols. Manchester, 1911.

in the Chaucer Society reprints. These are not utterly reliable, but they perform the essential service of reproducing punctuation.

If only one of the modern editions is available, go through a page or two marking the half-line divisions and try to get used to the phrase-movement that follows. (Then if you can see Hengwrt or Cambridge Dd.4.24 after all, compare your half-line divisions with those of an intelligent scribe, and realize how much better he read Chaucer than we do.) But most importantly, keep constantly in mind that poetry is the test of metre, and that in the poetry alone metre lives—or not, as the case may be. If your reading gives you a lifeless Chaucer there is something wrong with it, probably that it belongs to one of the academic traditions which demonstrate a real power by removing the life from the most consistently vivid English poet. If on the other hand your reading is lively there is something right about it even though there will certainly be room for improvement.

As to pronunciation and stress: give the necessary -e's metrical value if that makes sense; stress most words as in modern English but always stress words whose simple form has three syllables ⁄ ◡ ⁄ even if the present accent-pattern is different. Do what you like about vowel-sounds if reading to yourself; if to friends try not to sound ridiculous. But whatever you do don't suppose that sounds matter in the way rhythms do, or that any of our sounds could have been offered to Chaucer without giving him cause for amusement.

Never trust an expert on metre unless he improves your reading of a poet: that is what his expertise consists in, if anything, for there is no special metrical expertise different from what we all acquire and test in reading. Apply all this good advice to the present work, and if it doesn't improve Chaucer, persevere no further.

9

Chaucer in his Age

I

In its rhythms as elsewhere, Chaucer's poetry is a gathering of, or a compound from, elements of different traditions. *The Canterbury Tales* gather through one unifying sensibility hitherto quite separate elements of courtly romance, fabliau, saint's legend, sermon, etc., into a literature. The metre I have proposed for *The Canterbury Tales* similarly draws together the separate traditions of French-influenced *rym* and native *geest* to make something quite new. It is one of the evidences of Chaucer's dominating position in his age that he should be the man to make and establish this new, compound metre; but naturally enough others were working in comparable ways, and this chapter is an attempt to make the most obviously useful comparisons.

One finds before and contemporary with Chaucer plenty of regular foot-verse (*The Ormulum*, for instance, or *Confessio Amantis*), plenty of traditional alliteratives, but also some mixtures of these traditions and even one or two other attempts to marry them. *The Bestiary* is an early mixture: it often uses regular verse in feet to translate Latin *rithmus* and alliteratives for Latin quantitatives. For instance the following translates a passage of *rithmus* (considerably expanding it: but the metrical intention is plain):

> List ilk lefful man her to.   & herof ofte reche.
> vre sowle atte kirke dure . ches hire crist to meche.
> he is ure soule spuse luue we him wið migte.
> & wende we neure fro him ward . be dai ne be nigte.[1]

But the adder, from quantitative Latin, is in free but recognizable alliteratives:

> An wirm is o werlde . wel man it knoweð.
> Neddre is te name . ðus he him neweð.

[1] *The Bestiary*, lines 585–8. *Selections from Early Middle English, 1130–1250*, ed. J. Hall, Oxford, 1920, p. 194.

ðanne he is forbroken & forbroiden . & in his elde al forwurden.
Fasteð til his fel him slakeð . ten daies fulle.[1]

There are even places where the translator seems to be trying for both feet and phrases at once: here for instance is a momentary anticipation of Skelton:

> ðer ðurg haueð mankin.
> boðen nið & win.
> golsipe . & giscing.
> giuernesse & wissing.
> pride & ouerwene.
> swilc atter i mene.[2]

The rhyming short lines are also plainly half-line phrases, the two stresses often separated by 'and'; in making these phrases out of traditional collocations of words the writer is working with 'pieces of speech' like the Anglo-Saxon authors with their set phrases, but is also after feet as well.

Laȝamon's *Brut* is another mixture of traditions nearly two centuries older than Chaucer's. Its long lines are often ordinary alliteratives, often alliteratives whose halves rhyme, but are sometimes made of feet. He begins:

1   An preost wes on leoden ⁚ Laȝamon wes ihoten.[3]

This looks like a hexameter but is probably just two longish rhyming and partly alliterative phrases.

2   he wes Leouenaðes sone ⁚ liðe him beo Drihten.

(alliterative, B plus A types)

3   He wonede at Ernleȝe ⁚ at æðelen are chirechen.

(irregular alliterative). But further on there are rhyming lines in foot-metre like:

719   ȝe doð þan kinge muchel scome ⁚ þer fore ȝe sculen han grome.

The total effect is a kind of *cadence* where all traditions mix.

But for Chaucer the main alternative to the long line of *The Canterbury Tales* was the short line of his early poems. This was

---

[1] Lines 106–9; *ibid.* p. 179.
[2] Lines 243–8; *ibid.* p. 183.
[3] Laȝamon's *Brut*, ed. G. L. Brook and R. F. Leslie, E.E.T.S. 1963; Cotton Caligula A. ix manuscript.

first thoroughly naturalized in English and made available for sophisticated poetry by the author of *The Owl and the Nightingale*, again a century and a half before Chaucer. The problem solved in this poem was how to make flexible anything so stiff as this metre usually was in the popular romances, how to make it the measure of a witty and frivolous poem acceptable to people of French cultivation. To do so the author pulled the metre in the direction of the spoken language by making his metrical lines also rhythmic units that might conceivably be spoken. (How many phrases there are to the line in *The Owl and the Nightingale* is a question open to lengthy discussion: my remarks are just suggestions.) The result is that many of the lines, while retaining an iambic flow, speak themselves very naturally as phrases, and might in some cases have served as half-lines in *The Canterbury Tales*:

711
> ʃi axestu of craftes mine.
> Betere is min on þan alle þine.
> Betere is o song of mine muþe.
> Þan al þat eure þi kun kuþe.[1]

Here one gets the very Chaucer-like effect of producing a phrase by making the metre: fitting 'betere' into the metre needs the effort which itself forms the rhythmic contours of the phrase. But often the poem's phrases seem to be two to the line, and we get hints of a possible half-line development:

1757
> An þurh his muþe and þurh his honde.
>
> Hit is þe betere in to scot londe.

Perhaps if the author had written as much as Chaucer he would have gone in the same direction.

It is not surprising that a language with so well established an alliterative tradition as English—a tradition whose phrasal rhythms are so much part of the ordinary working of the language— should make *rym* at home by adding phrase-metre to it. Throughout the Middle English period verse in *rym* can occasionally be seen moving towards *geest*. In the metrical romances this may be just the result of careless writing—phrases are easier than feet—but often enough the result justifies itself. The phrases of *geest* belong to the poetic language and cannot be kept out. Like this:

---

[1] *The Owl and the Nightingale*, ed. Grattan and Sykes; Cotton manuscript.

> Sum tyme an Englisch schip we had
> Nobel hit was and heih of tour
> Þorw al Cristendam hit was drad
> And stif wolde stande in vch a stour
> And best dorst byde a scharp schour...[1]

The first two lines here have a simple iambic beat, but the third extends the metre over a suspiciously free-looking phrase, and by the last quoted one we have two sharply balanced phrases, made by the monosyllabic fourth foot and the alliteration.

Chaucer himself in *The Book of the Duchess* and *The House of Fame* makes rhythms comparable with those of *The Owl and the Nightingale*. The very attractive conversational feeling of Chaucer's early poems is expressed in a similar conjunction of regular metre with speech-phrasing. Here too the line is often a natural-sounding phrase:

BD 76	Now for to speken of his wyf...
153	This messager tok leve and wente
HF 111	Of Decembre the tenthe day...
68	With special devocion

But sometimes Chaucer seems to be anticipating Donne by controlling phrases of lengths unrelated to metrical structure:

BD 77	This lady that was left at hom
	Hath wonder that the king ne com
	Hom, for it was a longe term
HF 492	'O Crist' thoughte I 'that art in blysse
	Fro fantome and illusion
	Me save' and with devocion
	Myn eyen to the hevene I caste

And sometimes he seems verging on a half-line movement:[2]

HF 2	For hyt is wonder be the roode
	To my wyt what causeth swevenes
HF 17	To knowe of hir signifiaunce
	The gendres neyther the distaunce

Several alliterative poets travel in the other direction and approach *rym*, whether in the complicated internally rhyming

---

[1] A poem quoted in Sisam's *Fourteenth Century Verse and Prose*, p. 157, lines 17–21.

[2] Some manuscripts including the important Fairfax 16 punctuate *The House of Fame* metrically with half-line marks, but I cannot myself feel that the half-line movement is important or consistent enough to count as part of the metre.

lines of the Wakefield master or the bobs and wheels of *Sir Gawain and the Green Knight*. *Pearl* sometimes achieves a coalition of metre with phrase very like the ones we have been discussing. In this poem too the alliterative phrase, somewhat longer than the usual half-line, is the same as the four-foot line; but here too the phrasal element is not regular enough to be called part of the metre, and many of the lines go better as halves. These lines are also phrases:

I Perle plesaunte to prynces paye
To clanly clos in golde so clere[1]

But the lines of the second stanza begin to look as if they should divide as halves:

14 Syþen in þat spot hit fro me sprange
Ofte haf I wayted wyschande þat wele

II

Chaucer's choice of the long line and its balances was his progress into full poetic seriousness. It is not merely that with *The Parliament of Fowls* 'the eternal note of sadness' joins the other tones of his poetry:[2] the development of the half-line movement gave him the command of the life of the language which he needed for full poetic expression. In Chaucer's long lines we have—further than seems possible in the work of one man—the full range of the power of his English, controlled into verse and, hence, a great release of energy into English poetry. Some such marriage of traditions as is expressed in balanced pentameters was needed for the first flowering after the Conquest of a fully English poetry. By his use of the quasi-alliterative phrase Chaucer is recognizing and drawing on the resources of the deep habit of the language—which, at the same time, would not have known what it was capable of without him. I wish finally to point this judgement in a comparison of Chaucer with Gower, the alternative to Chaucer in the eyes of his contemporaries and for a hundred years afterwards. Gower tried to write English verse whose metre had no phrasal

[1] *Pearl*, ed. E. V. Gordon, Oxford, 1953.
[2] One of the astonishing things about *The Owl and the Nightingale* is that it can achieve real solemnity in the four-foot metre: see, for example, lines 1191–212.

element; and one aspect of his failure compared with Chaucer is his inability to see the need for Chaucer's rhythmic development.

Gower is at the other end of a scale from Langland. His rhythms answer, more or less, to the establishment account of Chaucer's. And here as elsewhere Gower is paradoxical in a way that will not seem strange to that very select band who are acquainted with his poetry: he is enormously ambitious and at the same time very timid. Gower is always trying hard to be a Great Poet (an affliction from which Chaucer made an almost complete recovery after *Anelida and Arcite*):

> *Conf. Am.* I, I I may noght strecche up to the hevene
> Min hand, ne setten al in evene
> This world, which evere is in balance

—but how he would have liked to! The form of Gower's works is always ambitious. He treats of the history of God, man, the earth, heaven and hell, giving a complete conspectus of human knowledge in polite verse in the best languages. His carefully designed tomb in what is now Southwark Cathedral has his effigy resting on the three ambitiously named works *Speculum Meditantis*, *Vox Clamantis* and *Confessio Amantis*, in French, Latin and English respectively. This heap of books is a sort of *summa summarum*.

But at the same time Gower is oddly lacking in some essential kinds of confidence, and his rigid control seems often to fail. The ambitions at the beginning of *Confessio Amantis* are confused:

> Prol. 4 Forthi good is that we also
> In oure tyme among ous hiere
> Do wryte of newe som matiere
> Essampled of these olde wyse
> So that it myhte in such a wyse
> Whan we ben dede and elleswhere
> Be leve to the worldes eere
> In tyme comende after this

But he goes on:

> Bot for men sein and soth it is
> That who that al of wisdom writ
> It dulleth ofte a mannes wit
> To him that schal it aldai rede
> For thilke cause if that ye rede
> I wolde go the middel weie
> And wryte a bok betwene the tweie
> Somwhat of lust somwhat of lore

Wisdom that dulls the intelligence is a peculiar notion, but read Gower and you will understand it. A poet who thinks such a middle way so easy to attain is likely to be neither amusing nor instructive. So too Gower's carefully planned, disinterested and dispassionate work only comes to life when it collapses into a quite embarrassing personality. The moral of *Confessio Amantis* is that Venus's kind of love is generally insufficient; but Gower seems only to argue with any force when he is talking about himself. The passage (VIII, 2726 ff.) where Cupid removes his dart is moving, but it is emotion gone wrong, run out of control. So far from achieving artistic impersonality by his ambitious schemes, Gower succeeds in writing well only about his own private and personal loathing of old age and about incest, for which he betrays a fascination surprising in a 'moral' poet. And unlike Hoccleve, Gower is only personal by accident, when he fails to do what he is trying to do.

Gower's rejection of half-line metre is just an aspect of his artistic timidity, his lack of confidence in English. He chose (with, I imagine, great deliberation) the short line for his Great English Work, *Confessio Amantis*. This line seems modelled on that of his French verse, but it is flatter and wearier. It has all the jog-trot of ordinary eighteenth-century verse without its confidence of movement and social gesture. In discussing Gower's metre there is no need to think of phrases at all.

Gower's short lines are units, but very artificial ones. They do not build phrases as we do when talking or reading Langland or Chaucer. The phrases in Gower are accidental, and his unconcern for them is an uninterestedness in the expressive resources of English. Even at his best, when he is writing on either of the subjects that arouse him to some signs of life, i.e. himself and incest, the metre seems to be flattening the language rather than co-operating with it.

Conf. Am. VIII 223   And forto se more of this thing ·
  The bible makth a knowleching
  Wherof thou miht take evidence
  Upon the sothe experience.
  Whan Lothes wif was overgon
  And schape into the salte Ston
  As it is spoke into this day
  Be bothe his dowhtres thanne he lay
  With childe and made hem bothe grete
  Til that nature hem wolde lete

> And so the cause aboute ladde
> That ech of hem a Sone hadde
> Moab the ferste and the secounde
> Amon of whiche as it is founde
> Cam afterward to gret encres
> Tuo nacions and natheles
> For that the stockes were ungoode
> The branches mihten noght be goode   etc. etc.

There are many good ways of describing the flatness of this verse; one is to say that it moves as it does for the sake of metrical convenience. Here the final -e does just what it is supposed to in Chaucer: it helps to make the lines metrical. But the metre has no expressive function whatever. Similarly it doesn't matter whether we read with variable stress or not:

> Til that nature hem wolde lete

is singsong,

> Til that nature hem wolde lete

rather halting, but the line is not very interesting in either case. All the verse does is to *be* verse and so to allow Gower to see himself as a poet.

But though, having traversed the frozen waste of the English Works, I have earned the right to make this severe judgement, it is also true, I think, that Gower can sometimes rise into a decorous but effective rhetoric, especially in his long-line poem *In Praise of Peace*. Here he goes some way to finding out what a metre might do for him. The long lines of this poem seem to be iambic pentameters with the usual freedom of trochaic substitution but without Chaucer's half-line movement. Here Gower can attain the decorum of the Second Nun or perhaps an even weightier impressiveness: but he is still quite lacking in Chaucer's or Langland's abundant and unpredictable vitality—or their precision of united sense and rhythm. Here are the poem's first two stanzas with sounded -e's and trochaic feet marked:

> O worthi noble kyng Henry the ferthe
> In whom the glade fortune is befalle
> The poeple to governe vppon this erthe
> God hath the chose in comfort of ous alle

> The worschipe of this lond which was doun falle
> Now stant upriht thurgh grace of thi goodnesse
> Which euery man is holde for to blesse
>
> The highe god of his justice allone
> The right which longeth to thi regalie
> Declared hath to stonde in thi persone
> And more than god may no man justefie
> Thi title is knowe uppon thin ancestrie
> The londes folk hath ek thy riht affermed
> So stant thi regne of god and man confermed[1]

Some of the marked places explain themselves, making a sense similar to the one they might have in Chaucer's verse. The sounded -e on *noble* has its usual effect of slowing movement and throwing back stress, with an obvious appropriateness here, and the emphasis is placed suitably on the king's name by the successive stresses of 'king Henry': *Henry* receives the stress of the inverted foot and the stress of the first stressed syllable of its phrase 'Henry the ferthe'. So too the first line of the second stanza has a fittingly majestical movement, achieved similarly by the -e on *highe* and by the inverted foot *justice*. Again, the three consecutive speech-stresses of 'Now stant upriht' are the result of an effective use of metre; and the last line really is a declaration because of its inverted last foot:

> Declared hath to stonde in thi persone.

But explanations of the other -e's and inversions, and of the many lines without either, throughout the works of Gower, would be exercises in critical ingenuity. What is the point of the trochaic substitution at 'governe'? We can ask such questions of many of Gower's rhythms without finding an answer. And sometimes he is worse than neutrally inexpressive; sometimes he places emphasis in the wrong places, perhaps in pursuit of a feeling of general grandeur.

> Which every man is holde for to blesse

---

[1] I quote from a photograph of the Trentham manuscript which was kindly made available to me by Mr John Fisher with the permission of the late Duke of Sutherland. The manuscript is very carefully written, and Macaulay's text is virtually a simple reprint with the addition of modern punctuation.

'Holde' is the stress-peak of that line because of its final -e and because of the following weak iamb, both of which throw back stress on to the word. But surely *holde* is not the word to benefit by this slowing and emphasis? 'Every' or 'blesse' could be defended as words perhaps specially important, but 'holde' unfortunately suggests an unpleasant duty. This misemphasis is a typical instance of Gower's vagueness, his wish rather to seem weighty than to say really weighty things.

190   To ʒive ous pes was cause whi Crist dide

It is possible to make this line quite strong by taking the last foot as a strong iamb: if 'Crist' is stressed, 'dide' will be even more stressed: but to do that takes a positive effort for which the metre seems to give little encouragement. It is more natural to go simply for Gower's ordinary jog-trot dignity, which puts a useless stress on *cause*:

        To ʒive ous pes was cause whi Crist dide

His successes are where there is a momentary fit between rhythmic movement and hortatory intent:

198   The righte feith to kepe of holy chirche

or   The firste point is named of knyghthode...

187   For Crist is more than was Moises

Sometimes Gower can seem dignified for three lines together:

169   In tholde lawe er Crist himself was bore
           Among the ten comandementz y rede
           How that manslaghtre schulde be forbore

—the genuine sententiousness there comes from the long build-up of sense created by the sustaining of the rhythmic movement over three lines. After the first emphasis at 'tholde lawe' the voice has to be sustained to the heavily didactic conclusion, where the shaking of the moral poet's finger is felt through the effective rhythms that follow from the stress on *schulde*. All the same, it is more typical for the verse to be mechanical and the emphases meaningless; and this is Gower's punishment for his lack of interest in his own language.

Chaucer then stands where we might expect him, on the central ground between Gower and Langland.

185

10

The English Chaucerians:
Hoccleve and Lydgate

The evidence for the belief that Chaucer's disciples forgot him is that they did not write iambic pentameters: 'But no steady tradition has brought down to the present the knowledge of Chaucer's accuracy [of metre]. His imitators in the fifteenth century did not understand his formal standards.'[1] This argument can be reversed: since Chaucer's imitators did not write modern iambic pentameter, Chaucer cannot have done so, either. If this argument were established, the literary history of our fifteenth century need no longer be incredible: but any attempt at understanding it must, of course, start from criticism of poems.

I

A few fifteenth-century eccentrics wrote medieval pentameters of the Gower kind, enjoying the usual freedom of trochaic substitution but not moving in half-lines. (We may notice these first not because they are important or common but as a matter of convenience.) All the verse of this kind is either eccentric, amateur, or written by foreigners. The French poet Charles duc d'Orléans wrote during his long captivity in England English verse which falls into this last class. Charles writes fluently in his smooth metre but cannot bring off the colloquiality he sometimes attempts. The phrase 'sett there a nayle'[2] is unusual enough to attract attention, and even there Charles cannot quite trust himself, and paraphrases the colloquialism in the next line:

Speke me no more therof y hertly pray.

---

[1] McJimsey, *Chaucer's Irregular -E*, p. 1.
[2] *The English Poems of Charles of Orleans*, ed. R. Steele, E.E.T.S. 1941, vol. I, p. 13, no. 6, line 354.

He has only one device to suggest the movement of speech within his rigid metre, and that is repetition. Some of his repetitions may be explained by the fact that he habitually translated French octosyllabics into English pentameters, but the repetitions are more frequent than that alone could explain and are, in effect, an idiom-substitute:

Hélas! et n'est-ce pas assés?	Allas allas & is this not y nough[1]
Vous, soiés la tresbien venue	Welcome and yit more welcome bi þis light[2]
Hélas! sire, pardonnez moy	Allas sir allas sir pardou*n* me[3]

Know ye not me / no / yes / nay certes nay[4]

As for farewel / farewel / farewel / farewel
And of farewel more þen a þousand skore[5]

The anonymous fifteenth-century translator of the *de Re Rustica* of Palladius Rutilius Taurus Æmilianus shares with Charles of Orleans a distance from the colloquial. *Palladius on Housbondrie*, a minor curiosity of fifteenth-century verse, was undertaken, the translator tells us, under the direct personal supervision of Duke Humphrey of Gloucester. Perhaps it needed a character as strong as Good Duke Humphrey to insist that Gower pentameter is the best medium for discussing, in an aureate way, the choice of boars:

> Now bores gladly brymmeth. Chese a bore
> Greet bodied, side, and wyde, eke rather rounde
> Then long, eke hipped greet, and wombed hoor,
> And huge snouted, shorte, his necke abounde
> With fattes feel, his stones greet and sounde.
> And from oon yere until he come att fyve
> He wol do wel ynough, and often wyve.[6]

This verse moves more like *The Spanish Gypsy* than *The Canterbury Tales*, and needs modern clause-punctuation—as may be shown by leaving it out:

---

[1] English *ibid.* p. 48, no. 40, line 1429; French from *Poésies*, ed. P. Champion, Paris, 2 consecutively paginated vols. 1923 7, p. 60.

[2] English *ed. cit.* p. 57, no. 47, line 1658; French *ed. cit.* p. 69.

[3] English *ed. cit.* p. 95, no. 76, line 2838; French *ed. cit.* p. 109.

[4] *Ed. cit.* p. 160, line 4781. No French.

[5] *Ibid.* p. 219, no. 121, lines 6504–5. No French.

[6] *Palladius on Housbondrie*, February, st. 151. I leave here the punctuation of Barton Lodge's E.E.T.S. edition, 1872.

I, st. 89
And for a cok beth hennes v ynowe
The Cok his eyron and his briddes hateth
Until the crest upon thaire hedes growe
And first in Feverer of love he prateth
And benes bake a lite his love abateth
Right nere adell yf that he ete hem warme
For thei wol rather his courage enarme

Trochaic substitutions are common enough in the Palladius translation, but they do not move the verse into half-lines; in the quoted stanzas the phrases are of arbitrary length and there need not be an expectation of two per line. To show the persistence of the Gower metre in Charles and the Palladius translator it will be enough to quote the first line of each, the former having two trochaic substitutions, the latter three:

The god Cupide and venus the goddes
Agriculture as in Nature and Art[1]

The Kingis Quair is another English poem apparently written by a foreigner in modern pentameter. (Even though the traditional ascription to James I of Scotland—which would allow a close parallel with Charles of Orleans—is now thought dubious, the poem is very obviously by a Scot.) Unlike the poems previously mentioned it does not sound eccentric and is at home with its idioms. *The Kingis Quair* is indeed a more distinguished example of Gower's metre than is to be found in Gower's works.

In hye unto the wyndow gan I walk
Moving within my spirit of this sight
Quhare sodeynly a turture quhite as calk
So evinly upon my hand gan lyght...[2]

The even flow of the last quoted line effectively enacts the meaning. Trochaic inversion of the first foot is also well used for a grandness of style different from Lydgate's:

st. 47
ther was wele I wote
Beautee eneuch to mak a world to dote.

---

[1] Wentworth Wodehouse Manuscript.
[2] *The Kingis Quair*, ed. W. Mackay Mackenzie, 1939, st. 177

Occasionally one finds lines with monosyllabic feet, usually with a clear enough rhetorical justification:

st. 8   The long nyght beholding as I saide.

st. 155   The pantere lyke unto the smaragdyne

                 The lytill squerell full of besyness

                 The slawe as, the druggar beste of pyne.

Both these examples involve words which could once have had a sounded -e: the effect is as if the movement caused by sounding the -e minimally is taken to the extreme of a monosyllabic foot. But *The Kingis Quair* is very unlike Lydgate, though contemporary with him. I think the explanation is simply that its metre is Scottish: foot-metres were very much better established in Scotland than England as proper for courtly verse, and Scotland never had the Chaucerian tradition of balanced pentameters.

As to amateurish writers of Gower metre, one could produce plenty of examples from the so-called Chaucer Apocrypha.[1] Much of the verse collected in volume VII of Skeat's Chaucer seems to be written by amateur dabblers easily distinguishable from the professionals of Chaucer's school by, among other things, their not attempting the mysteries of balanced pentameter.

What one cannot find after Gower in England is his regular octosyllabics or pentameters used normally by the professional courtly writers. In fifteenth-century England Gower-metre is always eccentric. The only plausible reason for this state of affairs in so claustrophobically conservative a literary tradition is the influence of Chaucer, whether directly or through Lydgate. Beyond the courtly pale there was a vast variety of other verse— alliteratives rhymed or unrhymed, lyrics in or out of foot-metres, carols, rhymed prose. But the disciples of Chaucer stand out for over a hundred years as a coherent if uninspired central tradition, one of the distinguishing marks of which is its metre, the balanced pentameter inherited from Chaucer. This, being so opposed to the traditional history, needs demonstration.

[1] I refrain from pursuing the Apocryphal writers because problems concerning manuscripts would need a longer treatment than the importance or interest of the subject warrants.

II

There are two good reasons for starting with Hoccleve: firstly he was closer to Chaucer than the other Chaucerians; secondly he is the most interesting of them. Here is the opening of Hoccleve's *Compleynt*:[1]

A fter that heruest Inned had his sheves
and that the broune season of myhelmesse
was come and gan the trees robbe of ther leves
That grene had bene / and in lusty fresshnesse
and them in to colowre / of yelownesse
hadd dyen / and doune throwne vndar foote
that chaunge sanke / in to myne herte roote.[2]

This is a use of Chaucer's metre for something Chaucer never attempted—intimately self-communing poetry. Its distinction is real, and will be apparent to anyone who has been convinced by the foregoing account of Chaucer's rhythms, for this verse expresses its very different purpose in similar ways: the most telling places, the ones that help us to define our sense of the verse, go best as balanced pentameter. 'Season' in line two has the usual effect of trochaic substitution in Chaucer: it points to a half-line phrase by its concentration of stresses. The stresses on 'broune season' are also intensified by the very light stresses earlier in the line, so that the half-lines go:

$$\text{and that the bró}\acute{\text{u}}\text{ne séason} / \text{of my}\grave{\text{h}}\text{elmesse}$$

The natural effect of this lingering stress on 'broune season' is to convey well 'the influence, so sweet and sad, of the autumnal months in the country'.[3] 'Lusty' has a comparable effect; its strong stress after the weak preceding ones brings a temporary flutter of life before the stanza settles into the true melancholy of its last line, that chaunge sanke / into myne herte roote

---

[1] I shall refer by this name to the connected series of poems in the Durham Cosin V. III. 9 manuscript, not merely no. XX in *Hoccleve's Works*, vol. I, ed. F. J. Furnivall, E.E.T.S. 1892, to which it is usually restricted. This manuscript is probably the poet's autograph and certainly a very good text, which did not prevent Furnivall from altering the punctuation frequently and without note.

[2] Supplied in the Durham manuscript by a later hand said by Furnivall to be John Stowe's. The older part begins with the lines of the next quotation.

[3] *Persuasion*, vol. I, Chapter 5.

There it is the final -e's that do the work, whether one sounds them or not: they (or the monosyllabic feet if they are quite silent) control the stresses that accumulate so effectively in the half-lines. 'That chaunge' is a strong iamb, a stressed first syllable followed by an even more stressed second; and the first half-line reaches its peak of stress with 'sank', which is separated from the first two stresses only by a final -e. This does seem to me to give an effectively plangent emphasis, and in the usual Chaucerian way, with the metre helping to control the speech-rhythms of the half-lines, and so creating tone.

The stanza is near to Chaucer and yet unlike Chaucer, as a real minor poet learning from a master ought to be. And that is the main observation to be made about Hoccleve; he learns from Chaucer how to express his own quite different, lesser, but real sensibility. Here are a few more stanzas of the same poem:

> More am I heuy now vp on a day
> Than I sum tyme was in dayes fyue
> Thyng þat or this me thoghte game & play
> Is ernest now / the hony fro the hyue
> Of my spirit withdrawith wondir blyue
> Whan al is doon / al this worldes swetnesse
> At ende torneth in to bittirnesse

> ([The fool thurgh loue of this lyf present
> Deceyued is / but the wys man woot weel
> How ful this world of sorwe is and torment
> Wherfore in it / he trustith nat a deel
> Thogh a man this day / sitte hye on the wheel
> To morwe he may be tryced from his sete
> This hath be seen often / among the grete

> How fair thyng / or how precious it be
> Þat in the world is / it is lyke a flour
> To whom / nature yeuen hath beautee
> Of fressh heewe / and of ful plesant colour
> With soote smellynge also and odour
> But as soone as it is bicomen drye
> ffarwel colour / and the smel gynneth dye[1]

It is difficult to understand how the writer of the first two lines of this passage can ever have been dismissed as an incompetent metrist. But the success of the pentameters where feet count more than half-lines (here, generally speaking, the unpunctuated

---

[1] Durham manuscript; cf. *Hoccleve's Works*, ed. Furnivall, vol. I, no. XXI, p. 119, lines 253–73.

lines) depends on their context amidst successful balanced pentameters. The characteristic *heaviness* at the beginning gets expressed
in the lagging regularity of the foot-metre, but other lines work
through the half-line stress-clusters, as usual often caused by
trochaic inversions and final -e's, like

To whom nature yeuen hath beautee

which gives the half-line balance

To whom nature / yeuen hath beautee

or by the second-foot trochee of

How fair thyng / or how precious it be

where the strong iamb followed by the trochee concentrates the
plangent stresses in the first half-line, 'How fair thyng', which
balances the run of weak stresses (including weak iambic fourth)
in the second half.

Hoccleve here is voicing one of the great medieval platitudes;
nevertheless it is not merely a platitude, because he says it as a
man talks of real experience. This too is a mark of a real minor
poet, the capacity to feel clichés freshly and so to turn them into
something else. Even so, Hoccleve is not quite so metrically easy as
Mr Mitchell in his useful new book wants to say:

The foregoing illustrations show that many lines by Hoccleve have no
instances of thwarted stress unless one presupposes that the poet wrote
iambic decasyllables with an invariable pattern of stresses...What
scholars have called his want of metrical skill is a value judgment that can
be traced back to an absurd theory of English pentameter line structure.
There is no thwarted stress in Hoccleve.[1]

I am, of course, in general sympathy with this attack on the old
establishment; but if there are no thwarted stresses in Hoccleve's
decasyllables he is still sometimes very far from what we recognize
as iambic pentameter, and the question could be asked sometimes
whether his verse is composed of feet at all—and, if not, why it
should be called verse. The answer to the question will involve
discussing the expressiveness of Hoccleve's rhythms in a way Mr
Mitchell doesn't attempt: as it stands, the dispute between Bock

---

[1] J. Mitchell, *Thomas Hoccleve, a Study in Early Fifteenth Century English
Poetic*, Urbana, 1968, p. 109.

(or whoever represents the older school) and Mitchell is at the level of assertion and counter-assertion.

I think I am right to call Hoccleve's metre by the same name as Chaucer's, but there is no denying that Hoccleve, as disciples are supposed to do, took his master's practice to an extreme.

> But as soone as it is bicomen drye

> ffarwel colour and the smel gynneth dye

It is more or less possible to mark like this the feet and the half-lines; and, setting aside temperamental considerations, it would be hard to assert at sight that these lines were not by Chaucer. But they would strike one as Chaucer at an extreme, carrying his manner further than elsewhere, for no very apparent reason. There is an iambic pattern to be seen, but weakly marked and very complicated; and the half-line divisions seem in danger of dissolving into real speech. Nevertheless, the grouping of stresses round the drawn-out 'the smel gynneth dye' is an effective use of Chaucerian balanced pentameter and the rhythms throughout the passage are not difficult to form with the aid of feet and half-lines. The difficulties in Hoccleve begin when he is less successful, when the complication of metre and feebleness of half-line grouping become more extreme and serve no rhetorical purpose. Even in the passage quoted there is

> The fool thurgh loue of this lyf present

How does that go? It looks like iambic pentameter with a monosyllabic fourth foot and trochaic fifth:

> The fool thurgh loue of this lyf present

which would give a half-line division

> The fool thurgh loue / of this lyf present

which has some point in the hectoring emphasis (Gower might have envied it) of the last phrase. But it is rather awkward; the line hasn't the naturalness of Chaucer's rhythmic control and one feels that the poet is pushing his metre hard, being too much of a metrical specialist. This is an impression which the reader of Hoccleve will often repeat.

In this way the line,

$$\breve{}\breve{}\,/\,|\,\breve{}\,\,/|\,/\,\,\,\breve{}\,|\,/\,|\,\breve{}\,\,/$$
But anoon to me telle out al thy gole[1]

is too precious in its deliberate search for metrical variety in preference to the surely more natural

But telle out al thy gole to me anoon

The deliberate preference for the laboured and artificial is very typical of the earlier Chaucerians, and one cause of any difficulty we may find in following their metres. Again,

for to taken heede
How for to gouerne hem in the vsage
Of armes / it is a greet auauntage
A man before him / to haue a mirour[2]

This is difficult to read well, though not difficult to shamble through, because nothing in the language, neither a firm foot-metre nor a plain half-line balance, tells us quite how to shape the rhythms. There is no best rhythmic pattern. Should *greet* or *auauntage* bear the primary stress of its half-line? If we don't know, the metre is failing in its primary function of controlling and stressing. Similarly

ffor him wolde han thoght þat swich a fyndynge[3]

—the half-lines are too weakly balanced to give any one effective reading.

But Hoccleve's rhythmic manner derives straight from Chaucer's, differing only in some exaggeration, the occasional reduction of Chaucer's manner to mannerism. Again and again one finds in Hoccleve rhythms thoroughly reminiscent of Chaucer.

What fool / took I thee nat out of prison /
No lenger hens / than yistirday / quod shee
In trust and hope / of thy correccion /
As thow swoor / and behightest vn to me
And now to thy folie and nycetee
Retourne woldest thow ˸ nay doutelees
It shal nat be / stynte and holde thy pees[4]

---

[1] *Hoccleve's Works*, vol. I, p. 159, line 545.
[2] *Ibid.* p. 131, lines 605–8. [3] *Ibid.* p. 173, line 944.
[4] Durham manuscript. In *Hoccleve's Works*, vol. I, p. 147, lines 204–10.

Here the rhythms are clearly indebted to the Chaucer of *The Wife of Bath's Prologue*. Two lines have Chaucer's device of 'pads'—line-fillers that concentrate emphasis on what goes before:

> No lenger hens / than yistirday   quod she

and

> Retourne woldest thow   nay douteleea

—compare such lines as

> And trouthe shal delivere   it is no drede[1]

or

B 1771   The white lamb celestial   quod she.

The more solemn Hoccleve, that is most of Hoccleve, is also occasionally reminiscent of the Chaucer of *The Man of Law's Tale*; and this passage reproduces the movement of parts of the *ABC*:

> Lady benigne / our souereyn refuyt
> Seur trust haue I to han by thy prayeere
> Of strength / & confort so vertuous fruyt
> That I shal sauf be / Crystes modir deere[2]

And there is at least one example of a mock-heroic rhythm in Hoccleve. This is from the poem beginning:

> Victorious Kyng our lord ful gracious
> We humble lige men to your hynesse
> Meekly byseechen yow o kyng pitous
> Tendre pitee haue on our sharp distresse
> For but the flood of your rial largesse
> Flowe vp on vs / gold hath vs in swich hate
> Þat of his loue and cheertee the scantnesse
> Wole arte vs three to trotte vn to Newgate[3]

The lowness of the line at the end following the conspicuously high style of the rest is expressed by the lurch into trochees after the surprising smoothness of the first half-line:

> Wole arte vs three to trotte vn to Newgate

This perhaps misses the arch extravagance of Chaucer's *Compleynt to his Purs*; nevertheless Hoccleve was an apt pupil; and this is shown above all by the success of his occasional creation of con-

---

[1] *Trouthe*, refrain. F. N. Robinson reads 'trouthe thee shal delivere'.
[2] *Hoccleve's Works*, vol. i, p. 68, lines 41–4.
[3] *Ibid.* p. 62, lines 1–8; perhaps a reminiscence of A 4402.

vincing speech in domestic situations. No English poet, not even
Chaucer, does this better than Hoccleve in the 'Dialogus cum
Amico', the second part of the *Compleynt*:

> And endyd my complaynt / in this manere
> one knocked / at my chambre dore sore
> and cryed a lowde / howe hoccleve arte thow here
> open thy dore / me thinkethe full yore
> sythen I the se / what man for gods ore
> come out / for this quartar I not the sy
> by owght I wot / and out to hym cam I
>
> This man was my good frynde / of farn a gon
> that I speke of / and þus he to me seyde
> Thomas / as thow me lovest tell a non
> what dydist thow / when I knocked and layde
> so fast vpon thy dore / And I obeyde
> Vnto his will / come in quod I and se
> and so he dyd / he streyght went in with me[1]

Thomas has to admit he has been at his poetry again. The Friend
is taken aback and (though he has never read a line of Hoccleve's
works) cautions him against publishing the *Compleynt*, but
eventually is persuaded into giving advice about how Hoccleve is
to satisfy a patron:

> ⟨ Now good freend / shoue at the cart I yow preye
> What thyng may I make vn to his plesance
> Withouten your reed / noot I what to seye
> ⟨ O / no pardee Thomas / o. no ascance
> ⟨ No certein freend / as now no cheuissance
> Can I / your conseil is to me holsum
> As I truste in yow mynystreth me sum
>
> ⟨ Wel Thomas / trowest thow his hy noblesse
> Nat rekke / what mateere þat it be
> þat thow shalt make of ⟨ no freend as I gesse
> So þat it be mateere of honestee
> ⟨ Thomas and thenne I wole auyse me
> ffor who so reed / & conseil yeue shal
> May nat on heed / foorth renne ther with al[2]

The Friend, after mature consideration, persuades Hoccleve to
amuse his patron with *Lerne Die*.

This verse is the achievement of a poet thoroughly in command
of his medium—perhaps a little too much 'in command'. This

---

[1] Durham manuscript; cf. *Hoccleve's Works*, vol. I, p. 110, lines 1–14.
[2] Durham manuscript; cf. *Hoccleve's Works*, vol. I, p. 132, lines 617–30.

mastery could only have come from an intelligent and sympathetic study of Chaucer. The humour of these passages is itself a debt to Chaucer by which Hoccleve saves himself from his perpetual danger of sinking in mere self-pity; it makes his wryness more interesting and more poignant than the misery which fills so many of his pages.

The break between Chaucer and Hoccleve is one not of technique but of temperament. If, as Professor Robertson says, 'medieval artists were not much concerned to express their private feelings',[1] Hoccleve was the most unmedieval poet imaginable, for his best things are all about himself, convincing creations of his own feelings of wretchedness. *The Compleynt* is just a first-person account of mental breakdown and gradual recovery, and I know nothing else at all like it in medieval literature. By calling Hoccleve's confessions convincing I bypass the question which interests some scholars, as to whether they are 'true'. Even Mr Mitchell spends time on this:

> Smith's observations [that Hoccleve's autobiographical poetry was 'more conventional and rhetorical, and of a pattern, than individual'] cannot be dismissed lightly. Much of what Hoccleve tells us about himself cannot be substantiated with any existing official records. In the Prologue to *The Regement of Princes* (vv. 1447 ff.) he tells the Beggar that he intended to be a priest and waited long for a benefice. When it seemed clear that none was forthcoming, he married, even though he had second thoughts about losing his freedom as a bachelor. In the *Dialogue with a Friend* he refers again to his wife. Yet there are no official records to back up his remarks regarding either his marriage or his thwarted intention to become a priest. What Hoccleve has said may be true, but we do not know for certain.[2]

But this concern with factuality is beside the point. What concerns us is poetry, not some hidden fact truer than poetry: perhaps Hoccleve's works are really first-person novels, but in any case the mode is autobiographical confession which works if the reader is convinced of its genuineness, in the way in which he may be convinced by any good poem. (But if we can't be convinced without raising the question whether Hoccleve is factually accurate it seems unduly sceptical to suggest without any evidence that Hoccleve was, in addition to his other misfortunes, a great liar.)

[1] D. W. Robertson, Jr, *A Preface to Chaucer*, Princeton, 1963, p. 13.
[2] *Thomas Hoccleve*, p. 3.

As has so often turned out to be the case, scholars here are too ready to abandon the real literary–critical interest in pursuit of some mysterious factual certainty. But the places in Hoccleve where the question of his sincerity is relevant are those where to ask it may help to understand the poems. For me the final touch to his character is the dubious sincerity of his poems about heresy and his political poems. Some of Hoccleve's comments on contemporary events are so odd as to have almost the air of *ambages* ('that is to seyen, double wordes slye'): he implies the opposite of what he seems to be passionately asserting.

This is especially so when he writes of heretics, a favourite subject, which perhaps fascinated him because it allowed him to express his dismay about the unsafeness of the world. Hoccleve's hatred and fear of heretics are obviously real; but at the same time he can sometimes betray a sympathy with the heretics. He chooses a most inappropriate moment to imitate Chaucer's refusal to speculate on the whereabouts of the souls of the departed:

> Lat þe diuines of hym speke & muse
> Where his soule is bycome or whider gone
> Myn vnkonyng of þat me schal excuse
> Of which mat*ere* knowleche haue I non
> But wolde god tho cristes foos echon
> That as he heelde were I-serued soo
> ffor I am seur þat þer ben many moo[1]

But if Hoccleve is so ignorant he would seem to admit the possibility that the souls of unrepentant heretics go to heaven, which is itself heresy. Again, the frequent appeals to *charity* and *pity* in these poems can ring very oddly:

> My lorde þe p*ri*nce god him saue & blesse
> Was at his deedly castigacio*un*
> And of his soule hadde grete tendernesse
> Thristynge sore his sauacio*un*
> Grete was his [the Prince's!] pitous lamentacio*un*[2]

and

> The laddre of heuene / I meene charitee
> Comandith vs / if our brothir be falle
> In to errour / to haue of him pitee
> And seeke weyes / in our wittes alle

---

[1] *Regement of Princes*, lines 323–9; in *Hoccleve's Works*, vol. III, p. 13.
[2] *Ibid.* p. 12, lines 295–9.

How we may him ageyn / to vertu call*e*
And in gretter erro*ur* / ne knowe I noon
Than thow [Oldcastle] þat dronke haast heresies gall*e*
And art from Crystes feith / twynned & goon[1]

Hoccleve then goes on to apply his moral by warning Oldcastle to
'Waar of the swerd of god / for it is keene'.[2] So too, it was hardly
tactful to say to Henry V

Our kyng Richard þat was / yee may wel see
Is nat fled from his remembrance aweye[3]

Well no, hardly. Hoccleve continues with another two lines that
could well be taken in a sense the opposite of the one intended:

My wit souffysith nat to peyse and weye
With what hono*ur* he broght is to this toun.

Hoccleve was unable

after Chaucer / to occupy the place

—but because of his character, not because he was overwhelmed
by linguistic change or artistic incompetence. He could never get
outside himself to anything like Chaucer's wonderfully dramatic
and impersonal creation of a world; even when he is not writing
directly about himself Hoccleve's poems are mainly of interest as
one individual's feelings about events. And one cannot help feeling
sorry for a man so well able to record his wretchedness and that
of his times (the feeling that one knows Hoccleve is one sign of his
success, but also of his limitation: we don't know Chaucer). His
place in history is not hard to understand: he was the heir of
Chaucer, and not unfitted in intelligence or sensibility to continue
the new tradition of English poetry. But he was crushed by the load
of responsibility; and the central figure of the age of English
poetry that follows Chaucer's is not Hoccleve but Lydgate.

III

Lydgate is generally agreed to be a harder nut to crack than
Hoccleve, and I think the reason is something else about which
until recently there was general agreement, that his kernel is less

---

[1] *Hoccleve's Works*, vol. I, p. 8, lines 1–8. My punctuation.
[2] *Ibid.* p. 11, line 88.   [3] *Ibid.* p. 48, lines 35–6.

worth the effort of extraction. But I do not think it is true that Lydgate is often hard to read rhythmically: his rhythms belong to the same tradition as Chaucer's and Hoccleve's and his lines (with some exceptions) only make one stumble if one comes to them with the wrong expectations.

The vast majority of the enormous bulk of Lydgate's lines in the E.E.T.S. editions of his works[1] are balanced pentameters. Here are a few picked at random from his addition to *The Canterbury Tales, The Siege of Thebes*:

> On whiche thyng / the kyng gan sore muse
> And cast he wolde / on that other side
> Agayn her doom / for hym silf provide
> Shape a way / and remedy to forn
> Biddyng the queene / whan the chyld were born
> With oute Mercy / or moderly pyte
> That he be ded / it may non other be
> And in al hast / lik as he hath sent
> She obeyed / his comaundement
> With wooful herte / and a pitous loke
> And face pale / her ʒonge sone she toke[2]

This is like both Chaucer and Hoccleve. If we give some final -e's metrical value and allow some trochees, the lines are recognizably pentameters, and they fall into halves in the usual way. A characteristic line in which the metre points to the half-lines is

$$\breve{}\ \acute{}\ |\breve{}\ \acute{}\ |\breve{}\breve{}\ |\ \acute{}\ |\breve{}\ |\acute{}\ |\ \acute{}\ \breve{}$$

With oute mercy or moderly pyte

Nevertheless this is unlike Chaucer as well. The half-line rhythms seem functionless. The first two quoted lines both have monosyllabic feet at the half-line, which in Chaucer is rather unusual and does not occur without good reason. It is an extreme way of enforcing the half-line division which ought to justify itself by some unusual expressive effect. But what sense is there in the resultant stressings in Lydgate's passage? The effect is to make

---

[1] No full investigation of the numerous Lydgate manuscripts has to my knowledge ever been made, and so one must bear in mind the possibility that the 'broken-backed' and other difficult lines are mere scribal corruptions. This seems, however, no more than a possibility (like Chaucer's having been rewritten to suit the taste of the age of Lydgate). Scribal corruption is normally directionless and Lydgate's rhythms are recognizably intentional.

[2] *The Siege of Thebes*, lines 400–10; ed. Erdmann, E.E.T.S. 1911, p. 19.

'And cast he wolde' a very important phrase, but there is no reason in the sense of the passage why it should be. Similarly,

> With wooful herte / and a pitous loke

puts an unusual stress on *and* of which it is hard to make any sense.

The difficulty here is not how to read the lines rhythmically; the metre of feet and half-lines is, like Hoccleve's, merely a Chaucerian extreme. The difficulty is to read these lines well. It has been the constant argument of this work that the test of a poet's metre is in the reading: if the metre indicates a good reading it is likely to be right. But the metre does not here lead to a good reading, so it may well be wrong? I acknowledge the possibility, but fear there is a more obvious reason why we cannot read these lines well, namely that they are bad verse. If Lydgate is not an artist even of Hoccleve's kind it is idle to expect artistic use of language from him. So here we must modify slightly the usual appeal from metre to poetry and ask not whether the metre leads to good poetry but whether it gives verse we recognize to be characteristic of the author. It will still, that is, be necessary to have some idea of what Lydgate's poetry is like.

But to call Lydgate a writer of bad verse is not to say with the established tradition that he is incompetent. He may, as Ritson remarked, be a prosaic and drivelling monk, but he is not incompetent to the task of writing metrically in English, which he did—I speak as one of the three living men to have read all 150,000 odd extant lines of Lydgate—all too fluently. Lydgate is not much of a poet, and one can object to his longwindedness and lack of concern for expressive language: but he is at least a *competent* hack, and perhaps a little more.

For instance Lydgate is a very competent imitator of Chaucer. His Canterbury Tale, *The Siege of Thebes*, seems to be his attempt to 'do Chaucer' for his own amusement. Lydgate, rightly enough a dismal figure in black, joins the pilgrims and is greeted by the Host:

> Her gouernour the host
> Stonding in halle ⸽ ful of wynde & bost
> Lich to a man / wonder sterne & fers
> Which spak to me / and seide anon 'daun Pers
> Daun Domynyk / Dan Godfrey / or Clement
> 3e be welcom / newly into kent'[1]

[1] *Ed. cit.* p. 5, lines 79–84.

and

96   'Daun Iohn' quod he / 'wel broke ȝe ȝoure name
            Thogh ȝe be soul / beth right glad & light
            Preiyng ȝou / soupe with vs to nyght
            And ȝe shal haue / mad at ȝoure devis
            A gret puddyng / or a rounde hagys
            A Franchemole / a tansey / or a froyse'

There are some signs that Chaucer is not the author of this—
Chaucer would hardly have had 'preying' for 'I preye' (a favourite
Lydgate locution) and the list of puddings is perhaps just a bit too
much Chaucer to be true—nevertheless this is an expert imitation
of the Host's famous colloquial familiarity. The Monk does not
shrink, either, in the cause of verisimilitude, from a mild Chaucerian vulgarity:

111   Tak a pilow / þat ȝe lye not lowe
            Ȝif nede be / Spare not to blowe
            To holde wynde / be myn opynyoun
            Wil engendre / Collikes passioun

This is no more than comic relief in Lydgate, whose habit is
aureate (in the same way he drags into the tale several references to
the roadside which might by analogy be called 'geographical
relief') and his tale is not really fit for the collection. But his
parrot-seizing of some of Chaucer's traits is impressive in the
sense that one would hardly have thought it could be done.

Lydgate's competence, at his own level, in the handling of the
balanced pentameter, seems to me obvious enough. He has fewer
lines of ten syllables than Hoccleve, both increasing and decreasing
the number of syllables, and the effect is to increase the importance
of the half-line element of the metre. But one can usually see how
they must go and find feet in them as well as half-lines, as a few
examples will make clear. Only one of these four lines from *The
Siege of Thebes* could cause much difficulty:

1171   And al the day / beholdyng enviroun
            He neyther saugh / castel toure ne toun
            The whiche þing / greued hym ful sore
            And sodeynly / the se began to Rore[1]

            [1] *Ed. cit.* p. 50.

The second quoted line has a trochaic third and monosyllabic fourth foot, but it is the next line that we may get wrong. Without the virgule it looks like an iambic tetrameter:

>   ˘   ′   ˘   ′ ˘ ′   ˘ ′
>   The whiche þing greued hym ful sore

but really it is a pentameter with two monosyllabic feet—an extreme very uncommon in Hoccleve or Chaucer:

>   ˘   ′ ǀ(˘) ′ ǀ ′ ′ ˘ ǀ ′ ǀ ˘ ′
>   The whiche þing greued hym ful sore

I am confident that this is the right reading both because it is indicated by punctuation and because that slow, halting movement expresses the sense better than the catchy tetrameter. At another extreme,

>   ′
>   Vn to my maistir / with humble affeccioun[1]

could be seen as a hexameter if 'humble' could be so stressed and if there could be a stress on 'with'. But the line again goes better as balanced pentameter, of a kind common enough in Hoccleve, with a trisyllabic foot spanning the half-line division:

>   ′ ˘ǀ ˘ ′ǀ ˘ ǀ   ′   ǀ ˘ ′ ǀ ˘ ′
>   Vn to my maistir with humble affeccioun

Cf.

>   ′ ˘ ǀ˘ ′ ǀ ˘ ˘   ′ ǀ ˘ ′ ˘ ′
>   Horryble dreedful and monstruous of sight[2]

Lydgate can also bring off effects even closer to one of Chaucer's manners:

>   Off God and kynde procedith al bewte[3]

This uses the trochaic inversion of the last foot in the way we are familiar with to produce a rather beautiful half-line balance:

>   ˘   ′ ǀ ˘   ′ ǀ ˘ ǀ˘ ǀ ′ ǀ ′ ˘
>   Off God and kynde procedith al bewte

But still Lydgate's flavour is very different from Chaucer's, especially in the high style which is the great mass of Lydgate.

[1] *The Churl and the Bird*, line 380; in Lydgate's *Minor Poems*, ed. H. N. MacCracken, p. 484.
[2] *St George*, line 41; in *Minor Poems*, p. 146.
[3] *Ibid.* p. 662, line 1.

Thetes which that is off waters chieff goddesse[1]

is grand enough, but the grandness comes from the stressing of *Thetes* and *chieff goddesse* at the two ends, contrasting with the run of unstressed syllables between: Chaucer, aiming at a similar grandness, might well have brought out the iambic pattern more simply.

Lydgate's odd little poem *The Kings of England sithen William Conqueror* devotes a stanza to each king, usually ending with the king's burial-place. The challenge of finding a different rhetorical formula for each king's tomb is one that Lydgate laboriously seizes, so producing a miniature catalogue of the variety of half-line rhythms and the extremes of metre available to his use of the balanced pentameter. I insert punctuation:

Beried at Seynt Swythynes / þe cronycle ye may reede[2]

(this has just about the limit of syllables beyond which a line could not be taken as pentameter).

21 At Malmysbury / list buried in his chest

28 Cronycles witnesse / is buried at Glastonbury

35 Edreed restith / in pesable memory

49 Buried at Glastonbury / as seith myn auctour

63 Deth for moordre / fynally was his meed

at Westmenster buryed was

91 Afftyr in þe chyrch yeerd of Danys / so stood þe cas

This line seems to have three feet of three syllables and only two of two, but we don't wholly lose the sense that they *are* feet.

105 Woundid to þe deth / buried at Waltham

---

[1] *Ibid.* p. 641, line 314.
[2] *Minor Poems*, ed. MacCracken, p. 710, line 14.

and even briefer:

<pre>
         /   ∪ I / ∪ I ∪ I /I∪ /I / /
154   Lith at Wircester / deied of poyson
</pre>

—which is, however, a pentameter whose metre is well used.

But some of these examples have been bringing us close to the notorious puzzle in Lydgate, how he means the lines which seem to have a resemblance to iambic pentameter while being plainly unmetrical. The most famous type is the 'broken-backed' line in which he leaves out a metrically stressed syllable. (In all the examples of monosyllabic feet so far quoted from the medieval poets the single syllable has been strongly stressed, i.e. capable of being seen as a beat.) For example any English reader will shape these lines of *The Black Knight* into some version of iambic pentameter:

> The grauel golde the water pure as glas
> The bankys rounde the welle environyng[1]

But the following line is

> And softe as veluet the yonge gras

What are we to do with that? There are more regular versions, but this seems to have two well marked half-lines,

> And softe as veluet / the yonge gras

but to have only four feet: or, alternatively, to have the stress of one foot missing:

<pre>
       ∪   / I ∪   /I ∪   ∪   /I ∪   /
or   And softe as veluet the yonge gras
</pre>

<pre>
       ∪   / I∪   /I ∪(/)I ∪ /I ∪   /
       And softe as veluet the yonge gras
</pre>

Alternatively if *the* could be metrically stressed and the -e on 'yonge' sounded we could get

<pre>
       ∪   / I∪   /I ∪ /I / / ∪I /
       And softe as veluet the yonge gras
</pre>

But all this is just scholarly ingenuity, which could lead to bewildering and useless discussions about time. The most natural reading is not iambic at all but leaves the line to organize itself

[1] Lines 78–9; *Minor Poems*, ed. MacCracken, p. 386.

only on the half-line division—which, as it happens, is effective enough. 'Broken-backed' lines like this almost always have a strong half-line organization, strong enough to make the line rhythmically unambiguous without the aid of feet.

I think the best explanation of such lines is that for Lydgate as for Hoccleve and perhaps Chaucer the long line consists normally of two half-lines and five feet but that sometimes the elements that went into Chaucer's compound come apart. If this is so it is itself evidence of the security of balanced pentameter: the half-line element was so much taken for granted that on occasion, as a normal variety of the line, it could do duty alone without the aid of feet. Lydgate can do smooth pentameters; he can also have a line that depends *only* on half-line balance. I do not see why this need be difficult to understand, given Lydgate's place in the Chaucerian tradition. Chaucer himself probably wrote some such lines, though his verse is usually a compound of feet and half-lines: but without Chaucer's force of genius to fuse the elements it is hardly surprising that Lydgate allowed them to separate. But whether the broken-backed lines are seen as unmetrical will depend on the conventions of the beholder. Half-line rhythms were an important part of Lydgate's sense of the rhythms of Chaucer's verse, so the broken-backed line belonged for Lydgate within the range of the metrically permissible—but only as a variety of the long line, belonging with others in which the feet were usually more important. (The range includes these extremes, but only as extremes of the range.)

The reason for accepting this account is that the broken-backed lines are hardly ever in themselves difficult to read. It is only if one is demanding that they should go in a different way—in feet—that they cause a stumble: they cause trouble if they are unexpected. But they shouldn't be unexpected. They are quite common, common enough to form part of the metrical expectation. So although the broken-backed lines are unmetrical in the sense that they are not organized in feet, they are certainly metrical in that they are organized in just the kind of half-lines we expect of the Chaucerians. They belong naturally with Lydgate's other lines, causing no difficulty to the experienced reader.

But my real confidence in this argument derives from the way these same broken-backed lines are also used by Wyatt, also in a context of balanced pentameters, because in Wyatt's case one can apply our usual test and find broken-backed lines part of the success of some of his greatest poems.[1]

This view of Lydgate as a pedestrian rather than a difficult or incompetent writer fits one's sense of his poetry. He writes competent uninspired balanced pentameters because he is a competent uninspired writer. He seems to have had no intelligent interest in Chaucer's poetry and to have learnt from Chaucer only the skeleton of his technical skill.

For Lydgate skill exists in the void, separate from anything a poet might have to say, and waiting to be exercised on raw material supplied by others He begins his *Fall of Princes*, the work which was to establish his reputation for over a hundred years, with this simile:

> Artificeres / hauyng exercise
> May chaunge and turne / bi good discrecioun
> Shappis / formys / and newli hem deuyse
> Make and vnmake / in many sundry wyse
> As potteres / which to that crafte entende
> Breke and renewe / their vesselis to a mende
>
> Thus men off crafft / may off due riht
> That been inuentiff / & han experience
> Fantasien / in their inward siht
> Deuises newe / thoruh ther excellence
> Expert maistres / han therto licence
> Fro good to bettir / for to chaunge a thyng
> And semblabli / these clerkis in writyng[2]

This is a very fair statement of Lydgate's position, though we might not grant that he always improves his material. It is as an 'expert maistre' of a craft, not as a creator, that we should think of Lydgate; one who alters and decorates rather than makes new. It was because Lydgate was properly so understood in his own day that he was thought a great poet: standards of taste alter. Professor Schirmer too sees Lydgate as above all a craftsman but in just the same way wants to make that a reason for calling him a poet.[3]

Lydgate's process of decorative translation is the making aureate of what are often quite simple texts. The original of the *Fall of Princes* is (by way of French) a work of Boccaccio's in Latin prose,

---

[1] Cf. below, Chapter 11, p. 232.
[2] *The Fall of Princes*, ed. H. Bergen, E.E.T.S. 1924, etc., vol. I, lines 8–21. I supply punctuation.
[3] W. F. Schirmer, *John Lydgate; ein Kulturbild aus dem 15. Jahrhundert*, Tübingen, 1952; English translation, 1961.

and *The Troy Book,* Lydgate's other great monument, is from a number of comparatively short and robust poems.

That material enters the Lydgate factory mud and leaves it terra-cotta. Lydgate's technique in the longer poems is always the application of beauties to a separately existing subject. In *The Fall of Princes* Lydgate doesn't even take the step of turning himself into the 'I' of the original. With a queer scrupulousness, the opposite of the artistic care of Chaucer or Wyatt which translates a text into the experience of the poet, Lydgate narrates the whole series of visions as happening to 'Iohn Bochas', and frequently reminds us that he is only reporting—a rebuke to Chaucer who never mentions Boccaccio's name? (I supply punctuation.)

470   Whan Iohn Bochas / considred hadde & souht
      The wofull fall / off myhti conquerours
      A remembraunce / entrid in his thouht. . .

1030   And certis / lich as Bochas in this book
      Remembrith first / off Adam the storye
      So next in ordre / he the storye took
      To speke off Nembroth. . .

1279   Wherfore Bochas / in despit off pride
      And in rebukyng / off al folkis proude
      Makyng his compleynt / crieth to hem ful lowde. . .

A poem once translated into English (the basic process in the Lydgate factory), pity, admiration, contempt, etc., are added by the narrator; for although Lydgate is so scrupulous about the independent existence of the poem, he is always there to comment in person as well. *Troilus and Criseyde* is not free from facile emotion: nothing can go wrong without Chaucer feeling ruth; but in Lydgate this tendency has settled down into a rhetorical habit of which it is quite impossible to take any serious notice. After the fall of each prince Lydgate laboriously records the appropriate woe or moral indignation.

The next process is the free expansion of the material and its inflation by the introduction of digressions, *exempla*, explanations and general encyclopaedic comment. A tree cannot be named without a catalogue of all the trees it isn't; the May-morning-green-mead scenes are never economized; we must have all the right birds and flowers and trees and the position of the sun and the strength of the wind. Fifty lines of the beginning of *The Siege of Thebes* paraphrase eighteen of Chaucer; this is about the usual proportion where no new matter is to be introduced.

The finishing process (no doubt this short account has left out many of the minor ones) is the addition of the machinery of dedications, prologues, epilogues, epistles, etc., at the devising of which Lydgate shows some considerable ingenuity. The most astonishing example is the *Secrees of Old Philisoffres*. The work to be translated takes the form of letters between Aristotle and Alexander: this opens up so many possibilities for machinery, all gravely taken by Lydgate, that the poem has not got going properly at all by the time Lydgate dies (at page 48 of the E.E.T.S. edition) and is succeeded by Benedict Burgh who, of course, opens with yet more machinery in the shape of a long double-ballade of apology for his incompetence.

Lydgate's aureate diction is a last careful polish of the finished product. Here too he seems conscious of his place as the decorator of something static. He sometimes cannot even trust us to take the force of his words from the way he uses them; instead he tells us what they are doing:

> And here vpon / to make no dellayes
> Mawgre ther myght / and ther Rebellyoun
> ffirst with my knyghthood / I wyl make Assayes
> To haue al perce / in subieccyoun
> Abydyng Oonly / for short Conclusyoun
> With your lettrys / for my Inpartye
> On this matere / pleynly to signeffye[1]

The last line is worse than mere padding: such additions are a kind of syntax-substitute, Lydgate labelling the functions of language as he needs them and piously hoping that they are in order. So too he loves synonyms and will never give one noun if he can think of two or three;[2] and his love of aureate diction is too well known to need any of our time. His guiding principle is always to use the longest and highest term available or, if nothing suitable occurs, to coin one.

But Lydgate's rhetoric, though so different from Chaucer's, is not by its own lights incompetent. Lydgate's rhetoric is the bricks in the ivory tower, the barrier between himself and life. But if

---

[1] *Secrees of Old Philisoffres*, lines 155–60; ed. R. Steele, E.E.T.S. 1894, p. 6.
[2] There is a fine collection in E. Sieper's edition of *Reson and Sensualyte*, E.E.T.S. 1901 and 1903, vol. II, pp. 46 ff.

poems really have to be manufactured in his way, and if style is
this kind of gilding the enamel lily, nobody can manufacture and
gild quite like Lydgate. And his mastery can often be shown in his
handling of the Chaucerian balanced line.

> As of hony / men gadren out swetnesse
> Of wyn and spices / is maad good ypocras
> Fro silver wellys / þat boyle vp with fresshnesse
> Cometh cristal watir / rennyng a gret pas[1]

Each of the first three lines has a marked half-line break after
which the second half is more straightforwardly iambic than the
first; but in the last line there is an obvious felicity in the way the
rhythm begins to run and bubble with the water by means of
the trochee that begins the second half-line. Similarly in the following passage all the lines but one (if we count the final -e's) have
the 'right' number of syllables:

> ⟨ The cely mayde / knelyng on hir kne
> Vn to hir goddes / maked hir preyer
> And St George / when he did it see
> To hir he sayde / with debonayre cheer
> Ryse vp a noon / myn owen doughter deer
> Take up þe girdell / and make þer of a bande
> And leed þis dragoun / boldly in þyn hande[2]

The one line with an extra syllable is

$$\text{/} \quad \cup \; | \; \cup \; \overset{/}{|} \; | \; \cup \quad | \quad \cup \quad \text{/} \quad | \; \cup \; / \; | \; \cup \; \text{/}$$
> Take up þe girdell / and make þer of a bande

which sets the verse off into the different rhythms of the end of the
quotation and changes the tone from piety to a very good imitation
of jollity. A different competence can often be found in the courtly
lyrics Lydgate mass-produced while tooling up for larger orders:

> Fresshe lusty beaute / ioyned with gentylesse
> Demure appert / glad chere with gouuernaunce
> Yche thing demenid / by avysinesse
> Prudent of speeche / wisdam of dalyaunce
> Gentylesse / with wommanly plesaunce
> Hevenly eyeghen / aungellyk of vysage
> Al þis haþe nature / sette in your ymage[3]

---

[1] *Minor Poems*, ed. MacCracken, p. 835, lines 1–4. My punctuation.
[2] *St George*, lines 106–12; in *Minor Poems*, ed. MacCracken, p. 149.
[3] *Minor Poems*, ed. MacCracken, p. 379, lines 1–7. My punctuation.

The sense of this gets worse as it goes along and by the end is mere courtly cliché; but the delicate variations in the half-line balances are not commonplace and tell us, at least, that the poem is the work of a skilled professional of the Chaucer school. This rhythmical variety may be of a rather deliberate sort (Lydgate of all poets was made not born) but it is not amateurish or accidental; all the symptoms of life are carefully painted on. And the dignity is not insincere; there need be no doubts about Lydgate's belief in his craft. If the emotions are stock-in-trade (with many a florin he the coloures bought) the courtiers who commissioned this kind of poem cannot have felt that their craftsman was giving bad value for money. Lydgate can even follow Chaucer in using padding for rhetorical effect:

> ⁋ And with that word the kyng lift vp his hede
> And abrayd / with sharpe sighes smerte
> And al this thing be ordre / gan aduerte
> Ceriously / be good avisement
> And by signes / cleer and evident
> Conceyueth wel / and sore gan repente
> It was hym silf / that Iocasta mente[1]

Here the *thou art the man* line derives its force from the thinness of the preceding lines, which as far as sense goes are close to non-existence. But let it be admitted that in Lydgate the reverse is more common: here, also from *The Siege of Thebes*, is Tydeus announcing his intention to be brief:

1901
> Sir quod he vnto ʒour worthynesse
> My purpoos is breefly to expresse
> Theffecte only as in sentement
> Of the massage why that I am sent
> It were in veyn / longe processe forto make
> But of my mater / the verrey ground to take
> In eschewyng of prolixitè
> And voyde away / al superfluytè
> Sith ʒoure silf best ought to vnderstond
> The cause fully / that we han on hond
> And ek conceyve / þentent of my menynge
> Of rightwisnesse / longgyng to a kynge

[1] *The Siege of Thebes*, ed. Erdmann, p. 41, lines 954–60.

IV

Something certainly went badly wrong with English courtly poetry after the death of Chaucer. Even Hoccleve does not recognize his real strengths and produces reams of aureate dullness, and Lydgate is a rather stupid writer: both fail, for instance, to follow through the promising interest in the mysterious which they get from the Chaucer of *The Man of Law's Tale*. The literary atmosphere of their time was certainly stultifying and in Lydgate's work comes out as an active disrelish for the life of the spoken language. It is ironical that the metre Chaucer developed for the lively speech of his poetry should have been fossilized by Lydgate to keep speech out. Things went wrong—but not in the way the scholars suppose. Lydgate did not forget Chaucer: he might have been a better writer if he had been able to do so.

Chaucer misused is the dominant force in fifteenth-century English poetry in Hoccleve, Lydgate and their lesser colleagues who also write balanced pentameters (Ashby, Bokenham, Burgh, Capgrave, and so on through the alphabet). They cannot escape from Chaucer, but for them Chaucer is the great rhetorical innovator, the man who introduced English poetic diction. This is not the emphasis we would give, and the remarks about Chaucer in Spurgeon's first volume make astonishing reading. Chaucer as the English Cicero, the importer of aureate words, is not the poet we read. But the Chaucerians were not factually mistaken. Chaucer *did* establish a way of writing English poetry, including his balanced pentameters, and it is in a tradition founded by Chaucer (if perverted by his successors) that the English Chaucerians write. What is more, they say so: the poets never tire of recording their admiration of Chaucer first, then Gower, then, later in the century, to Lydgate, as a sort of courtly trinity of which Chaucer is the father.

I reserve for another occasion the question of what possible sense there might be in this unanimous praise of Chaucer for the wrong reasons: my immediate point is the undoubted existence of a Chaucer tradition with Hoccleve and Lydgate at its head. If *they* could not read and imitate Chaucer's rhythms there is small hope for us.

11

The Last Chaucerians: Hawes, Skelton, Barclay, Wyatt

The English Chaucerians form the longest-lasting literary establishment we have yet achieved. The present chapter does not aim to explain this remarkable fact; such an explanation would take a volume and different methods. But I wish to make a few comments which will help us to see the later Chaucerians as at once genuinely descending from Chaucer and, in their different ways, quite different from him. If we can see the relationship of some of the poets to Chaucer and their attempts to relate themselves to their own time, we may be closer to satisfying the minimum criterion for a literary history of the century (above, Chapter 3), that it be credible. For the purposes of this essay the fifteenth century continues until about 1530. We are not now in danger of underestimating the importance of the changes that took place under Henry VIII, but I wish to show some neglected truths about the continuity of the poetry of his court with that of the courts of the preceding century.

The English Chaucerians fall naturally into two main groups, the first consisting of Hoccleve, Lydgate and their friends and acquaintances, immediate contemporaries of Chaucer, and the second the poets I shall be calling the last Chaucerians, happily surviving over a hundred years later in the early Tudor age.

This second group certainly are Chaucerians. Skelton makes the traditional appeal to Chaucer, Gower and Lydgate as part of his poetic credentials in *The Garlande of Laurell*; Wyatt is full of echoes from Chaucer; and Barclay, I believe, read *The Canterbury Tales* carefully after writing *The Ship of Fools* and before writing the *Egloges*: but the main sign of belonging to the Chaucerian tradition, and the one that particularly concerns us, is that all these poets (as well as many others) still write balanced penta meters. Reading the work of this group presents us with just the same problems as reading Hoccleve or Lydgate, and we solve them in the same way by allowing a half-line movement as well as a succession of feet.

To stress the continuity of Skelton or Wyatt with earlier English writers is still not wholly commonplace, and of course both are, in different ways, characteristic figures of the Renascence. Wyatt belongs, in most of our minds, with Surrey, leaving the Middle Ages decisively behind as he imports the sonnet with its Italian smoothness of metre, and as he translates from the fashionable Renascence writers. Skelton too may seem a very post-medieval figure, self-consciously a poet, proud of his honorary degree and even, apparently, wearing a special poetical uniform, in a manner that would have been uncongenial to Lydgate or Hoccleve.

Yet all these poets are equally moulded by the older English court traditions. Wyatt translates, but, at his best, into lines that move like Chaucer's. Skelton launches off, very deliberately, into inspiration, which may seem the extreme opposite of Lydgate's worship of authority; but Skelton when genuinely inspired always expresses feelings thoroughly at home in the medieval tradition.

I particularly mention Skelton, Barclay and Wyatt because they seem to me the only English Chaucerians except Hoccleve who might still be worth some of the time of a curious common reader. They are the ones to whom the reader of Chaucer might go on with some pleasure. To show that will be the same as showing how their verse moves and also the same as showing their place in the Chaucerian tradition.

But as well as Skelton, Barclay and Wyatt there are still, around 1500–20, hordes of lesser imitators of Lydgate, one of whom we will notice briefly to stand for the rest. The Chaucer tradition reached a sort of terminal perfection in the work of Stephen Hawes, who revised the usual fifteenth-century trinity to make Lydgate greater than Chaucer.[1] Hawes's line is pure Lydgate pentameter, but done with a wooden sameness that Lydgate was too much of a craftsman to fall into. Hawes's best-known poem, *The Pastime of Pleasure* (a name the modern researcher will greet wryly but which was perhaps justified by the work's original

---

[1] *The Pastime of Pleasure*, ca. xiii. Skelton's is the only other revision I know: in *Phyllyp Sparowe* he makes Jane Scroupe stand up for Chaucer but criticize Gower and Lydgate adversely.

popularity), is a last complete autobiography-with-dreams, supplying everything demanded by the Chaucerians' market— first person love in the quest of Labell Pucell (as in the *Romance of the Rose*, Gower, Charles of Orleans, etc.), giants and knight-errantry like the romances (Hawes varies the interest of his giant episodes by varying the number of heads per giant), battles as in Malory, morality and devotion like the pious side of Lydgate, and copious scholarly information including a complete tour of the trivium and quadrivium, the whole peppered with dreams and allegories and half-baked in Lydgate high style. It is all quite dead. Even the comic relief supplied by the character of Godfrey Gobylyue, a deformed dwarf who lays his grievances against his repulsive love before Venus, the excuse for a very crude diatribe against women, seems very half-hearted and put in because tradition demands it. By it Hawes proclaims a debt to *The Canter-bury Tales*, even going over into couplets for the occasion: I do not know of a more stupid tribute to Chaucer. High style in Hawes goes with dead dream-techniques, dead courtly attitudes, and is expressed in deadly balanced pentameters. Here he is, for example, entertaining his Tudor audience by his account of his meeting with Dame Grammar:

> Madame quod I / for as moche as there be
> Viii. partes of speche / I wolde knowe ryght fayne
> What a nowne substantyue / is in his degre
> And wherfore it is / so called certayne
> To whome she answered / ryght gentely agayne
> Sayenge alwaye / that a nowne substantyue
> Mygh stande / without helpe of an adiectyue
>
> The latyn worde / whiche that is referred
> Vnto a thynge / which is substancyall
> For a nowne substantyue / is well auerred
> And with a gendre / is declynall
> So all the eyght partes in generall
> Are laten wordes / annexed properly
> To euery speche / for to speke formally[1]

Hawes will present no difficulty to anybody who can read Lydgate. The difficult questions would be why the Lydgate metre survived so long in this dead-and-alive state and why anyone read Hawes. (The contemporary amateur Nevill's *Castell of Pleasure* is comparable and somewhat less dull.) The latter question is beyond

---

[1] *The Pastime of Pleasure*, ca. v, lines 582–95; ed. Mead, pp. 27–8.

our scope, but I can offer a hint or two about the former. The Chaucerian pentameter survived so long partly for want of anything better but also partly because it justified itself in the early years of the sixteenth century in a way not to be guessed at from reading Hawes: it and developments of it were the medium of some very interesting poetry.[1]

If one takes Hawes as the dead centre, Skelton, Barclay and Wyatt are interestingly divergent, in metre as in other ways.

Poeta Skelton

Skelton's main rhythmic innovation was, of course, the short line in rhyming groups of arbitary length—Skeltonics. This line is not the short line of simple foot-metre to be found in many contemporary lyrics including some of Skelton's own. I will suggest instead that Skeltonics are half-lines of balanced pentameters made to stand independently. This seems more probable than the other theories of the genesis of Skeltonics, and to account better for their

---

[1] There are two principal developments; one is Skeltonics, discussed below, the other a line longer even than Lydgate's pentameter usually is and, I think, a kind of fattened version of it, perhaps with five beats per line. This longer line works in half-lines in the usual way but is not confined even approximately to ten syllables. It is not common or important enough to be mentioned again but is found for instance in Skelton's *Garlande of Laurell* and in Barclay's last poem *The Mirour of Good Maners* where the increased length is symptomatic, I think, of a relaxation of the poet's intelligence. I want to call such lines as this 'fatty pentameter':

Wherfore haue done (Reader) address thee to vertue

In whose cause and quarell be bolde to stande and fight

Thy blinde carnall lustes of frayle members subdue

Be ready for to dye for Justice truth and right

Despise all iniury so seemeth Christes knight

Subdue this false world it is but vanitie

Then thinke thy selfe stabled in magnanimitie

—*The Mirour of Good Maners*, Spenser Society reprint, Manchester, 1885, p. 45. I think these lines go better as pentameters than hexameters but if pentameters they are certainly fatter than the Chaucerians' we have considered.

vigour. It is an idea put forward in different words by Guest and also mentioned by Mr H. L. R. Edwards in his list of possible sources.[1]

The alternatives are the theories of Messrs Berdan and Gordon, and Mr Edwards's suggestion that Skeltonics arose from the division of Latin hexameters.[2] Berdan's view need not be discussed because it was decisively refuted by Professor Nelson,[3] whose own idea is more attractive. He believes that Skeltonics are derived from Latin rhymed prose, and when he shows Skelton writing rhymed prose in Latin and English, and going easily from rhymed prose to Skeltonics, he is initially convincing. But two objections are to be made. The first follows from Mr Edwards's demonstration, using just the same argument, that Skeltonics come from Latin hexameters: he quotes a sentence that Skelton begins in Latin hexameter and ends in English Skeltonics. For that matter Skelton can be found doing the same with smooth English verse. All this can only prove that Skelton liked to break from one form to another, and it can surely emphasize the unlikeness of forms as much as the likeness. (Nevertheless there is a real resemblance between some of the rhymed Latin prose and Skeltonics.) The other objection to Mr Nelson's idea, implicit in the first, is that the rhymed prose is *prose*. To see a simple development from it to Skeltonics he has to argue that ' Clearly, there is no great difference between Skelton's poetry and Skelton's prose, nor did the poet

---

[1] Cf. Edwin Guest, *A History of English Rhythms*, ed. W. W. Skeat, 1882, pp. 396–7; H. L. R. Edwards, *Skelton*, 1949, p. 88.

[2] I have not seen B. S. Kendle, *The Ancestry and Character of the Skeltonic*, unpublished Ph.D. dissertation, University of Wisconsin, 1961. According to *Dissertation Abstracts* (Ann Arbor, Michigan, 1961, vol. XXI, p. 3090) this work says that: ' The complex ancestry and character of the Skeltonic are suggested by the many conflicting theories concerning its origin. An eclectic position, stressing the divergent literary backgrounds available to Skelton, is therefore necessary to account for the varying traditions operative in his verse.' This account does not mention the Chaucerian pentameter as one of Skelton's backgrounds but does also report that ' The Skeltonic may be the result of the breaking of the fourteenth-century alliterative line'.

[3] Cf. W. Nelson, *John Skelton, Laureate*, New York, 1939, pp. 88–9. Berdan's idea (J. M. Berdan, *Early Tudor Poetry 1485–1547*, New York, 1920, pp. 166 ff.) that Skelton was imitating Latin in a way initiated by certain French and Italian writers is not substantiated by his example, a perfectly smooth poem; and his example from Trevisa, though not metrically so regular, does not resemble Skeltonics. The fact that Caxton's modernization of Trevisa is in places rather Skeltonic merely emphasizes the fact that Skeltonics do not appear before the last part of the fifteenth century, and that the verse was not Skeltonic before it was altered.

erect a high wall between them.'[1] But the evidence adduced is the *Replicacioun*, where Skelton is at pains to distinguish verse and prose. And in any case the assertion that Skeltonics are some kind of verse surely needs little defence?

I suggest that the reason so many plausible models have been found for Skeltonics is that many scholars have observed that each short line is a speech-phrase, and finding forms built of speech-phrases has not been difficult. But surely the most natural source was the balanced pentameter Skelton frequently wrote.

'Balance' is an important element of the Chaucerian long line; Skelton's use of one half of this line might be expected to destroy the balance, and his short lines are in fact a series of unbalanced half-lines. In the absence of the second half-line to balance the new impetus of the first, Skelton's lines go off like a series of rockets, at a cracking, jerky pace not quite like anything else in English. Part of their force comes from a sort of fission: the enormous unbalanced energy comes in part from an expectation of balance.

There are two kinds of Skeltonics: one of two and one of three feet. In both cases the metrical stresses are also phrase-stresses, so that Skeltonics, unlike balanced pentameter, is a beat-metre. The speech-phrase of which the line consists is shaped just like the parent half-lines by a co-operation of foot and two- or three-beat unit. For example the two-beat line:

> Her lothely lere
> Is nothynge clere
> But vgly of chere
> Droupy and drowsy
> Scuruy and lowsy
> Her face all bowsy
> Comely crynklyd
> Woundersly wrynkled
> Lyke a rost pygges eare
> Brystled wyth here[2]

The metre here enforces the 'pieces of speech' in the way we are by now familiar with; the verse is the opposite of difficult to read rhythmically. Parts of *Phyllyp Sparowe* are in three-beat Skeltonics, equally easy to read:

[1] *John Skelton, Laureate*, p. 100.
[2] *Elynour Rummynge*, lines 12–21. In *The Poetical Works of John Skelton*, ed. A. Dyce, 2 vols. 1843; vol. I, p. 95.

O cat of carlyshe kynde
The fynde was in thy mynde
Whan thou my byrde untwynde
I wolde thou haddest ben blynde
The leopardes sauage
The lyons in theyr rage
Myght catch thé in theyr pawes
And gnawe thé in theyr iawes
The serpentes of Lybany
Myght stynge thé venymously[1]

That Skelton's verses are not mere accident is shown—for anyone who has persevered thus far in the belief that it needs demonstration—by a passage of *Magnyfycence* where a foot-metre is played off against Skeltonics for dramatic effect:

FELYCYTE:	Wolde it please you then
LYBERTE:	Vs to informe and ken
MEASURE:	A ye be wonders men
	Your langage is lyke the penne
	Of hym that wryteth to fast
FELYCYTE:	Syr yf any worde haue past
	Me other fyrst or last
	To you I arecte it and cast
	Therof the reformacyon
LYBERTE:	And I of the same facyon
	Howe be it by protestacyon
	Dyspleasure that you none take
	Some Reason we must make
MEASURE:	That wyll not I forsake
	So it in Measure be
	Come of therfore let se
	Shall I begynne or ye
FELYCYTE:	Nay ye shall begynne by my wyll
LYBERTE:	It is Reason and Skyll
	We your pleasure fulfyll
MEASURE:	Then ye must bothe consent
	You to holde content
	With myne argument
	And I muste you requyre
	Me pacyently to here
FELYCYTE:	Yes Syr with ryght good chere
LYBERTE:	With all my herte intere[2]

The passage begins in three-beat Skeltonics, into which Measure is at first carried away, but he protests that Felycyte and Lyberte

---

[1] *Phyllyp Sparowe*, lines 282–91. *Ed. cit.* I, 59–60.
[2] *Magnyfycence*, lines 87–113; ed. R. L. Ramsay, E.E.T.S. 1908, pp. 4–5.

are 'lyke the penne Of hym that wryteth to fast' (i.e. like Skelton),
and in his second speech uses non-Skeltonic iambic trimeter,
which has an obvious appropriateness to his character. Felycyte
and Lyberte again reply in Skeltonics; Measure replies with an
exaggeration of his foot-metre, and they enact their submission by
concurring and also abandoning Skeltonics.

To show how right Skelton was to practise his own metre, and
to show that it was not merely rumbustious, one need only compare
the lyrics in *The Garlande of Laurell* in Skeltonics with the ones
from the same poem in strict foot-metres. 'To Maystres Margaret
Hussey' gives the impression, as Skelton always does at his best,
of complete spontaneity. It has the air of being the first thing that
came into his head—but the first thing is a beautiful, conventional
poem:

> Mirry Margaret
> As mydsomer flowre
> Ientill as fawcoun
> Or hawke of the towre[1]

Even if 'gentle' has nothing of its modern meaning, and even
though 'hawke of the towre' needs an explanatory note, there is
something striking and immediately perceptible in this image; it
feels original and genuine but manages to sum up an ideal implicit
in many medieval poets. The poem has lines that are padding, if
not simply meaningless:

1007
> With solace and gladnes
> Moche mirthe and no madnes
> All good and no badnes...

But they don't spoil it; such lines are the condition of Skelton's
inspiration. He has to wait for it to revive and send new good lines.
'To Maystres Isabell Pennell' is even freer and ends quite
successfully with a few lines of birdsong. 'To Maystres Margery
Wentworthe', too, is excellent:

910
> Plainly I can not glose
> Ye be as I deuyne
> The praty primrose
> The goodly columbyne

Here the sentiment is altogether conventional, from what one may
think of as the dead centre of the courtly tradition which had for

[1] *Poetical Works of John Skelton*, ed. Dyce, vol. 1, p. 401, lines 1004–7.

the whole age symbolized female beauty as a flower. But Skelton can say Miss Wentworth is a primrose and a columbine (he disdains mere simile) as if he were the first poet in the world to think of it. This power is given to him by his command of rhythm in the delicate half-line constructions of the last two quoted lines.

All these poems are more delicately alive than the smooth ones in the same work. 'To Mastres Margaret Tylney' is comparatively wooden and stupid:

926
> I yow assure
> Ful wel I know
> My besy cure
> To yow I owe
> Humbly and low
> Commendynge me
> To yowre bownte
>
> As Machareus
> Fayre Canace
> So I iwus
> Endeuoure me
> Yowr name to se
> It be enrolde
> Writtin with golde

Skelton is an extreme and quite explicit believer in inspiration and describes in a stanza of *The Garlande of Laurell* his ideal of bursting into poetry without the least idea of what will result:

829
> As a mariner that amasid is in a stormy rage
> Hardly bestad and driuen is to hope
> Of that the tempestuows wynde wyll aswage
> In trust wherof comforte his hart doth grope
> From the anker he kuttyth the gabyll rope
> Committyth all to God and lettyth his shyp ryde
> So I beseke Ihesu now to be my gyde

Skelton is always cutting the cable rope and committing all to God. In places this leads to a writing-on-and-on-and-on style which is totally uninspired, as in *Ware the Hawk*, an exception to the odd rule that Skelton's best poems are about birds—which is spun out in a way that practically eliminates meaning. But at least the style is always an attempt to be true to impulse and escape the merely predictable. A minor poet who believes in absolute inspiration is, however, peculiarly at the mercy of the tradition he finds himself in, and cutting the cable rope is not for Skelton a way of escaping from the Chaucerian tradition. This is true even in *Speke Parrot*, Skelton's most original poem. This used to be an obscure poem: Ritson called it a 'farrago of nonsense' and Saintsbury's opinion was not much different: 'It is the most incoherent of all his poems and, in parts, absolutely unintelligible.'[1] The poem comes clear once one realizes that Parrot is a very appropriate type of Skelton's crotchety muse (an interpretation of the poem first publicly made, I think, by Mr Edwards, and worked out in meticulous detail by Mr Fish).[2]

In its *sensus litteralis Speke Parrot* is a poem in which the Parrot appears as a real bird, full of life, and in Skelton's best vein:

> With my becke bent / my lyttyl wanton eye
> My fedders freshe / as is the emrawde grene
> About my neck a cyrculet / lyke the ryche rubye
> My lyttyll leggys / my feet both fete and clene
> I am a mynyon / to wayt vppon a quene
> My proper Parrot / my lyttyl pretty foole
> With ladyes I lerne / and go with them to scole[3]

The parrot then goes on to speak odd phrases in all the European languages, and the poem ends with five envoys, after the last of which it starts again with pronouncements by Parrot on various subjects. At first sight it really can look mystifying.

But the random utterances in half a dozen languages are simply examples of Skelton's ideal of perfect freedom of inspiration. *Speke Parrot* is therefore a poem about writing poetry: in it Skelton's galloping inspiration is made to consider itself. The suggestions that this is what the poem is all about are plain enough once one begins to look for them:

94
> Suche shredis of sentence / strowed in the shop
> Of auncyent Aristippus / and such other mo
> I gader togyther / and close in my crop
> Of my wanton conseyt / *unde depromo*
> *Dilemmata docta* / *in pædagogio*
> *Sacro vatum* / whereof to you I breke
> I pray you / let Parot haue lyberte to speke

---

[1] *The Cambridge History of English Literature*, vol. III, p. 76.
[2] S. E. Fish, *John Skelton's Poetry*, New Haven, 1965, pp. 135 ff.
[3] *Speke Parrot*, lines 17–23; *Poetical Works of John Skelton*, ed. Dyce, vol. II, p. 2. My punctuation.

or

108   Parrot / Parrot / Parrot / praty popigay
              With my beke I can pyke / my lyttel praty too
              My delyght is solas / pleasure / dysporte and pley
              Lyke a wanton / whan I wyll I rele to and froo
              Parot can say *Cæsar ave* also
              But Parrot hath no fauour / to Esebon
              Aboue all other byrdis / set Parrot alone

What could be fitter figures of Skelton's poetry and its predicament? And the relation of Parrot, courtly poetry, to the courtly lady, is caught in action. There is a commentary by a courtly voice:

118   Gedeon is gon / that Zalmane vndertoke
              Oreb *et* Zeb / of *Judicum* rede the boke
              Now Geball / Amon / and Amaloch / harke harke
              Parrot pretendith / to be a bybyll clarke

Parrot is requested to speak on various matters and replies on others or speaks in riddles, just like the Muse. But when at last he does speak it is in a satire of the most traditional kind, though in a metre a little fatter than Lydgate might have approved:

           So many morall maters / and so lytell vsyd
           So myche newe makyng / and so madd tyme spente
        So myche translacion / in to Englyshe confused
           So myche nobyll prechyng / and so lytell amendment
           So myche consultacion / almoste to none entente
           So myche provision / and so lytell wytte at nede
           Syns Dewcalyons flodde / there can no clerkes rede[1]

Skelton has within his limits a liveliness we cannot find in Lydgate: but the limits are largely those of the Lydgate tradition, without which Skelton would have been lost.

Alexander Barclay

Alexander Barclay uses in his *Egloges* an easily comprehensible development of the balanced pentameter. As Mr Pyle points out,[2] the second halves of Barclay's lines are normally smoother than the

---

[1] *The Poetical Works of John Skelton*, ed. Dyce, vol. II, p. 22.
[2] F. Pyle, 'The Barbarous Metre of Barclay', *The Modern Language Review*, vol. XXXII, 1937.

first. (This applies too to the fat lines quoted above, p. 216.) In the *Egloges* we know we are reading pentameters, but Barclay is almost always careful to avoid the simplest iambic pattern in the first half-line (◡/◡/◡/(◡/)) by introducing an indefinite number of extra syllables.[1] But he seems to like to settle into more obvious iambic movement later in the line. We still find in Barclay the twin controls of feet and half-lines: what makes him stand out from the other practitioners of the metre is that he has a real poetic feeling for rhythm. In my opinion—though in crossing the Chaucerian desert one is prone to see mirages—Barclay is a much underrated poet. And he could have achieved the very attractive verse-movement of the *Egloges* in no other way than through his balanced pentameter.

Barclay is really a one-poem writer (there is regrettably no time to make the survey of his *œuvre* which would substantiate the judgement) but in the *Egloges* at least, almost anywhere we test them, we find a delight in life, of however severe a kind, that is quite beyond the reach of Lydgate or Hawes. The description of Ely cathedral, where Barclay was a monk, has an individual quality of gaiety where Lydgate would certainly have been ponderous:

> There was I lately about the middest of May,
> Coridon his Church is twenty sith more gay
> Then all the Churches betwene the same and Kent,
> There sawe I his tome and Chapell excellent.
> I thought fiue houres but euen a little while,
> Saint Iohn the virgin me thought did on me smile,
> Our parishe Church is but a dongeon
> To that gay Churche in comparison.
> If the people were as pleasaunt as the place
> Then were it paradice of pleasour and solace.[2]

But the *Egloges* are possibly unique in English as being about real shepherds, who have real disputes in which the end is not always foreseeable. The evocation of the hard peasants' winter is wonderful in such places as this:

> The winter snowes, all couered is the grounde,
> The north wind blowes sharpe & with ferefull sound,

[1] Miss B. White, the excellent editor of the *Egloges* (E.E.T.S. 1928) found one regular line, rather reminiscent of Pope, and was so pleased she annotated it:
Unapt to learne, disdayning to be taught
(p. 166, line 703) Note, 'An unusually successful line'.
[2] *The Eclogues of Alexander Barclay*, ed. B. White, E.E.T.S. 1928, p. 17, lines 533–42.

The long ise sicles at the ewes hang,
The streame is frosen, the night is cold & long,
Where botes rowed now cartes haue passage,
From yoke the oxen be losed and bondage,
The ploweman resteth auoyde of businesse,
Saue when he tendeth his harnes for to dresse,
Mably his wife sitteth before the fyre
All blacke and smoky clothed in rude attire,
Sething some grewell, and sturring the pulment
Of pease or frument, a noble meat for lent.[1]

Though this is a translation from a (rather thinly elegant) Latin
original, the winter is certainly English. (One of the traditional
reproaches to Barclay is that his shepherds aren't pastoral enough.)
Yet Barclay can make the hard life of the peasants sound, despite
everything, worthwhile; and the force of the sober advice to them
to stay put rather than go off to town comes from his full knowledge of the wretchedness of the country.

If God (as men say) doth heauen and earth sustayne,
Then why doth not he regarde our dayly payne?
Our greeuous labour he iustly might deuide,
And for vs wretches some better life prouide.
Some nought doth labour and liueth pleasauntly,
Though all his reason to vices he apply:
But see with what sweat, what busines and payne
Our simple liuing we labour to obtayne:
Beholde what illes we shepheardes must endure
For flocke and housholde bare liuing to procure,
In feruent heate we must intende our folde,
And in the winter almost we frese for colde:
Upon the harde ground or on the flintes browne
We slepe, when other lye on a bed of downe.
A thousande illes of daunger and sicknesse
With diuers sores our beastes doth oppresse:
A thousande perils and mo if they were tolde
Dayly and nightly inuadeth our poore folde.
Sometime the wolfe our beastes doth deuour,
And sometime the thefe awayteth for his hour:
Or els the souldiour much worse then wolfe or thefe
Agaynst all our flocke inrageth with mischefe.
See howe my handes are with many a gall,
And stiffe as a borde by worke continuall,
My face all scoruy, my colour pale and wan,
My head all parched and blacke as any pan,

[1] *Ibid.* pp. 182–3, lines 63–74.

My beard like bristles, so that a pliant leeke
With a little helpe may thrust me throw the cheeke,
And as a stockfishe wrinkled is my skinne,
Such is the profite that I by labour winne.[1]

The presence of such passages makes the final morality more
acceptable:

CORIDON

But tell me Cornix one thing or we departe,
On what maner life is best to set my harte?
In court is combraunce, care, payne, and misery,
And here is enuy, ill will and penury.

CORNIX

Sufferaunce ouercommeth all malice at the last,
Weake is that tree which can not bide a blast,
But heare now my counsell I bid thee finally,
Liue still a shepheard for playnly so will I.

CORIDON

That shall I Cornix thy good counsell fulfill,
To dye a shepheard established is my will.

CORNIX

So do, or after thou often shall repent,
Poore life is surest, the court is but torment.[2]

My point is Barclay's dependence for these real successes on the
balanced pentameter of the Chaucerian tradition. How much
duller many of these lines would have been if they had appeared
in the simple foot-metre in which it is easy to rewrite them:

Or else the soldier, worse than wolf or thief,
Against our flock enrageth with mischief.
See how my hands are sore with many a gall
And stiff as boards with work continual;
Scurvy my face, my colour pale and wan,
Parched my head and black as any pan;
My beard so bristly that a pliant leek
With little aid may thrust me through the cheek...

Barclay's lines are simply more energetic, serious and expressive.
And the power to command the language is given to him by the
metre.

---

[1] *Ibid.* pp. 7–8, lines 213–42.
[2] *Ibid.* pp. 138–9, lines 811–22. In Cornix's first speech, as often in Barclay,
sentence leads naturally on to proverb.

The half-line rhythms in Barclay are so clearly marked that it makes very little difference whether the lines are metrically punctuated (as in the unique sixteenth-century edition of his *St George*) or punctuated only with occasional commas, like the early editions of the *Egloges*. It is surely easy enough to follow his rhythms provided we do not insist on his lines being modern pentameters.

Sir Thomas Wyatt

Wyatt has received better critical attention than the other poets considered in this chapter; the merit of his poetry has always been more widely recognized. And the first effort of modern criticism has had to be to show that Wyatt is not the clumsy writer our elders (including so intelligent a leader of the opposition as Nott) thought him. Mr Thompson quotes, 'Wyatt was the pioneer who fumbled in the linguistic difficulties that beset him',[1] and when such things can be believed of a sensitive poet criticism has to begin by clearing the ground. The old view was that this 'fumbling' of Wyatt was towards iambic pentameter and other smooth metres, unfortunately forgotten by Chaucer's disciples. It is obviously true that some of Wyatt's poems are in what I have called foot-metres, and it used to be generally assumed that these came later, as his fumblings became gradually more experienced. A handy collection of examples of this point of view is to be found in the 'Critical Comments' prefixed to Professor Muir's edition of Wyatt's poems;[2] and such is the force of scholarly tradition that Muir himself, for all his editorial caution, is led astray into the same belief in the course of making what I believe to be a critical misjudgement: 'None of the sonnets, not even the late ones which are comparatively smooth, can be ranked among Wyatt's best poems.'[3] There we see the traditional belief that smoothness is virtue.

But it is not true that Wyatt's career is a progress towards smoothness of metre. He was a habitual metrical experimenter and went on writing time-metres (e.g. poulter's measure), foot-metres (many of the lyrics) and half-line metres to the end of his life. Mr Mason[4] presents much of the evidence, and in addition to his

---

[1] J. Thompson, *The Founding of English Metre*, p. 16.
[2] *Collected Poems of Sir Thomas Wyatt*, ed. Kenneth Muir, 1949 (The Muses' Library).   [3] *Ibid.* p. xxi.
[4] H. A. Mason, *Humanism and Poetry in the Early Tudor Period*, 1959.

thoughtful and helpful book there has recently been a very fine dissertation, already cited,[1] which as well as gathering together what is known interprets the knowledge as a way of reading Wyatt's poems.

Wyatt wrote a range of metres, and the best modern criticism has been at pains to show that he is often at his most effective when least smooth. Professor D. W. Harding's essay[2] has been a great influence on the whole of the present investigation and is, I believe, profoundly right in its basic argument about the way Wyatt works with speech-phrases. Mr Mason follows and elaborates Harding's point of view, as Mr Raymond Southall has also done more recently;[3] and Miss Endicott has specifically enquired into the connections of Wyatt's rhythmic movements with his uses of metre. As Professor Baldi puts it:

La rivalutazione odierna dell'opera del Wyatt ha sormontato la maggiore difficoltà della prima critica (l'asprezza del pentametro giambico del Wyatt) con una rivoluzione di gusto: ciò che era ieri un difetto è considerato oggi uno dei massimi pregi.[4]

All I can add to the discussion is an attempt to show, by speaking of Wyatt in the context of this study, that his rhythmic strength is a traditional one, coming in an unbroken line from Chaucer. And that may perhaps correct a popular imbalance: Wyatt is certainly a renascence poet as he is always thought to be, but an English renascence poet and in resonance with the English tradition. His best things are translations from the writers of the new age—but into English balanced pentameters.

Writing in the early sixteenth century, Wyatt presumably pronounced no final -e's that are mute for us. But his verse often moves very like Chaucer's where Chaucer has a minimally sounded -e. Many of Wyatt's lines are iambic pentameter with one monosyllabic foot; and especially frequent is the line beginning ∪ / | / | ∪ / :

I, I   Behold love thy power how she dispiseth[5]

I, 2   My great payne how litle she regardeth

---

[1] Endicott, *Metrical Effects*.
[2] 'The Rhythmical Intention in Wyatt's Poetry', *Scrutiny*, vol. XIV, 1946.
[3] R. Southall, *The Courtly Maker*, Oxford, 1964.
[4] Sergio Baldi, *La Poesia di Sir Thomas Wyatt*, Florence, 1953, p. 91.
[5] The text is quoted and poems numbered from Muir's edition, minus punctuation.

ᵕ　／　｜／　｜　ᵕ／
4, 1　　The longe love that in my thought doeth harbar

be redy there

ᵕ　／｜　／　　｜　ᵕ／
27, 10　　At all howres still vnder the defence

ᵕ　／　｜／　　｜ᵕ　　／｜
Of tyme trouthe and love to save the from offence

The rhythmic effect is just what it would have been in Chaucer; the line is slowed and the half-line phrase deliberately formed. All these examples are obviously successful; Miss Endicott cites many more.[1] Monosyllabic feet can also work well elsewhere in the line:

／　ᵕ｜ᵕ　／　｜ᵕ　　／　｜／｜ᵕ／　ᵕ
44, 2　　Have I so much your mynd then offended

This movement creates, as in Chaucer, some particular shade of tone or feeling.

ᵕ　　／　｜　ᵕ　／｜ᵕ　／｜　ᵕ　／　｜／
196, 51　　And skorne the story that the knyght tolld

ᵕ／　｜ᵕ　　／　｜ᵕ／｜　ᵕ／　｜／
200, 42　　The hete doth strayt forsake the lymms cold

Wyatt similarly uses trochaic substitutions in a Chaucerian way to help the half-line rhythms:

ᵕ　　／｜　／　ᵕ｜
8, 22　　O small honye muche aloes and gall

In bitternes have my blynde lyfe taisted

ᵕ　／｜　／　　ᵕ｜
24　　His fals swetenes that torneth as a ball

ᵕ　／　｜／　ᵕ　｜ᵕ　／｜／　ᵕ｜ᵕ／
12, 2　　A swete languor a great lovely desire

ᵕ　／　　｜ᵕ／｜　ᵕ　／　｜／｜ᵕ｜　／　ᵕ
8, 66　　And doeth the same with deth daily thretyn

／　ᵕ｜ᵕ／｜ᵕ　／｜　／　ᵕ｜ᵕ　　／
207, 1　　Rew on me lord for thy goodnes and grace

Whether or not Wyatt sounded Chaucer's final -e's, such lines as these indicate that he understood the rhythmic movement of final -e's and trochaic inversions.

One may easily see how much the success of Wyatt's best poems depends on the expressive resources of balanced pentameter.

[1] *Metrical Effects*, pp. 84–5.

37, 1   They fle from me that sometyme did me seke
           With naked fote stalking in my chambre
           I have sene theim gentill tame and meke
           That nowe are wyld and do not remembre
           That sometyme they put theimself in daunger
           To take bred at my hand; and nowe they raunge
           Besely seking with a continuell chaunge.

The first line is the smooth variant, perfect modern pentameter without half-line division, but line two at once goes into expressive half-lines because of the third-foot trochee, putting stress on the right word, *stalking*. Line three is the headless variant; line four again goes into half-lines because of the monosyllabic third foot. Line five's monosyllabic second foot gives half-lines which well express, by emphasizing 'sometyme', how melancholy the change is. Line six has a second-foot trochee. The next line, though recognizably in foot-metre, is more like Hoccleve than Chaucer in its strongly-marked halves and weakly-marked feet:

$$ \acute{}\,\smile\smile\;\acute{}\,\smile\;\;|\;\;\acute{}\,\smile\smile\smile\;\acute{}\,\smile\smile\;\;\acute{}\, $$
Besely seking   with a continuell chaunge

One could go all through the poem—one could almost say all the way through Wyatt—showing how thoroughly Chaucerian his best things are. To avoid tedium I will only comment on one more line of 'They Fle from Me', the startling opening of the last stanza:

37, 15   It was no dreme I lay brode waking

Tottel's *Miscellany*, of 1557, in which Wyatt's poems were re-phrased to suit the metrical tastes of a later age, makes havoc of this poem and in particular this line, which appears as:

It was no dreame: for I lay broade awakyng.[1]

Why is that smoother version so much weaker than Wyatt's? Wyatt's line is still iambic pentameter, though close to losing its feet entirely to the half-lines. The first four syllables are two iambic feet, a weak one (two lightly stressed syllables) and a strong one; these make the first half-line. The line's effect of startled wakefulness depends on the repeated half-line rhythm of increasing stress, and that comes largely from the monosyllabic fourth foot (which,

---

[1] *Tottel's Miscellany*, ed. Edward Arber, 1870, p. 40.

sure enough, could have had a sounded -e in Chaucer) and the
trochaic fifth which together put three stresses next to each other:

᷄ ⏑ / ⏑ ˘ / | ⏑ / ⏑ / / / ⏑
It was no dreme ⏐ I lay brode waking

This line is still foot-metre as well as half-lines; and the remark
is worth making because I find myself here partly in disagreement
with Miss Endicott and Mr Thompson. The latter offers a list of
lines which Tottel's *Miscellany* left irregular, and says, 'Some of
these lines cannot be brought into any relation with an iambic
metrical pattern' and that they 'resist any attempt at explanation'.[1]
I am naturally tempted to explain and so will consider some of
Mr Thompson's examples *seriatim*:

1.

       Rather than to liue thrall vnder the awe

This is regular with weak iambic second foot, strong iambic third
foot and trochaic fourth foot:

/ ⏑ ⏐ ⏑ /•/ / ⏐ / ⏐ / ⏑ ⏐ ⏑ /
Rather than to liue thrall ⏐ vnder the awe

2.

       With innocent bloud to fede my selfe fatte

Regular: trisyllabic second foot, monosyllabic fifth:

⏑ / ⏐ ⏑ ⏑ / / ⏐ ⏑ / ⏐ ⏑ / ⏐ /
With innocent bloud ⏐ to fede my selfe fatte

3.

       And he that suffreth offence withoutt blame

Almost the same: trisyllabic third foot, monosyllabic fifth.

4.

       Rather then to be outwardly to seme

This looks like a sort of trochaic version of the second line of
a poulter's measure:

/ ⏑ / ⏑ / / ⏑ / ⏑ /
Rather than to be [one-foot pause] outwardly to seme

[1] *The Founding of English Metre*, p. 25.

and perhaps that is how it is meant to go in the *Miscellany*. But it can also just about be taken as pentameter if the first two feet are trochees and the third a strong iamb:

$$/ \; \cup \; | \; / \; \cup \; | \; \cup \; / \; | \; / \; | \; \cup \; | \; \cup \; /$$

Rather than to be   outwardly to seme

5.

$$\cup \; / \; | \; \cup \; / \; | \; \cup \; / \; | \; / \; | \; \cup \; | \; \cup \; /$$

She cheered her with how sister what chere

This is perfectly regular with a fourth-foot trochee, whose function is to give the convincingly colloquial opening of a speech with two stresses, 'How, síster...'

6.

$$\cup \; / \; / \; \cup$$

To freate inward for losyng such a losse

Regular with trochaic second foot.

7.

Seke still thy profite vpon thy bare fete

Trochaic (or strong iambic?) first foot, trisyllabic third foot, monosyllabic fifth foot after missing final -e:

$$/ \; \cup \; | \; \cup \; / \; | \; \cup \; \cup \; / \; | \; \cup \; / \; | \; /$$

Seke still thy profite vpon thy bare fete

Similarly, Mr Thompson's first example of an unmetrical line in Wyatt is the already discussed

It was no dreme: I lay brode waking.

I certainly agree with his comment that there is 'a certain effect... as of the speaking voice',[1] and I would say that part of the control of the speaking voice is the half-line metre: but another part is the feet.

But it is true that Wyatt, like Lydgate and perhaps Chaucer, sometimes controls a line *only* by its half-line movement. These lines moreover are often amongst his best, and belong very naturally with ones where we can see a foot-metre.

4, 12   What may I do when my maister fereth
But in the feld with him to lyve and dye
For goode is the liff ending faithfully

[1] *Op. cit.* p. 15.

To count as iambic pentameter the last line would need the impossible stressing:

$$\breve{} \quad / \quad \breve{} \quad / \quad \breve{} \quad / \quad \breve{}$$
For goode is the liff ending

(Possibly it could be a strong iamb followed by a weak iamb then another strong iamb: but I don't naturally perceive any such pattern.) Surely it just goes in the half-lines:

$$/ \qquad\qquad / \quad / \qquad\qquad /$$
For goode is the liff / ending faithfully

(Sievers B plus A type without alliteration.) There is no rhythmic ambiguity about this powerful line. I would say that where Wyatt abandons feet he takes particular care, like Lydgate in similar situations, to make the half-line rhythm unmistakable; and the lines where the half-lines are all-powerful always have two beats per half.

Sometimes we can see Wyatt making a sense of the broken-backed line which could have been got in no other way (which is the chief reason for believing in broken-backed lines). In the instance just quoted the line without feet seems wholly right in its place at the end of the sonnet, an invocation of the phrasal extreme of Wyatt's metrical range for a tone at once serious and intimate, the tone, almost, of proverb, naturally expressed in phrases. That very great poem 'Who so List to Hount' works by a similar rhythmic progress from balanced pentameter to pure half-line movement:

7   Who so list to hount / I knowe where is an hynde
            But as for me / helas I may no more
            The vayne travaill / hath weried me so sore
        I ame of theim / that farthest commeth behinde
        Yet may I by no meanes / my weried mynde
            Drawe from the Diere / but as she fleeth afore
            Faynting I folowe / I leve of therefore
        Sins in a nett / I seke to hold the wynde
        Who list her hount / I put him owte of dowbte
            As well as I / may spend his tyme in vain
            And graven with Diamonds / in letters plain
        There is written / her faier neck rounde abowte
        Noli me tangere / for Cesars I ame
        And wylde for to hold / though I seme tame[1]

        [1] My punctuation.

One of the ways of showing how this poem is so much more than a development of the coarse idea (so popular at Henry VIII's court), of courtship as the hunt, is to discuss its rhythms. The tone is at risk until the last two lines. Before that there is enough feeling to rescue the poem from the necessary coarseness of the image, but the danger of collapse is always present.[1] Wyatt needs this figure of the hunt to express his hopeless weariness; it is the right figure: but it necessarily gives the chance throughout the poem that it will collapse into the nastiness and jollity of the other hunt-poems

> There she gothe! Se ye nott,
> How she gothe over the playne?
> And yf ye lust to have a shott,
> I warrant her barrayne. Etc.[2]

Instead Wyatt gives us a highly individual emotion in which that un-Tudor feeling, tenderness, is an element. He can only do so by going at last into two lines without feet which work wholly by half-line balance:

> *Noli me tangere* for Cesars I ame
> And wylde for to hold though I seme tame

The half-line rhythms are quite unambiguous: nobody will miss the finely enforced stress on *wild*, which repeats not any foot-pattern, but the half-line rhythm of the line before. This line in fact works by its deliberate contradiction of foot-metre: it is deliberately not

And wyld[e] for to hold though I seme tame

It is:

And wylde for to hold / though I seme tame

Where else than the Chaucerian tradition could Wyatt have gone for this possibility of release from stereotyped feeling into something individual? It is a strength permitted to him by the Lydgate line, typical of the poet and common enough in his work.

---

[1] Cf. Mason, *op. cit.* pp. 188–9: 'As I see it, there is a certain tight-rope element in it, an avoidance by a narrow margin of falling into one of two inviting but inferior attitudes: the pretty-pretty or external idealization of Petrarch and the grossness in popular usage of the animal equation running through the sonnet.'

[2] Quoted from Henry VIII's manuscript in John Stevens, *Music and Poetry in the Early Tudor Court*, 1961, p. 400.

All this is not to deny that Wyatt sometimes shows a certain amateurishness that would have been surprising in Lydgate. Some of his lines are difficult or rhythmically ambiguous:

19, 1   Thou hast no faith of him that hath none
              But thou must love him nedes by reason
              For as saieth a proverbe notable
              Eche thing seketh his semblable

There might be some point in the movement of these first two lines, and even the second pair might be made easier by the poet's punctuation; but I do not know, as they stand, which of the various rhythmic possibilities is best. Perhaps Wyatt would have written differently if he had had a public in mind: this looks as if it needs performance by the author himself. It is, not surprisingly, one of Wyatt's poems on which Tottel's editors made no attempt.

But one can certainly distinguish in Wyatt between the best things which are normally a use of the Chaucerian balanced line, and the ordinary, uninteresting lyrics in smooth foot-metres without half-lines. Contrast the engaging, lagging stress of

4, 1   The longe love / that in my thought doeth harbar
           And in myn hert / doeth kepe his residence
           Into my face / preseth with bolde pretence
           And therin campeth / spreding his baner...

                              [my punctuation]

with things like

5, 1   Alas the greiff and dedly wofull smert

or

51, 1   At moost myschief
                    I suffre greif
                    For of relief
                      Syns I have none
                    My lute and I
                    Continuelly
                    Shall vs apply
                    To sigh and mone.

Differences of rhythm are here differences of sincerity. Wyatt's achievement is his use of balanced pentameter—and of translation—for a really individual utterance. Telling the truth is never easy: if Wyatt is a love poet, if he tells some truth about love, it is because he manages to speak a language of love, which has nothing to do with lutes, sighs, and such props. The Chaucerian tradition gave him a rhythmic language he could not find in the smoothness of the lyrical metres. The lyrics show Wyatt confined within cliché. It may be, as Muir says, that they 'came to him as naturally as the leaves to a tree'.[1] Clichés often do. But Mr Mason shows well how completely these poems are constructed out of a shuffling of common phrases. They are almost *forms* rather than poems. Perhaps they had some point in particular situations; perhaps Wyatt charged them with the meaning of a particular emotion. But there is no knowing: whatever they meant to him has not got into their language, and so is not expressed for us.

Wyatt's plight—the wish to be truthful and new at Henry's court—involved him in the search for a poetic language. And that meant the resuscitation of the Chaucerian line. It had to be rescued from the aureation of Lydgate and his admirers; but such a refinement was the only possibility, and Wyatt's success shows that the possibility was enough. He did, of course, go back quite consciously to Chaucer. 'Under the aureate poets language had become turgid to the point of hypertrophy, and was often unrecognizable as language. With Wyatt, however, began an entirely new idiom. Aided by Pynson's edition of Chaucer, which appeared opportunely in 1526, he was able to evolve a poetic diction that was new because it was deliberately old.'[2]

Renewing contact with Chaucer was Wyatt's way of drawing on the resources of spoken English, because in Chaucer's pentameter Wyatt found a way of bringing into metrical verse 'pieces of language'. If Wyatt was an archaiser it was because he was a searcher for the life of the spoken language. Wyatt's success is the great compliment to the balanced pentameter: he needed it.

The great break in English poetic history comes not after Chaucer's death but after Wyatt's. (Barclay lived through it in a rather bewildered way: anybody who has difficulty in believing in the reality of the reformation in England should compare Barclay's last work with his earlier ones.) The new age made itself felt by sweeping away the old language of poetry in favour of strict time-metres, poulter's measure and the common metre of Sternhold and

---

[1] *Collected Poems*, p. xxi.
[2] Veré L. Rubel, *Poetic Diction in the English Renaissance, Revolving Fund Series of the Modern Language Association of America*, XII, 1941, p. 47.

Hopkins's psalms. (It is ironical that poulter's measure, Wyatt's only completely unsuccessful experiment, should have been the one to catch on.) The development of these metres is the subject of Mr Thompson's book, to which I have nothing to add; the continuing influence of the new tradition is part of the reason for the need for the present work. We still inherit the different sense of metre brought about, quite decisively, within the twenty years or so after 1530.

But anybody who has been in sympathy with the foregoing comments on the last Chaucerians will agree that the new regularity of metre was not a simple improvement on the earlier situation. Tottel's *Miscellany* did not improve Wyatt. Expression was decisively changed, but not by men of genius; and if the Chaucerian tradition was not prolific of great poetry it was not as decisive a stifler of talent as the metres that immediately followed it. The rhythmic revolution after Wyatt virtually killed English poetry for fifty years. It was not until the new metres were forced to make some compliance with speech, not, that is, until the reintroduction—above all in Shakespeare's blank verse—of something akin to the phrasal element of Chaucer's metre, that there were again real poets in the land.

It may perhaps be agreed, whether or not we agree that Barnabe Googe is as dead as a doornail, that there was real strength in a rhythmic tradition that gave Wyatt the chance to write 'They Fle from Me' and 'Whoso list to hount'. And it is by further exploration of the successes of the Chaucerian tradition that we might one day find it and its dark century not, after all, wholly obscure.

The complex of problems centring on the rhythms of Chaucer and his followers is not one that can be solved; indeed the idea that if enough life and science is spent everything here can be neatly tied up has always been at the heart of the established confusions. We shall always be able to improve our knowledge of the rhythms of our medieval poets. But if they *are* ours we may be able to do better than the nineteenth-century scholars: by giving Middle English the chance to be still alive in our reading in the present. This, of course, is the demonstration that the medieval English poets do belong to our language, that we have the essential continuity of being able to read them which is an important part of what is meant by 'a literature'.

The better we read Chaucer the more we shall understand the movement of his verse and his relationship to his disciples; the more we understand the movement of Chaucer's verse and his relationship to his disciples the better we shall be reading Chaucer. I offer this as a circular argument more useful than the ones I began by criticizing, because it rests on the process of familiarization which is the way we get to know any language or literature. It is an argument that points back to the poetry and our developing sense of it, and therefore has no neat conclusion. I could only take it further by more extensive literary criticism for which this is not the place.

Appendix: Foreign Determinants and Parallels

Discussion of French and Italian rhythms has been noticeably absent from the present work, and in this respect at least it is wholly original, for all previous scholarship from Tyrwhitt to Southworth has devoted major effort to the attempt to understand the relation of Chaucer's metres to French and Italian ones. If Chaucer did imitate French and/or Italian, and if we understood what he imitated, we could certainly be in a strong position to work from French and Italian to a reading of Chaucer. Nevertheless I do not regret my omission and must briefly explain why. The explanation is the more necessary because I am here opposed simultaneously by establishment and opposition. To quote only the latter, Professor Southworth writes, 'Any study of Chaucer's prosody that can lay claim to validity must do certain things...it must examine the possible models available to the poet.'[1] One could retort that Southworth is here involving us in an infinite regression (how do we understand the possible models without going back to *their* possible models?) but I will consider only the more practical objections, which are three in number.

The first was so well used by Southworth that it alone would go far to invalidate his insistence on the need to inspect Chaucer's possible models. It is merely that the attempt to come to Chaucer from French has never succeeded in improving anyone's reading of Chaucer; Southworth's attack on all the important works that argue from French to Chaucer is convincing and even scholarly.

The second objection is that the attempt to argue from French always makes Chaucer not only deeply influenced by French, which is obvious, but determined and controlled by it, which is untrue: Chaucer's individuality survives and shapes a great many traditions and does so, moreover, in English, which means that whatever rules he was following they could not have been simply transferred from another language. So in any case anything we

---

[1] *Verses of Cadence*, p. 7.

could learn from French would need to be taken in conjunction with the main evidence, which would remain our sense of English.

But the third and main objection is that these attempts share the weakness of the established theories of final -e and variable stress in that they establish one unknown by comparing it with another, but with the air of dealing in plain and incontrovertible fact. 'Chaucer's early handling of the measure was according to the model of the French decasyllable', says one scholar, as if that makes all plain.[1] Ten Brink can settle a fine point in Chaucer by a confident appeal, in parenthesis: 'If we assume apocope, elision and slurring to the same extent at the caesura as in other positions in the verse (which we are perfectly justified in doing, as proved above all by the example of Italian verse)....'[2] The language appealed to by ten Brink is a different one, but the fallacy is just the same. In either case 'This is *ignotum per ignocius*'. By asserting that the French (or Italian) practice was so and so and Chaucer's the same, the argument begs all the formidable questions we discussed in Part I, above. All real knowledge of poetry is a working within a language; only a really inward comparison with foreign poems could be of any use here: the French rules, whatever they are, have their sense in relation to French poems, and cannot be abstracted from them.

And even at the present day the rhythms of French poetry are notoriously difficult for the Germanic reader to understand. The English reader is inveterately inclined to read Racine in foot-metres of an English sort even though the French assure him that

Le vers français ne se rhythme pas, comme celui de toutes les autres langues, par un certain entrelacement de syllabes brèves et longues. Il est seulement l'assemblage d'un certain nombre régulier de syllabes, coupé, dans certains espèces de vers, par un repos qui se nomme *césure*, et toujours terminé par un son qui ne peut exister à la fin d'un vers sans se trouver reproduit à la fin d'un autre ou de plusieurs autres vers, et dont le retour se nomme LA RIME.[3]

An English version of the same position goes,

In order to scan French verse, one must be able:
   I. To count the number of syllables.
   II. To recognize the occurrence of the caesuras.

---

[1] Enid Hamer, *The Metres of English Poetry*, 4th edition, 1951, p. 46.
[2] Ten Brink, *Language and Metre*, pp. 216–17.
[3] T. de Banville, *Petit Traité de Prosodie Française*, Paris, n.d. p. 10.

III. To know the rules that govern hiatus.
IV. To understand the laws of rhyme and assonance.[1]

It is *not* necessary, that is, to know anything about stress, which is always indispensable to scansion in Germanic languages. On the other hand Kastner says, 'Yet French verse is in a measure accentual in so far that the last sounded syllable of the line must be a stressed syllable, as also the last sounded syllable immediately preceding the caesural pause. The place of the other accents, however, is free'[2] and 'To sum up, the fundamental principles of French verse are (1) syllabism, (2) rime and (3) *to a certain extent* accentuation.'[3] But to *what* extent is the puzzle to those whose first language is English. A *very* good knowledge of French would be necessary for anybody who wanted to use it to illuminate Chaucer.

My own French is not good enough. And if I can without too much shame confess uncertainty about the metres of a literature I can read fairly easily and with pleasure, how much more uncertain must I be about the same matter taken back to Chaucer's age. Moreover, how am I to know Chaucer's French was any better than mine? May he not have found French metres equally tricky?

The argument from French or Italian, moreover, has always had to be based on simple notions of their versification which have to some extent been justified by the way the elder scholars, especially the French, spoke of the matter. But traditional French prosody is now being strongly challenged by attitudes much closer to the ones in the present work; so it may be that we have been inadvertently bringing Chaucer close to French, but only in so far as the French would have been unacceptable to the ten Brink school. The alexandrine can now be called a *tetramètre* with four *temps forts* per line[4]—which certainly puts it into a class of mixed metre comparable with the Chaucerian balanced pentameter. And it may be that Chaucer's use of final -e is rather like that of French verse—but because in French too the question of whether or not to sound it is open, and to be settled by the expressive effect on the verse. A native of Toulouse would sound the -e's in a line of

---

[1] L. M. Brandin and W. G. Hartog, *A Book of French Prosody*, 1904, p. 1.
[2] L. E. Kastner, *A History of French Versification*, Oxford, 1903, p. 5.
[3] *Ibid.* p. 2. My italics.
[4] Cf. the brief but illuminating remarks in Alan M. Boase, *The Poetry of France*, 1964, etc., vol. I, pp. cvi ff. and vol. III, pp. lxvi ff.

Racine that are silent for the Parisian; but the latter may still take metrical note of the -e and allow it to affect the movement by lengthening its syllable.

Further, the fourteenth-century situation is complicated by the existence of Norman French. If Chaucer's rhythms are imitations of French, was the French Paris French or Stratford atte Bowe French or Norman French? And what was the rhythmic habit of the last? (It is said that Norman French was greatly influenced by the accents of English: this might suggest the possibility of getting at the English by way of the French and then at the Norman French through the English.)

In any case, if Chaucer's metres are determined by some non-English influence, how do we know that it was the influence of French? Ten Brink and Skeat thought of this and found Italian as well: but Chaucer also knew, of course, quantitative Latin. The long Latin line (frequently found with metrical punctuation) seems at least as likely a progenitor of balanced pentameter as anything in fourteenth-century French or Italian. How quantitative Latin was read in medieval England must, perhaps, remain for ever unknown: but that is not to say it was not the source of Chaucer's metrical practice. Did not Gascoigne say that Chaucer 'hath vsed the same libertie in feete and measures that the Latinists do vse'?[1] And does not Mr H. L. R. Edwards find the genesis of Skeltonics in the break-up of Latin hexameters? Gower, of course, wrote Latin long lines, and Gower told Chaucer what to write. None of this shows that quantitative Latin had the slightest influence on Chaucer but it does suggest how easy and useless the whole train of argument can be.

The attempt to determine Chaucer's metre by reference to foreign metres must fail; but there may be point in comparing Chaucer's fusion of feet and half-lines with similar rhythms in other literatures. This work has not made such comparisons only because other things were more urgent and because I am not confident enough in the relevant literatures to make pronouncements about how verse should go. All that can be done here is to throw out the suggestion, which I have never seen used in our study, that the history of German poetry may be more useful in giving us a perspective than either French or Italian. (The parallel with German ought also to be usable in the study of sounded

---

[1] Quoted in Spurgeon, I, p. 110.

final -e. The idea that Chaucer sounded -e (as French verse is supposed to) as part of an artificial system of versification unconnected with speech, is surely untenable: the German -e that is part of the standard language ought to be more useful to contemplate.)

The history of German metres as of English shows the displacement of alliteratives by foot-metre; in Germany too the process was long and not a simple immediate change. Problems similar to the ones we have been discussing occur, and tend to be settled in similar ways. H. G. Atkins says this of some lines of Hans Sachs: 'The great question is the part played in them by the natural prose accentuation of the words. It is obvious that they cannot all be read with natural prose accent *and* regular alternation, though by no means all the lines present any difficulty in this respect...According to Saran, Hans Sachs has only 75·7 "difficulties" for each hundred lines.'[1] There are various solutions to this problem, proposed by different scholars,

'(1) Some investigators have held that they are to be read with regular alternations, which implies violation of the natural prose accentuation of the words.'[2]

'(2) Another school...holds that the lines have four lifts, but are to be read with the natural prose accentuation.'[3]

'(3) Another school...reads the lines with the natural accentuation of the words, as in prose speech, but with a variable number of lifts...'[4]

'(4) There remains a fourth possibility...'[5] On this I merely wish to observe that this is where we came in.

There are striking likenesses, but we cannot follow them here; we must also neglect the other Germanic literatures which went through the change from half-lines to feet, and perhaps the intervening stages, much later. But I do think that *that* comparative literature would be more promising than the attempt to come to Chaucer from French; and as far as I know nobody has tried to do it since A. J. Ellis, who got it wrong.

[1] H. G. Atkins, *A History of German Versification*, 1923, p. 146.
[2] *Ibid.*   [3] *Ibid.* p. 147.   [4] *Ibid.* p. 149.
[5] *Ibid.* Cf. also J. G. Robertson, *A History of German Literature*, Edinburgh, 1931, p. 34, for a theory that Otfrid was forced to abandon alliteration by linguistic change, and J. Knight Bostock, *A Handbook of Old High German Literature*, Oxford, 1955, p. 125, for a condemnation of lines of the *Muspilli* on the grounds that they do not conform to the rules of older verse.

Bibliography

An exhaustive bibliography would be perhaps three times as long as the following, which is merely a list of the works I have found most useful, together with a few whose uselessness can be explained in a brief note.

Babcock, C. F. 'A Study of the Metrical Use of the Inflectional -E in Middle English', *PMLA*, vol. xxix, 1914.

Baldi, S. *La Poesia di Sir Thomas Wyatt*, Florence, 1953.

Baum, P. F. 'Chaucer's Metrical Prose', *The Journal of English and Germanic Philology*, vol. xlv, 1946.

Chaucer's Verse, Durham, N.C., 1961.

Bond, G. *The Factors Governing the Pronunciation of Chaucer's Final -E*, University of Michigan Doctoral Dissertation, 1946.

Borroff, M. *'Sir Gawain and the Green Knight', a Stylistic and Metrical Study*, New Haven and London, 1962.

Brink, B. ten. *The Language and Metre of Chaucer*, second edition, revised by F. Kluge. Translated by L. Bentinck Smith, 1902.

Brusendorff, A. *The Chaucer Tradition*, Copenhagen and London, 1925.

Child, F. J. See Ellis.

Clemoes, P. *Liturgical Influence on Punctuation in Middle English, Occasional Papers Printed for the Department of Anglo-Saxon*, Cambridge, 1952.

Crosby, R. 'Oral Delivery in the Middle Ages', *Speculum*, vol. xi, 1936.

'Chaucer and the Custom of Oral Delivery'. *Speculum*, vol. xiii, 1938.

Danielsson, B. *Studies on the Accentuation of Polysyllabic Latin, Greek and Romance Loan-words in English*, Stockholm, 1948.

Dante Alighieri, *De Vulgari Eloquentia, Opere Latine*, Florence, 1878–82.

Daunt, M. 'Old English Verse and English Speech Rhythm', *Transactions of the Philological Society*, 1946.

'Some Notes on Old English Phonology', *Transactions of the Philological Society*, 1952.

Dobson, E. J. *English Pronunciation 1500–1700*, 2 vols., second edition, Oxford, 1968.

Donaldson, E. T. 'Chaucer's Final -E', *PMLA*, vol. lxiii, 1948.

A note after J. G. Southworth's rejoinder to the above, *PMLA*, vol. lxiv, 1949.

Edwards, H. L. R. *Skelton*, 1949.

Ellis, A. J. *On Early English Pronunciation*, 5 vols., E.E.T.S. 1867–89. (This includes reprints of the work of Payne, Child et al.)

Endicott, A M. *A Critical Study of Metrical Effects in the Poetry of Sir Thomas Wyatt, with Some Reference to Analogous Effects in Elizabethan Poetry*, London M.A. Dissertation, 1963.

BIBLIOGRAPHY

Epstein, E. L. and Hawkes, T. *Linguistics and English Prosody, Studies in Linguistics, Occasional Papers*, no. 7, Buffalo, 1959.

Faral, E. (ed.). *Les Arts Poétiques du XIIe et du XIIIe Siècle*, Paris, 1924.

Gordon, I. A. *John Skelton, Poet Laureate*, Melbourne, 1943.

The Movement of English Prose, 1966.

Hammond, E. P. 'The 9-Syllabled Pentameter Line in some post-Chaucerian MSS', *Modern Philology*, vol. XXIII, 1925.

(ed.). *English Verse between Chaucer and Surrey*, Durham, N.C., 1927.

Harding, D. W. 'The Rhythmical Intention in Wyatt's Poetry', *Scrutiny*, vol. XIV, 1946.

Harrison, T. C. *Chaucer's 'Measure', a Study in Moderation*, University of Virginia M.A. Dissertation, 1929. This work has made its way into bibliographies of prosody but is really a disquisition upon the Golden Mean in Chaucer, and so may now disappear from them.

Haswell, R. E. *The Heroic Couplet before Dryden*, University of Illinois Doctoral Dissertation, 1932. This is listed by Griffith but has only incidental references to Chaucer.

Hill, M. A. 'Rhetorical Balance in Chaucer's Poetry', *PMLA*, vol. XLII, 1927. This essay is *not* about rhythm.

Hughey, R. 'The Harington Manuscript at Arundel Castle and Related Documents', *The Library*, vol. XV, 1934.

Ing, C. M. *Elizabethan Lyrics, A Study in the Development of English Metres, and their Relation to Poetic Effect*, 1951.

Kittredge, G. L. 'Make the Metres...', *Modern Philology*, vol. VII, 1910.

Kurath, H., Kuhn, S. M. *et al.* (eds.). *Middle English Dictionary*. Ann Arbor, 1952–. (In progress.)

Learned, H. D. 'The Accentuation of Old French Loan-Words in English', *PMLA*, vol. XXXVII, 1922.

Lewis, C. S. 'The Fifteenth Century Heroic Line', *Essays and Studies*, vol. XXIV, 1938.

'Metre', *A Review of English Literature*, vol. I, 1960.

Licklider, A. H. *Chapters on the Metric of the Chaucer Tradition*, Baltimore, 1910.

Luick, K. *Historische Grammatik der englischen Sprache*, issued in parts, Leipzig, 1914–40.

McJimsey, R. B. *Chaucer's Irregular -E*, New York, 1942.

Manly, J. M. and Rickert, E. (eds.). *The Text of 'The Canterbury Tales' Studied on the Basis of All Known Manuscripts*, 8 vols., Chicago, 1940.

Mari, G. 'Terminologia Ritmica Medievale', *Studi di Filologia Romanza*, vol. VIII, 1901.

(ed.). *I Tratti Medievali di Ritmica Latina*, Milan, 1899.

Mason, H. A. *Humanism and Poetry in the Early Tudor Period*, 1959.

Mitchell, J. *Thomas Hoccleve, a Study in Early Fifteenth Century English Poetic*, Urbana, Illinois, 1968.

Morgan, M. M. 'A Treatise in Cadence', *The Modern Language Review*, vol. XLVII, 1952.

Nelson, W. *John Skelton, Laureate*, New York, 1939.
Nöjd, R. *The Vocalism of Romanic Words in Chaucer*, Uppsala, 1919.
Nott, G. F. 'Dissertation', in vol. I of *The Works of Henry Howard, Earl of Surrey, and of Sir Thomas Wyatt, the Elder*, 2 vols., 1815.
Pyle, F. 'The Barbarous Metre of Barclay', *The Modern Language Review*, vol. XXXII, 1937.
Reger, H. *Die Epische Cäsur in der Chaucerschule*, Bayreuth, 1910. (Useful for numerous examples.)
Robertson, S. 'Old English Verses in Chaucer', *Modern Language Notes*, vol. XLIII, 1928.
Rubel, V. L. *Poetic Diction in the English Renaissance, Revolving Fund Series of the Modern Language Association of America*, no. XII, 1941.
Schick, J. Introduction to *The Temple of Glas*, E.E.T.S. 1891.
Schipper, J. *Englische Metrik in historischer und systematischer Entwickelung dargestellt*, 2 vols., Bonn, 1881–8.
A History of English Versification, Oxford, 1910.
Schultz, J. R. 'Barclay and the Later Eclogue Writers', *Modern Language Notes*, vol. XXXV, 1920. (An essay that usefully shows there is *no* connection between Barclay and the later eclogue writers.)
Shapiro, K. *A Bibliography of Modern Prosody*, Baltimore, 1948.
Simpson, P. 'The Rhyming of Stressed and Unstressed Syllables in the Sixteenth Century', *The Modern Language Review*, vol. XXXVIII, 1943.
Southall, R. *The Courtly Maker*, Oxford, 1964.
Southworth, J. G. 'Chaucer's Final -E in Rhyme', *PMLA*, vol. LXII, 1947.
'Chaucer's Final -E', *PMLA*, vol. LXIV, 1949. (A retort to Donaldson; the same volume has a brief re-rejoinder.)
Verses of Cadence, an Introduction to the Prosody of Chaucer and his Followers, Oxford, 1954.
The Prosody of Chaucer and his Followers, Supplementary Chapters to Verses of Cadence, Oxford, 1962.
'Chaucer: A Plea for a Reliable Text', *College English*, December, 1964.
Spurgeon, C. F. E. (ed.). *Five Hundred Years of Chaucer Criticism and Allusion, 1357–1900*. 3 vols., Cambridge, 1925.
Stevens, J. *Music and Poetry in the Early Tudor Court*, 1961.
Swallow, A. 'Pentameter Lines in Skelton and Wyatt', *Modern Philology*, vol. XLVIII, 1950.
Tatlock, J. S. P. *The Harleian Manuscript 7334 and Revision of the 'Canterbury Tales'*, Chaucer Society, 1909.
Tatlock, J. S. P. and Kennedy, A. G. *A Concordance to the Complete Works of Geoffrey Chaucer*, Washington, 1927.
Thompson, J. *The Founding of English Metre*, 1961.
Tydeman, W. M. *Wyatt and the English Tradition*, Oxford B.Litt. Dissertation, 1965.
Tyrwhitt, T. 'Essay on the Language and Versification of Chaucer', prefixed to his second edition of *The Canterbury Tales*, 2 vols., Oxford, 1798.

BIBLIOGRAPHY

I have not seen the following:

Hamer, R. C. *The Poetry of Sir Thomas Wyatt,* Harvard Doctoral Dissertation, 1952.

Malone, K. 'Chaucer's Double Consonants and the Final -E', *Medieval Studies* (Toronto), 1957.

Seeberger, A. *Fehlende Auftakt und fehlende Senkung nach der Cäsur in der Chaucerschule,* Bayreuth, 1911.

Wager, W. J. *A Study of Chaucer's Development in his Use of the Decasyllabic Line,* New York Doctoral Dissertation, 1919.

Index

249